OLIGOPOLY, COMPETITION AND WELFARE

OLIGOPOLY, COMPETITION AND WELFARE

Edited by

P. A. GEROSKI
L. PHLIPS
A. ULPH

Basil Blackwell
published in cooperation with
The Journal of Industrial Economics

© *The Journal of Industrial Economics*, 1985

First published 1985

Basil Blackwell Ltd
108 Cowley Road, Oxford OX4 1JF, UK

Basil Blackwell Inc.
432 Park Avenue South, Suite 1505,
New York, NY 10016, USA

All rights reserved. Except for the quotation of short passages for the purposes of criticism and review, no part of this publication may be reproduced, stored in a retrieval system, or transmitted, in any form or by any means, electronic, mechanical, photocopying, recording or otherwise, without the prior permission of the publisher.

Except in the United States of America, this book is sold subject to the condition that it shall not, by way of trade or otherwise, be lent, re-sold, hired out, or otherwise circulated without the publisher's prior consent in any form of binding or cover other than that in which it is published and without a similar condition including this condition being imposed on the subsequent purchaser.

British Library Cataloguing in Publication Data

Oligopoly, competition and welfare: some recent developments.
1. Oligopolies
I. Geroski, P. A.   II. Phlips, Louis
III. Ulph, A. M.
338.6'048   HD2731
ISBN 0-631-14479-X

Library of Congress Cataloging in Publication Data

Main entry under title:

Oligopoly, competition, and welfare.

Proceedings of a joint meeting of the E.S.R.C. Industrial Economics Study Group and the E.S.R.C. Economic Theory Study Group.
  Bibliography: p. 173
  Includes index.
  1. Oligopolies—Congresses.   2. Competition, Unfair—Congresses.   3. Welfare economics—Congresses.
I. Geroski, Paul.   II. Phlips, Louis.   III. Ulph, Alistair.   IV. E.S.R.C. Industrial Economics Study Group.   V. E.S.R.C. Economic Theory Study Group.
HD2757.3.044   1985   338.8'2   85-11200
ISBN 0-631-14479-X

Typeset by Advanced Filmsetters (Glasgow) Ltd
Printed in Great Britain by T. J. Press, Padstow

CONTENTS

P. A. GEROSKI, L. PHLIPS and A. ULPH
Oligopoly, Competition and Welfare: Some Recent Developments — 1

RAY REES
Cheating in a Duopoly Supergame — 19

KEVIN ROBERTS
Cartel Behaviour and Adverse Selection — 33

ROBERT H. PORTER
On the Incidence and Duration of Price Wars — 47

JONATHAN B. BAKER and TIMOTHY F. BRESNAHAN
The Gains from Merger or Collusion in Product-Differentiated Industries — 59

DAVID EASLEY, ROBERT T. MASSON and ROBERT J. REYNOLDS
Preying for Time — 77

CHRISTOPHER HARRIS and JOHN VICKERS
Patent Races and the Persistence of Monopoly — 93

HUW DIXON
Strategic Investment in an Industry with a Competitive Product Market — 115

NORMAN J. IRELAND
Product Diversity and Monopolistic Competition under Uncertainty — 133

G. K. YARROW
Welfare Losses in Oligopoly and Monopolistic Competition — 147

THOMAS von UNGERN-STERNBERG and CARL CHRISTIAN von WEIZSÄCKER
The Supply of Quality on a Market for "Experience Goods" — 163

Bibliography — 173

Author Index — 185

Subject Index — 189

PREFACE

THIS VOLUME stems from a Conference on "Oligopoly Theory" held at St Anne's College, Oxford, on 21st–22nd March, 1984. The Conference, jointly organized by P. Geroski and A. Ulph (with the assistance of J. Cubbin and T. Sharpe), was a joint meeting of the E.S.R.C. Industrial Economics Study Group and the E.S.R.C. Economic Theory Study Group, and was kindly supported by the Economic and Social Research Council through their annual grants to these two study groups. The papers in this volume by R. Rees, N. Ireland, G. Yarrow, C. Harris and J. Vickers, and D. Easley *et al.* were all presented at the Conference, together with a related paper by K. Roberts and one by O. Hart (which will appear elsewhere).

One of the more active and encouraging supporters of the initial idea of holding such a conference was Donald Hay. He is largely responsible for bringing *The Journal of Industrial Economics* into the venture, organizing the whole enterprise under the current editorial team. Subsequent to the Conference, the Editors decided to supplement the Conference programme by inviting several further papers in related areas of work. We are most grateful to H. Dixon, T. Bresnahan, R. Porter, T. von Ungern-Sternberg, and C. von Weizsäcker for their prompt replies and the useful papers that they offered us. At the insistence of the Editorial Board of the *Journal* and with Donald Hay's active encouragement, the Editors agreed to introduce the volume with a survey on recent developments in the area of Oligopoly and Imperfect Competition.

An enterprise such as this necessarily runs up formidable debts to various assistants who are roped into the proceedings, frequently in times of crisis and high panic. We would like to record our sincere thanks to a group of referees who provided first-class reports in considerably less than the usual amount of time. Sarah Rollason and Tim James organized and produced the Bibliography, all the while maintaining a sense of humour against considerable odds.

P. A. GEROSKI
L. PHLIPS
A. ULPH

OLIGOPOLY, COMPETITION AND WELFARE: SOME RECENT DEVELOPMENTS*

P. A. Geroski, L. Phlips and A. Ulph

I. INTRODUCTION

In this essay, we wish to highlight three particular areas in the enormous literature on oligopoly where, we believe, recent work has proved particularly productive and illuminating. One recent development of interest has been the application of game theory to the well known "interdependence of expectations" problem. While interesting in its own right, it has also had a major impact in clarifying thinking about rational strategic choice, and the role of information in affecting outcomes. Our view is that the information structure of the oligopoly problem plays a crucial role in conditioning the nature of its solution, and this is the first topic that we propose to discuss. These developments in theory have occurred in tandem with and, indeed, have stimulated empirical work. One important empirical problem is that of identifying the exercise of monopoly power in practice, and recent work has focussed on the problem of inferring conduct from observed price-output configurations. This obviously has a high order of policy importance, and it constitutes the second topic in our discussion. Rational strategic choice involves, *inter alia*, the use of various types of competitive weapons, and such modes of rivalry produce outcomes which differ substantially from competition in simple homogeneous goods markets. We wish to briefly highlight these, and then turn to one of the more interesting features of such competitive processes. When firms can strategically invest and pre-commit themselves to markets, the timing of competitive movements becomes important. A recent body of work has focussed on pre-emption, and the likelihood that monopoly positions—however created—can persist for long periods of time. This material is of major importance for those concerned with market dynamics, and we shall close this essay by highlighting some of the recent work on this topic.

II. OLIGOPOLY AND IMPERFECT INFORMATION

A number of interesting new developments on the oligopoly front can be traced back to Stigler [1964] who examined the relationship between collusion and the information structure of an oligopolistic market. He argued that the basic problem in colluding to maximize joint profits is that of policing the agreement (rather than joint profit maximization as such; see Roberts [1985] on this

---

* We are obliged to Beth Allen, Tim Bresnahan, Jean Jaskold Gabszewicz, and Bentley MacLeod for comments on various portions of early drafts. The usual disclaimer applies.

second issue). This is a problem in the theory of information, since secret price cutting must be detectable for retaliation to be possible, or for a threat of retaliation to be credible. Given this framework, subsequent research has tried to clarify a number of questions, three of which we shall consider in some detail.[1]

First, how much information (among rivals) is needed for collusion to be possible?

Second, does less information (among rivals) promote "active competition" or more frequent "price wars"? Interpreting "active competition" as a move from the profit frontier to a non-cooperative Nash equilibrium, this question can be reformulated as: does a non-cooperative Nash equilibrium require perfect information? If not, related questions are: (a) do duopolists, taken individually, wish to acquire more information in a non-cooperative equilibrium?; (b) do they wish to share information in such an equilibrium?

Third, can price wars or "active competition" be shown to result from (intertemporally) rational behaviour, rather than the result of a myopic pursuit of self interest? That is, can one define a non-cooperative equilibrium that includes both episodic price wars, as well as periods of effective collusion?

(i) *The Prisoners' Dilemma and Imperfect Information*

Credit should be given to Osborne [1976] for unveiling the information structure that is required for a group of oligopolists to come to a workable collusive agreement which maximizes joint profits on the one hand, and which deters cheating on the other. The basic dilemma is that whatever the point chosen on the profit frontier (see Figure 1), each member finds it profitable to produce more than the quota allotted to him and so has an incentive to cheat whether the other members cheat or not. The situation is that of the familiar prisoners' dilemma[2] in which each player has two strategies (observe the agreement or cheat) and the profits are such that for each player, cheating is a dominant strategy—i.e. the best strategy no matter what strategy the other player chooses. However, the strategy pair (cheat, cheat) is off the profit frontier (since profits to both firms could be increased by both observing the agreement), and so is "Pareto dominated" (it could be a Cournot–Nash equilibrium; see section (ii)). The other three strategy pairs are on the profit frontier (or "Pareto optimal"), since one firm's profit cannot be increased without decreasing others'

---

[1] We do not discuss oligopoly with asymmetric market information, such as badly informed buyers (see Nermuth [1979], Stahl [1982] and von Ungern-Sternberg [1984a, Chapter 5]) or badly informed sellers (see de Palma *et al.* [1983]). We will also not discuss the question of how firms may systematically mislead their less well informed rivals. Such signalling models have recently featured in discussions of entry; see, for example, Milgrom and Roberts [1982a] and [1982b], Kreps and Wilson [1982b] and Easley *et al.* [1985].

[2] Shubik [1982, p. 254] formulates the usual verbal scenario as follows: "Two prisoners who are suspected of having committed a crime are interrogated separately by the police. If both maintain silence, at most they can be booked on a minor charge. Each is encouraged to incriminate the other with a promise of leniency if he is not himself incriminated. If they double-cross each other, they are both in trouble."

profits. Explicit pooling of revenue agreements has long been thought to be the only way out of this problem, so that tacit collusion and explicit collusion without pooling seemed doomed to failure (see Patinkin [1947]). Osborne showed that the dilemma can be solved without explicit pooling if each firm is assigned an operating rule incorporating a deterrent to cheating. This "best reply" rule to cheating involves loyal firms increasing their output in the same proportion as the cheaters increase theirs.[3]

However, it should be realized that everything hinges on the information that is available to the players. To begin with, to locate their Pareto optimal strategy pairs, the members of an agreement should know the production of non-members. In addition, they should have adequate and compatible information on the payoff matrix itself, which implies compatible forecasts about future developments in the market and compatible time horizons. In short, they should be well informed about the rules of the game itself; i.e. their information should be "complete" (in the terminology of Selten [1982]). Clearly, this difficulty can be overcome, but it is likely to become more severe as the number of players increases. The detection of cheating also raises problems of "imperfect" information. For example, to deter cheating with quotas, information on the actual output of the players is essential. In order to be able to use Osborne's operating rule, either the output of each player or the total output of all players should be known. (In the latter case, the rule could be modified by supposing that the cheater has an average quota, but this would not deter small cheaters.)

At this point, an important caveat is in order. Osborne's rule is *not* a theoretical solution to the prisoners' dilemma as defined above: that dilemma occurs in a one-period game and remains without solution, while Osborne's rule implies the passage of time, with some cheaters increasing their output first and other firms reacting to this subsequently. Osborne's rule thus refers to a game in which history matters, and a satisfactory theoretical treatment should consider it as a strategy in a supergame (see section (iii)).

(ii) *Cournot–Nash Equilibrium and Imperfect Information*

Suppose information is incomplete and sufficiently imperfect for the players to be off the profit frontier. Is even a non-collusive equilibrium possible under these conditions? The answer is: yes. A non-cooperative game with "incomplete" information can be redefined as a game with complete information in extensive form, i.e. with all possible decisions, and the sequence of these decisions fully described.[4] The possibility of writing a game in extensive form

---

[3] Holahan [1978] has shown that this rule may leave loyal members worse off if sufficiently large differences exist between the profit functions of loyalists and cheaters. Rothschild [1981] identifies conditions under which loyal firms are worse off than they would have been if they had stood pat, even when all firms have identical profit functions.

[4] The classic reference is Harsanyi [1967–8]; Selten [1982] explains (in a not too technical way) how this can be done using fully worked out examples.

solves the problem of imperfect information analytically through the use of "information sets" which describe the lack of information at each stage of the game for each player.

A series of experiments have suggested much the same answer.[5] Experimental games conducted by Hoggatt ([1959], [1967]), Fouraker and Siegel [1963], Friedman ([1963], [1969], [1970]), Dolbear et al. [1968] and Sauermann and Selten [1967] show that when information about competitors is limited, and in the absence of communication between players, (posted) prices actually tend to a competitive equilibrium when Bertrand price strategies are played, even with very few players. With quantity decisions, the outcome is most often a non-cooperative Cournot–Nash equilibrium.[6] The accuracy of the joint maximization model was found to decrease with a reduction of information about other agents' actions, but joint profit maximization was the outcome under perfect information with experienced players (Stoecker [1980] and Friedman and Hoggatt [1980]). These results suggest that under imperfect information

> "the number of sellers becomes a very important treatment variable in that an increase in the number destroys the accuracy of the joint maximum model. In duopoly markets, significant (but less than perfect) cooperation occurs but, with an increase in the number of firms, it vanishes almost completely and the Cournot model is very accurate by comparison." (Plott [1982], p. 1516–1517).

These experimental results are compatible with the theoretical and econometric findings of Spence [1978] on tacit coordination and imperfect information. Spence introduces both *event uncertainty* (for example unforeseen changes in demand) and *imperfect information* (firms do not observe their competitors' behaviour directly but receive market signals, such as changes in total industry output or market shares), so that the reaction functions have market signals as arguments. These signals are, in turn, functions of the competitors' outputs and of the states of nature. Spence defines signalling equilibria (in terms of these reaction functions) such that no firm has an incentive to cheat when it takes the probability of being detected (and punished) into account, and the Cournot–Nash equilibrium turns out to be such an equilibrium; i.e. it has the property that the expected profit if one does not cheat is always larger than the expected profit if one cheats. To these equilibria correspond a region of payoffs (represented by a circle in Figure 1) around the Cournot–Nash equilibrium payoffs inside the profit frontier (Π_1 and Π_2 are their respective profits. m_1 and m_2 are the profits after penalties are inflicted on player 1 or 2 when a deviation from the equilibrium is detected).

---

[5] Excellent reviews of experiments in this field can be found in Selten [1979] and Plott [1982].

[6] The distinction between Bertrand price strategies and Cournot quantity strategies appears as less fundamental once it is realized that the Cournot outcome is also a perfect equilibrium in a two stage game in which the players choose their capacity in the first stage and compete in prices in the second stage, as shown by Kreps and Scheinkman [1983]. See also MacLeod [1984], and Dixon [1985].

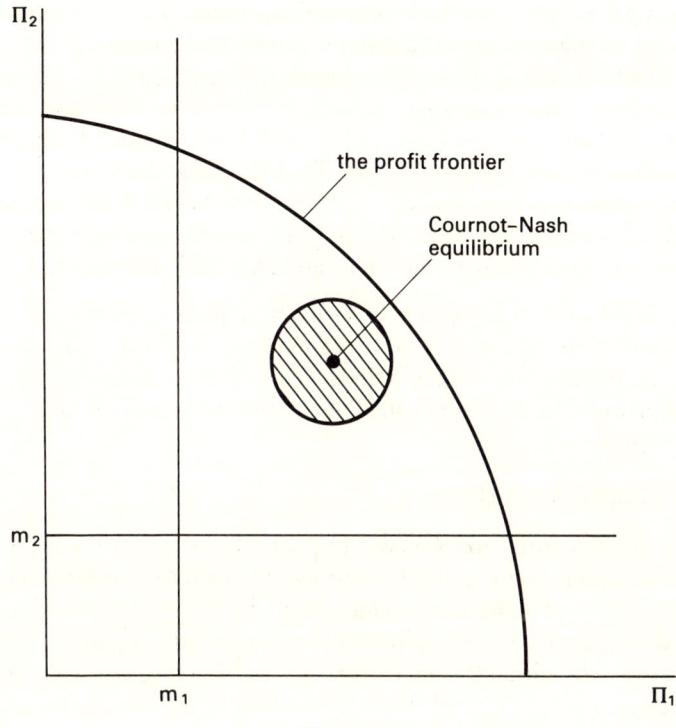

Figure 1

Thus, perfect information seems not to be a necessary ingredient of Cournot–Nash equilibria. This leaves open the question of whether non-cooperating oligopolists care about acquiring more private market information, and whether they are indifferent to sharing it. Novshek and Sonnenschein [1982] argue that they do want more information but are indifferent about sharing it if they have access to the same information set. Clarke ([1983a], [1983b]) shows that, if a crucial assumption made by Novshek and Sonnenschein is dropped, they do not wish to share information. The assumption is one of "fulfilled expectations". Expectations are "fulfilled", when, given the equilibrium, the expected joint evolution (the joint distribution) of a signal and the random variable on which it provides information is correct. The signal provides information about the value of the (random) intercept of the (linear) market demand equation, and each signal is defined as the simple average of observations on the intercept drawn from a sample owned by an independent information agency. Each firm's profit is defined in terms of these observations. It turns out that the profit of a firm increases with the information acquired by itself (or by a competitor if the latter pools some of it), but is the same whether all information is kept private or pooled. In a signalling Cournot–Nash equilibrium, players are thus indifferent with respect to information pooling.

However, total welfare (consumer surplus plus producer surplus) increases with the amount of information acquisition *and* with the amount of information release. Clarke ([1983a], [1983b]) replaces this *ex post* fulfilled expectations assumption by a "Bayes–Cournot" assumption, that firms make their quantity decisions based on their best Bayes estimates of their opponents' information. Using results obtained by Basar and Ho [1974], Clarke finds that in all cases where expectations are not actually fulfilled, firms would prefer not to share information[7] (even if they have less accurate information than their rivals) unless they will cooperate once the information has been shared.[8]

> "This situation is unfortunate as society's welfare is maximized only when firms share information, but act competitively. Thus society faces a dilemma. Information pooling is good if firms behave competitively, but shared information makes anticompetitive agreements easier to construct." (Clarke [1983b, p. 383]).

The policy implication is clear:

> "If all industry firms are observed to pool information without paying each other compensation, they must be setting quantities cooperatively on the basis of the homogenized information. Hence information-pooling mechanisms like trade associations can be considered *prima facie* evidence that firms are illegally cooperating to restrict output. This result strengthens Posner's [1976] informal analysis of the desirability of information-sharing agreements. On the other hand, lack of information-pooling mechanisms can be taken as fairly good evidence that cooperative behaviour is impeded." (Clarke [1983b, p. 392]).

(iii) *Tacit Collusion, Price Wars and Imperfect Information*

Having discussed the informational requirements of a collusive equilibrium and of a non-cooperative Cournot–Nash equilibrium, it seems natural to ask whether the two could not constitute the components of a non-cooperative Nash equilibrium in a "supergame". Not surprisingly, time now explicitly enters the picture: players are now viewed as playing (stationary) repeated game (also called "supergame") with an infinite horizon. The strategic variables are either quantities or prices and Osborne's instantaneous operating rule is replaced by the following intertemporal strategy. In the first period of the game, all players choose the collusive Pareto optimal quantities q_1^* (or prices). In any subsequent period, they continue to do so if, in all past periods, all players were loyal. If, however, this is not the case, then all players shift to the Cournot–Nash

---

[7] See also Crawford and Sobel [1982] and Palfrey [1982]. Empirical evidence on the exchange of information and collusion can be found in Eisenberg [1980].
[8] Gal-Or [1982] and Vives [1983] find this result to hold only if the goods produced are substitutes, and to be reversed for the case of Bertrand price competition (with substitutes).

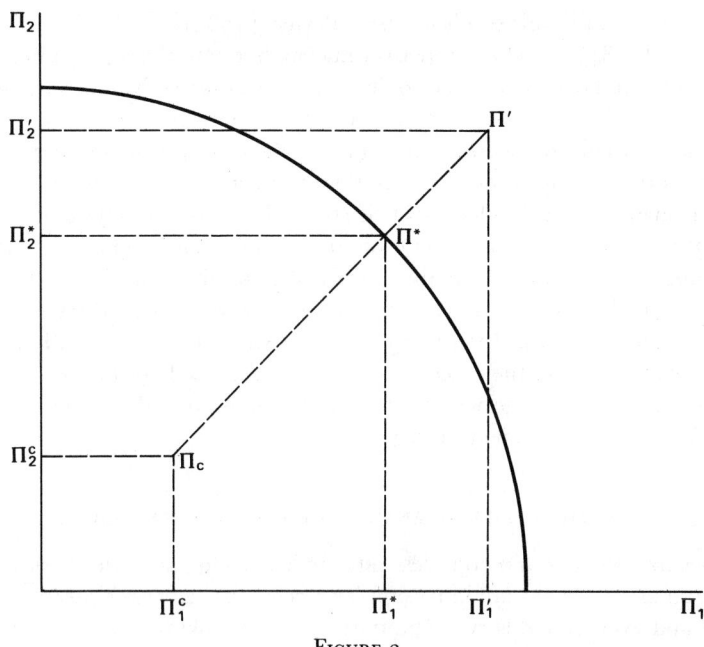

FIGURE 2

quantities q_i^c. The profit possibilities for a single period are represented in Figure 2.[9] Π^* represents the collusive profits and Π^c represents the profits when all firms have shifted to the Cournot–Nash equilibrium. It turns out that the collusive payoff Π^* can be obtained without an explicit agreement; "tacit collusion" can thus be defined in game-theoretic terms as the non-cooperative achievement of the collusive outcome.

To understand this, suppose the intertemporal strategy defined above is not played by a firm j in period t. Then its immediate profit is Π'_j. However, in period $t+1$ all rivals will switch to q_i^c, so the cheater's profit will be reduced to the level associated with the Cournot–Nash equilibrium. A tacitly collusive outcome occurs if the discounted flow of j's profits when j cheats is smaller than the discounted flow of profits when nobody cheats. This inequality will be satisfied if the discount factor $(1/(1+r))$, is close to one, i.e. if the rate of interest is sufficiently small. The discount factor plays such a crucial role because the important comparison for form j is between the immediate additional profit due to cheating $(\Pi'_j - \Pi_j^*)$ and the present value of subsequent per period losses of $(\Pi'_j - \Pi_j^c)$. This supergame approach gives a precise meaning to the concept of "tacit collusion" but solves the prisoners' dilemma too well: no firm ever has an

---

[9] These arguments were first presented by Friedman [1971] following an idea by Aumann [1960], and then included in his 1977 textbook (chapter 8); see also Friedman and Hoggatt [1980, chapter 1], Friedman [1972], Rees [1985], and, for a survey, Fudenberg and Tirole [1984].

incentive to cheat in this equilibrium![10] Porter ([1983a], [1983b]) and Green and Porter [1984] introduce imperfect information into the supergame, allowing for random shocks in demand so that firms are imperfectly informed on their rivals' output. An observed price decrease may then be blamed on the demand shock rather than on cheating, and this may give rise to some cheating. An intertemporal strategy that combats this problem is to switch to the Nash equilibrium as soon as the observed price is less than some "trigger price" which depends, *inter alia*, on the extent of uncertainty. The collusive quantities pertaining to this strategy are above their joint-profit-maximizing levels, but tend towards this level as the variance of the unobserved disturbance term (of demand) goes to zero. Interestingly, price wars now occur with positive probability; however, their occurrence is not the result of cheating, but of unusual demand shocks to which firms must respond in order to maintain the credibility of the punishment strategy.

III. THE EMPIRICAL ANALYSIS OF PRICING BEHAVIOUR

After several decades and countless inter-industry regressions, empirical work has begun to turn from examining simple correlations between industry concentration and average industry profitability towards looking more closely at the pricing behaviour underlying them. This recent work seeks to make inferences about existence of monopoly power from observed data on costs, demand, and equilibrium prices and quantities, and we wish to highlight some of its features here.[11]

(i) *Testing Price-Taking Behaviour*

Easily the simplest exercise one can perform is to attempt to test whether firms appear to be price takers. In general, however, an integral feature of the problem is the need to simultaneously estimate a marginal cost function and detect significant differences between it and prices at observed outputs.[12] With data on inputs and input costs, one can do this in a straightforward fashion by jointly estimating the parameters of a production function and the marginal revenue curve, and testing to see whether the latter is horizontal (one may date

---

[10] Price wars can occur only when the inequality just defined is reversed, and thus only a change in the interest rate could take an industry back into a non-cooperative equilibrium. Furthermore, with a sufficiently small interest rate, tacit collusion is likely to occur only in certain types of markets, such as geographically segmented markets (of the Loschian type—see MacLeod *et al.* [1984]) or markets with no rapid growth or slow technical progress, in which Friedman's inequality is relatively easy to compute in practice.

[11] The precise relationship between the work to be reviewed below and these earlier studies becomes evident when the profits-concentration link is written out in precise form; e.g. see Cowling and Waterson [1976]. For further remarks on this relationship, see Geroski [1982a].

[12] This is the natural way of dealing with the well known ambiguity of interpreting profit-concentration correlations as indicators of monopoly power or of superior efficiency (e.g. Demsetz [1974]). For other empirical work on this problem, see (*inter alia*) Caves and Pugel [1980], Mueller [1981] and Clarke *et al.* [1984], and the discussion in Scherer [1980].

this approach at least as early as Rosse [1970]; Appelbaum [1979] is a good recent example). However, testing for price-taking behaviour becomes considerably more complex when industry outputs cannot be reasonably taken as homogeneous. In this case, one must carefully specify and estimate the parameters of the demand functions for the products produced before one can examine whether the associated marginal revenue functions are horizontal.

Bresnahan [1981] attempted such an exercise for the U.S. Automobile industry in a cross-section study for 1977 and 1978. The basic simplification he used was to take products as being vertically differentiated. Consumers were modelled as differing in their valuation of product quality, and the demand for each product was built up from the demands of those consumers in its "quality segment" of the market. The cost side of the model was characterized by multiproduct production, and equilibrium was assumed (but not tested) to be Nash in prices. Using the first order conditions for equilibrium prices and quantities together with observed data on prices, quantities, and so on, enables one to infer the parameters of the unobserved cost and demand functions. Departures of prices from marginal costs can then be gauged by inspection (the statistical testing of this difference seems all but impossible given the complexity of the model). Bresnahan observed markups of the order of 10% over marginal cost, with higher markups observed for higher quality models, perhaps due to higher product bunching and more extensive foreign competition at the lower quality end of the product range.[13]

Since these exercises are rather data expensive, it is worth remarking that one can dispense with *precise* characterizations of equilibrium and the associated high demand for data. By inspecting these first order conditions, it is clear that the change in equilibrium prices and quantities induced by a perturbation of any of the exogenous variables will differ depending on pricing conduct (or, solution concept). It ought to be possible, then, to make some inferences about solution concepts by observing the responses of firms to outside shocks. Sumner [1981] (see also the comments of Bulow and Pfeiderer [1983]) and Just and Chern [1980] report interesting exercises of this variety, looking at the effects of taxes and technical changes respectively. However, it does seem to be exceedingly difficult to do more than observationally distinguish the responses of price takers from those of non-price takers without being very precise about characterizing equilibria, and this would seem to limit the appeal of this approach. Baker and Bresnahan [1985] have, however, developed a technique for assessing the change in market power (say, due to a merger) from pre-change data alone, without looking at post-change pricing conduct explicitly, and this

---

[13] This varying distortion of prices from marginal costs leads to some distortion of consumer purchases away from preferred models, and Bresnahan's estimates of this source of welfare loss suggests that it dominates conventional dead-weight loss, both of which sum to an aggregate loss of about 8% of industry revenues. It should be added that there are some doubts about the statistical significance of his loss estimates (deriving at least in part from the unsatisfactory estimates of the product quality scalar).

may turn out to be a data cheap way of predicting potential changes in monopoly power.

The importance of the work discussed thus far lies not so much in what it yields by way of conclusions on pricing conduct, but in the light it sheds on other, familiar empirical exercises. It is standard practice to use observed prices and quantities to make inferences about the parameters of costs (or production functions) and demand, and there seem to be no good grounds for believing that estimating these cost and demand parameters conditional on the assumption of price taking behaviour will yield unbiased estimates.

(ii) *Estimating Conjectural Variations*

In order to make progress and to develop a more detailed analysis of industry conduct, it is necessary to specify marginal revenue functions in a precise way. A natural way to parameterize various oligopoly solution concepts is by using conjectural variations—the expected change in rival's (or total industry) output consequent upon a change in the output of firm i.[14] Including these amongst the parameters to be estimated opens up the possibility of estimating and evaluating more precisely the departure of price from marginal cost (see Bresnahan [1982] on identifying conjectures). This is the focus of Iwata's paper [1974]. He generated extraneous estimates of cost and demand functions for the Japanese Flat Glass industry and then, using the first order conditions describing output choice together with observed prices and outputs, solved directly for the implied values of the conjectural variations. The sources of statistical uncertainty in the demand and cost functions were then used to develop confidence intervals around these calculated conjectural variations under various null hypotheses about their values. A very similar approach was taken by Cubbin [1975] in an examination of the U.K. Car industry, who used the equilibrium relation between price-cost margins and the elasticity of demand to make some inferences about changes in conduct over the period 1956–69 by (in effect) solving for the implied values of conjectural variations.[15]

The most elaborate exercise of this type is the study done by Gollop and Roberts [1979] on firms in the U.S. Coffee Roasting industry. They attempted to estimate a *pattern* of conjectural variations (together with production function parameters[16]) across rival firms i rather than either a single conjectural vari-

[14] It is often argued that conjectural variations are hard to interpret in the one shot games characteristic of static oligopoly theory, since the action-reaction sequence posited by such conjectures has no meaning (e.g. see Friedman [1983]). This is not a very compelling criticism of the work we are discussing here. Our lack of knowledge of solution concepts can, as a matter of econometric convenience, be parameterized as a lack of knowledge about conjectures. It is then natural to think of such conjectural variations parameters as *describing* the different equilibrium positions which may have generated the data, but not necessarily as *explaining* them in a theoretically satisfying manner.

[15] An alternative way to reach much the same goal is to try to estimate a "conjectural variation elasticity" (e.g. Dickson [1982], Geroski [1983], and Applebaum [1982]).

[16] Gollop and Roberts used an extraneous estimate of the elasticity of demand which is extraordinarily low and, in particular, rules out the possibility that pricing behaviour could be cooperative. It appears (footnote 15, p. 322) that their estimates of the values of the conjectural

ation parameter for firm i vis-à-vis all rivals, or a single summary number aggregated across all firms i. Since there are $N(N-1)$ such cross conjectural variations between i and j in an N firm industry, they imposed an *a priori* structure expressing the conjectures of all firms in terms of those of certain "benchmark firms", thus dramatically shrinking the set of parameters to be estimated. This procedure naturally enables one to consider asymmetric models of oligopoly, and Gollop and Roberts were able to reject Cournot and price-taking behaviour in favour of something reminiscent of Dominant Firm or Stackelberg models.[17]

The main difficulty with all of these studies is that the results are, in a sense, difficult to interpret, for the numbers estimated differ from those corresponding to the familiar solution concepts of oligopoly theory (e.g. zero conjectural variations correspond to Cournot and conjectural variations equal to minus unity correspond to price-taking behaviour). Clearly, it would be useful to estimate conjectures subject to the constraint that the estimates are interpretable in the light of familiar oligopoly models. The important point to grasp is the fact that different solution concepts place precise restrictions on the values of conjectural variations.[18] Thus, for each solution concept taken in turn, conjectural variations are not an unknown parameter to be estimated; rather, they can be expressed as a number or in terms of the fundamental underlying parameters of costs and demand, depending on the details of the particular oligopoly model under consideration.

A start has been made on this problem by Geroski [1982b] and M. Roberts [1983], using the Gollop and Roberts [1979] database. Both authors examine several solution concepts (including Price-Taking, Cournot, Stackelberg, Collusion, Dominant Firm, and Consistent Conjectures Models) and conclude that the Dominant Firm model best describes the data. There is some disagreement about the size of the Dominant Firm group in the two papers (the leading five or two firms respectively), and a puzzle about precisely how to explain the very high levels of concentration in this industry,[19] but there is no doubt that there

---

variations (though perhaps not their pattern) are rather sensitive to the precise value of the demand elasticity used.

[17] Slade [1984] and Anderson [1984] both push this type of exercise one step further, and try to explain the variations in conjectures across firms they observe by a variety of firm specific factors. Spiller and Favaro [1984] look at the effects of entry regulation on pricing conduct, in the process comparing a Stackelberg model to others somewhat in the manner of the studies discussed immediately below.

[18] This is easiest to see in the case of Cournot and price-taking behaviour where the conjectural variations are just numbers. In the case of the Stackelberg model, the followers are Cournot while the conjectural variations of the leader are equal to the slope of the follower's reaction function. Much the same is true in the Dominant Firm model, where the followers in this case are Price-Takers. Consistent Conjectures, to take a final example, are defined at an equilibrium where each firm correctly conjectures the slope of its rival's reaction functions.

[19] A basic problem applying to almost all the work discussed thus far is to explain the degree of concentration in the industries studied. The usual practice of assuming that all firms in the industry operate on a common production frontier implicitly assumes (in a homogeneous goods industry) that variations in factor prices and/or asymmetry in conjectures adequately explain the observed distribution of output across industry members.

are fairly strong grounds for believing that this oligopoly model is a superior description of the U.S. Coffee Roasting industry to most of the well known alternatives.

(iii) *Varying Conduct Models*

The studies that we have examined are useful for the positive and precise information that they yield about industry conduct. However, their value is clearly dependent on the stability of conduct patterns. To the extent that conduct is stable over time in industries, then the knowledge of conduct in some year t can be used to predict and evaluate industry performance in the future.[20] This observation, in turn, suggests that it is important to develop models which allow for systematic conduct change over time. The gain here comes not only from testing the proposition that conduct is stable, but also from developing models capable of explaining price wars, cartel formation, pricing behaviour over the business cycle, and so on.

Porter [1983b] provides one example of this type of work (see also the extension in Lee and Porter [1984], and Porter [1985]; Bresnahan [1981] is also interesting in this regard).[21] His model posits discrete shifts in industry conduct between cooperative and non-cooperative pricing regimes, the trigger shifting the industry into a "price war" being an unexpected drop in demand (see section II above). Applying his model to the Joint Executive Committee, a cartel controlling freight shipments from the East Coast of the U.S. at the end of the last century, he estimated demand and cost functions with a varying parameter indicating whether an industry wide conjectural variations term varied from price-taking values to something less than full collusive values.[22] He observed that cooperative periods were, in fact, characterized by Cournot prices (giving the cartel added 11% higher revenue in cooperative periods), that non-cooperative periods lasted about 10 weeks on average, and that two of the three "price wars" observed occurred following significant entry. Whether it was, in fact, demand which triggered the price wars (which were identified by using trade reports of the time which identified whether a war was occurring) is a little unclear since they did not appear to occur in periods of low demand. In any case, it does seem clear from his results that significant shifts in conduct occurred.

[20] Perhaps through the use of "industry-performance gradients" (e.g. Dansby and Willig [1979]; see the computations of M. Roberts [1983] for the U.S. Coffee Roasting industry), or the construction of "appropriate" indices of concentration (see Geroski [1983] for the U.S. Cigarette industry).

[21] By contrast, Geroski and Ulph [1984] parameterized the conduct of the oil producing nations in terms of "co-efficients of cooperation" (see Cyert and DeGroot [1973]) rather than conjectural variations. These were taken to shift in a continuous fashion depending on an assortment of factors, including past conduct, financial needs and capacity. Their model easily outperformed a "constant conduct" version in accounting for the 1973 and 1978 price "shocks".

[22] His model suggests that, because of uncertainty, cooperative prices will be below full joint profit maximizing levels, and he regards the evaluation of just how high they are to be part of the goals of estimation.

IV. NON-PRICE STRATEGIC COMPETITION

Textbook models of non-cooperative behaviour with homogeneous products give rise to a presumption of competitive outcomes when markets are "large enough" and economies of scale become negligible (Novshek and Sonnenschein [1980] and others) or when conduct is Nash in prices. However, this presumption does not survive the introduction of non-price competition (see Marris and Mueller [1980] who develop this theme). Non-price strategies weaken the impact of price competition by partially isolating any one firm's product from the effects of a price cut by other producers, and by providing a richer set of strategies for firms to consider. Further, in these more complex competitive processes, one is led to focus on issues and types of analyses rather different from those used in homogeneous goods industries.

(i) *Product Differentiation and the Localization of Competition*

From the viewpoint of oligopoly theory, the introduction of non-price competition (especially product or locational differentiation) substantially complicates the expectations that firms must form. In a homogeneous goods industry, it is only the *aggregate* response of rivals' outputs that matters to any particular firm; with differentiated goods, the firm not only has to weigh the likely price or output response of *individual* rivals, but also must consider how a change in the equilibrium set of prices or outputs will in turn affect the choice of advertising, production, location and so on. Indeed, non-price competition may so successfully blunt the impact of price competition that, at the level of price/output choice, firms can quite legitimately ignore the effect they have on other firms.[23] These effects, however, are somewhat mitigated if firms are only concerned with a relatively small number of (possibly "local") rivals.

Here one can usefully distinguish two approaches in the literature to modelling product differentiation. The first approach is that of *horizontally differentiated* goods. This arises when all goods offered at the same price are ranked differently by different consumers because they value the characteristics in these goods differently. An important further distinction here is between *symmetric* and *asymmetric preferences*. With asymmetric preferences (e.g. Phlips and Thisse [1982], Lancaster [1979], and others), there is an ordering of goods such that if a consumer has a strong preference for good i he will also have strong preference for goods close to i; with symmetric preferences (see Dixit and Stiglitz [1977], Perloff and Salop [1983], Sattinger [1983], and Hart [1983], amongst others), a consumer's preference for good i tells one nothing about his preference for goods $i+1$. All spatial models generate asymmetric preferences and, by analogy, one conjectures that as long as the number of characteristics is small relative to the number of goods, one is likely to have asymmetric preferences.

[23] This latter insight may be useful in rationalizing certain solution concepts such as Nash or Bertrand (Hart [1983]).

However, if one believes that the number of characteristics is very large compared to the number of goods, then symmetric preferences may be more plausible (Hart [1983]). With symmetric preferences, as the number of firms grows, the influence of any one firm on others diminishes and the appropriate equilibrium notion is monopolistic competition.[24] This corresponds roughly to the kind of presumption found in textbook stories. With asymmetric preferences, however, even if the number of firms becomes very large, each firm has a small number of close neighbours who are affected by the price it sets (Salop [1979b], Lancaster [1979], Stern [1972], Schmalensee [1978]). Competition is thus localized within the industry, and individual firms still face a downward sloping demand curve.

The second approach to modelling product differentiation can be found in the work of Shaked and Sutton on natural oligopolies ([1982], [1983a], [1983b]). Here the framework is that of *vertical product differentiation*: if all goods were offered at the same price, consumers would unanimously select only the "highest quality" good. In this case, all the characteristics of the different goods can be aggregated into a single "quality" index. Shaked and Sutton show that if the *variable* costs of production rise only slowly with quality then there is a limit on the number of firms that can exist irrespective of how product quality is chosen. Once this number of firms is reached, then no further reduction in fixed costs or expansion of the market could increase the number of firms in equilibrium, and hence these markets will remain "naturally oligopolistic". As with the asymmetric preferences case, the usual limiting arguments about competition will fail to apply. This, of course, eliminates the presumption that markets will reach a perfectly competitive equilibrium outcome.

(ii) *Sequential Competition, Pre-emption and First Mover Advantage*

Non-price competition not only blunts the effects of price-competition, but, also widens the set of weapons available to firms. At the very least, this means that decisions on price and non-price variables need to be taken simultaneously, recognizing the interaction they have on each other and recognizing the variety of responses rivals may make to price changes (Lambin *et al.* [1975]). But, there is a more important point. The weapons of non-price competition (choice of product, advertising, R&D level, capacity investment) often have the characteristic of involving sunk and irreversible investment, and this gives these weapons a powerful additional role to play as commitments that make threats against rivals credible (see Salop [1979a]; Dixit [1982] and Encaoua *et al.* [1984]). The area in which this effect has played a most prominent role is that of entry, where the weapons of non-price competition can be used as pre-emptive investments by incumbents to bias post-entry outcomes against en-

---

[24] Indeed, not only do cross price effects become negligiblé, but own price effects may become so large that equilibrium tends towards perfect competition; see Perloff and Salop [1983].

trants, and so enable incumbent monopolists to persist (Geroski and Jacquemin [1984]).

The simplest context in which to analyse the role of non-price competition in creating credible commitments is that of capacity (Spence [1977], Dixit [1980] and the extension by Ware [1984], Spence [1979], Eaton and Lipsey [1980] and [1981], and Salop [1979a]). A threat by incumbents to maintain high output in the face of entry (i.e. the "Sylos" postulate) is not a credible one, for output decisions are easily reversed. After entry occurs, it is generally more profitable for the incumbent to cut output and share the market than to maintain output at pre-entry levels, the potential entrant can calculate this, and so will not be rationally deterred by such empty threats. Such threatened actions by the incumbent to make entry unprofitable for the entrant often damage the incumbent as well and, to make it credible that the incumbent will carry out such actions post-entry, the incumbent will have to alter the nature of the post-entry game in a way that makes it profitable to carry out his threat (the classic reference on "self-crippling" strategies is Schelling [1960]). Such actions taken pre-entry to alter the payoffs in the post-entry game are called pre-commitments, and by the argument just advanced, they must be irreversible to be credible. The use of *capacity* as a threat is promising because once the incumbent has sunk his capital costs,[25] it is only the *variable* costs of production that are relevant to the incumbent. The entrant must incur both fixed and variable costs, and so suffers a disadvantage. Similar analyses can be carried out in which the variable chosen at the first stage is not capacity, but product specification. Assuming that there are *sunk* costs of product choice, then a strategy of carefully scattering products throughout the product space will leave no gaps for subsequent entrants to profitably exploit (Eaton and Lipsey [1978], Schmalensee [1978], Hay [1976], Prescott and Visscher [1977], Lane [1980]). One interesting consequence of this is that the clustering result of the original Hotelling [1929] spatial model does not appear in general (Eaton and Lipsey [1975] and [1976] and Shaked and Sutton [1982]).

A rather different type of first mover advantage emerges in the discussion of pre-emptive patenting as an entry barrier (Gilbert and Newbery [1982], [1984a] and [1984b], Reinganum [1981], [1983] and [1984], Lee and Wilde [1980], Loury [1979], Dasgupta and Stiglitz [1980] and, for a survey, Dasgupta [1984]). Here the notion is that an incumbent seeks to protect an existing monopolized market from the development of a close substitute product by a potential entrant. If the incumbent patents the substitute first, he will be able to maximize profit across both markets, whereas if the entrant develops it, the resulting equilibrium will be a duopoly. Since total profit across both products will be lower under duopoly than monopoly, the patent is worth more to the

---

[25] Much of the analysis assumes infinitely lived capital (see Eaton and Lipsey [1980] and [1981]). When investments are not sunk, markets may become contestable (see Baumol *et al.* [1982]), in which case monopolists can be completely disciplined by entry threats.

monopolist than the entrant, and so the incumbent will "outbid" the entrant, and pre-empt.[26] One rather special patent race occurs where firms seek a new process to produce an already existing product at the same cost. In this case, the incumbent has no interest in the patent *per se*, but he still wants to prevent the potential entrant winning the patent because that will erode his monopoly position. Obviously, the patent will be left "sleeping" by the incumbent if he develops it first. This case is discussed by Gilbert and Newbery [1982] and emphasized by Harris and Vickers [1985]. Harris and Vickers also introduce the notion that R&D may involve many stages of expenditure. If this is the case, then, in a perfect equilibrium, the incumbent may be able to gain a winning advantage very early in the race and force the entrant to retire. Note that, in the R&D context, one does not necessarily have to impose some first mover advantage on the game to observe pre-emption; the asymmetry that produces the result arises solely from the fact that a monopoly already exists and so the monopolist has more to lose if he does not gain the patent than just the cost of the R&D.

Two final points should be mentioned. Much of the discussion so far has been focussed on the context of the entry problem, in which some asymmetry between incumbent and entrant was assumed. Some work has been done on multi-stage strategic games without asymmetries—e.g. models of capacity choice by Kreps and Scheinkman [1983] and Dixon [1984]. They show that if all firms choose capacity at the first stage and in the second stage prices are set either in a competitive market (Dixon) or as a Bertrand equilibrium modified to take account of capacity restrictions (Kreps and Scheinkman), then the final outcome is identical to a one-stage Cournot equilibrium. This is a move towards trying the solution concept employed in the price setting game more closely to the outcome of the strategic competition. Work on symmetric models of strategic competition is more prevalent in the R&D literature (see Dasgupta [1982] for a survey). There the link between the market structure that prevails in the output stage of the model and the level of strategic competition is addressed directly (although no notion of causality is implied). Second, the notion of credibility employed in the above literature effectively assumes that there is perfect information—the entrant needs to know the characteristics of the incumbent so that it can compute rational behaviour by the incumbent in the post-entry game, while the incumbent needs to know the characteristics of the entrant to choose the level of entry-deterring precommitment. In the context of entry, the assumption of perfect information seems especially in-

---

[26] Reinganum [1983] shows that this asymmetry in favour of the incumbent can be eroded if there is some uncertainty in the R&D process. If there is some uncertainty about the date at which a given investment of R&D resources will yield results, then, by bidding a bit less, the incumbent only marginally reduces his chance of winning the patent, but extends the likely time before the product is patented, and hence lengthens the period over which his existing market earns monopoly profits. There is a rather confused debate about whether the original Gilbert-Newbery result also depended on first move advantage, but the fact that the problem can be viewed as a bidding game suggests that move order is not crucial (Reinganum [1984], Gilbert and Newbery [1984]).

appropriate,[27] but the problem is more pervasive than tha', and requires some fairly extensive modifications along the lines mentioned in section II above.

(iii) *Welfare Implications*

As is well known, with horizontally differentiated products, one has to consider not only the familiar welfare losses arising from suboptimal levels of production by oligopolistic firms, but also the question of whether the range of products provided is socially optimal. One of the important developments in the recent literature has been a careful treatment of the problem of optimal product variety, for which Spence [1976], Dixit and Stiglitz [1977], Lancaster [1975] and Meade [1974] are the seminal sources. What gives the issue bite is increasing returns to scale. If there were non-increasing returns, the first best solution would be to price each variety at marginal cost and produce every variety for which there was a positive demand at marginal cost. With increasing returns, it will pay to reduce the range of products offered in order to reap economies of scale on those that are produced. The first best can be achieved by price discrimination (Spence [1976], Phlips [1983]), since this will achieve both the right quantity setting rule (marginal price equals marginal cost) and the right product choice rule (produce all products with non-negative profits). This option is attractive if there are 100% profit taxes and lump sum handouts to deal with the surpluses. An alternative is to have marginal cost pricing (which achieves the right output rule), and some calculating by the government of consumer surpluses to decide which products to produce and hence subsidize. However, the design of lump sum taxes to finance these subsidies is a delicate matter (Brown and Heal [1979]). Obviously first best policies are not of much interest for the usual reasons, but only rather limited forms of constrained (or second best) analyses are available (for example, Dixit and Stiglitz [1977] examine optimal product variety under the constraint of average cost pricing). Usually authors compare the product variety selected by the market with that in a first best (or very simple second best) equilibrium. The interesting result is that there is no general conclusion about whether markets achieve too little or too much product variety. Again, textbook presumptions about the beneficial workings of free markets fail to carry through.

When goods are vertically differentiated, a rather different set of welfare issues arises, for there is now no intrinsic consumer benefit from variety (*ceteris paribus* all consumers would prefer to have the highest quality product).[28] If

---

[27] A discussion of what form credibility constraint should take in the absence of perfect information (together with an analysis of the resulting equilibria) can be found in Geroski, Ingham and Ulph [1984].
[28] One topic of some importance is the analysis (positive and normative) or markets where consumers are unsure of product quality (e.g. von Ungern-Sternberg and von Weizsäcker [1985], Grossman and Shapiro [1984], Ireland [1985], and Wolinsky [1983] [1984]). Once again, this calls for further development of models involving information acquisition and evaluation along the lines discussed above.

there are identical constant costs of producing each quality, only the best quality would be produced (compared with horizontal differentiation where *every* variety would be produced), and economies of scale only add to the argument for concentrating on one product. What gives rise to the need to produce different qualities is inequalities in the distribution of income and this introduces a wider set of welfare concerns.[29]

Finally, let us turn briefly to the welfare aspects of strategic competition. The issues are not unrelated to those just discussed in the debate on optimal product variety, and once again we would expect the results to be ambiguous. Two broad forces are at work. Unless perfect price discrimination is practised, the private gains from strategic investment will be below social gains and this will be a factor leading to too little investment. For example, if R&D can be easily imitated despite patents, then there will be no private incentives to innovate, though social gains may be large (e.g. Kamien and Schwartz [1982]). On the other hand, the value of strategic investment as a precommitment suggests that there will be overinvestment and a "dissipation of rents". In the R&D context, having more than one firm do R&D may create waste (Dasgupta [1984]). Waste can occur if one firm pre-empts but leaves the resulting patent "sleeping", and there may still be overinvestment in that all the profits of the potential entrant are eliminated in R&D expenditure. How these factors balance out in practice will be a matter of empirical investigation; Yarrow [1985] provides some orders of magnitude to suggest that conventional measures of welfare loss may be substantial underestimates.

P. A. GEROSKI AND A. ULPH,
Department of Economics,
The University,
Southampton SO9 5NH,
U.K.

and

L. PHLIPS,
CORE,
Université Catholique de Louvain,
34 Voie du Roman Pays,
1348 Louvain-la-Neuve,
Belgium.

---

[29] At first sight, it might appear that moves to equalize income distribution would work in the *same* direction as cost minimization by justifying only producing one quality of good. However, Beath and Ulph [1984] argue that if the cost of producing higher quality products rises quite slowly with quality (precisely the condition needed to generate natural oligopolies), then the indirect utility of income may not be concave (essentially because this may cause a sharp increase in the quality people choose as income rises). Then, even if one has a welfare function which has inequality aversion (except only extreme Rawlsian inequality aversion), it may be desirable to have an unequal distribution of income with low income households consuming low quality goods and high income families consuming high quality goods.

CHEATING IN A DUOPOLY SUPERGAME[1]

RAY REES

I. INTRODUCTION

THIS PAPER examines an approach to oligopoly theory, first proposed in a relatively neglected paper by George J. Stigler [1964]. Suppose that the firms in an oligopoly have achieved, tacitly or explicitly, a collusive agreement, and that open defection, in a sense to be made more precise below, does not pay. Given that the other firms observe the agreement, it pays any one of them to cheat, that is, to make secret price cuts to selected buyers in order to secure sales it may not otherwise have made. Stigler then sets out to define the likely extent of the gain a cheat can make without detection and to relate this to observable market parameters. This would allow prediction of the probable incidence of cheating in a market and hence of the effectiveness of the collusive agreement.

Stigler first argues that in a purely deterministic world, there could be no scope for cheating. Each firm's sales could be fully anticipated and any deviation from the expected level would be immediate evidence of cheating, which becomes, in effect, open defection. Implicit in this, of course, is the assumption that firms can observe each others' outputs at negligible cost—a reasonable assumption which will be maintained throughout the rest of this paper. If the world is not in fact deterministic, then scope for cheating may arise. Suppose that in each period any one buyer buys from any one seller with a probability between zero and one. Then, each seller's sales in each period are a random variable and it is possible that a seller may attribute to chance a well above average sales level which in fact was due to cheating. In deciding whether to accept this, the other sellers are involved in hypothesis testing and the critical level of this test will determine how far a cheat dare go.

Stigler's development of this idea in a formal model is open to a number of specific criticisms. McKinnon [1966] criticized the excessively simplistic decision-theoretic basis of Stigler's model. In deciding whether a rival has gained above average sales by cheating or simply by chance, a firm is assumed to use a standard significance test with conventional critical levels, the choice of which is entirely unexplained in the model. There is also an unnecessary separation of tests according to the precise source of the buyers won by cheating—previous customers of the cheat, other firms' customers or newly-

---

[1] Earlier versions of this paper have been presented at seminars at Exeter, Hull and Southampton Universities in the U.K., and at the Center for Mathematical Studies in Economics and Management Science, Northwestern University, Evanston, Illinois. I am grateful to participants in those seminars for many helpful comments, and in particular to Ray Deneckere, Peter Dolton, Paul Geroski, and Alistair Ulph. A referee made some especially helpful comments. I am also very grateful to Neil Manning for help in carrying out the simulations reported in section III of the paper.

entered buyers. To these criticisms, I would add the observation that Stigler's model is internally inconsistent. In calculating the gains from cheating, Stigler appears to assume that the cheat is able to control precisely the total number of buyers he receives so as to remain below the critical level at which the hypothesis of no cheating would be rejected. This explains the implication of Stigler's model that cheating is always profitable, and also the absence in the model of any specific analysis of retaliation to detected cheating, or of an enforcement mechanism. Consider, however, the following description of the market. At the collusive price, there is a given population of buyers with given probabilities of buying from each seller. A seller cheats by approaching some subset of these buyers and offering each of them, secretly and individually, a price cut if they will buy from him for sure. However, the cheating firm will also still receive, at random, some of the buyers to whom it does *not* offer secret price cuts and there is no guarantee that, given the level of cheating, the sum of the cheating sales and the sales made by chance will not exceed the critical level. Thus, a cheat can never be sure that he will get away with cheating, and the question of detection, retaliation and enforcement becomes a relevant one.[2]

Perhaps the main criticism of Stigler's model is, however, that it does not specify the equilibrium outcome in the market. Stigler is content to tabulate the gains from cheating as a function of market parameters with resulting behavior left implicit. But, what precisely will be the market outcome when each firm knows that there are gains to cheating, and knows the others know, etc? Does Stigler's basic insight, that randomness permits cheating, have interesting and well-defined implications for market equilibrium? This paper sets up a simple formal model to explore these questions, using the concept of a "supergame".

A supergame consists of an infinitely repeated "constituent game". In the following section, a constituent game is constructed which embodies Stigler's main ideas. It is shown that viewed in isolation, or in single-play terms, this game is uninteresting. It yields the conclusion that whenever cheating is profitable, the collusive agreement will collapse. This can be viewed as simply an illustration of the difficulty of rationalizing collusive behavior in a single-period oligopoly model—adherence to a collusive agreement which maximizes joint profits is not a best response for one firm to the strategy of adherence by the others. In the supergame, on the other hand, adherence to the collusive agreement can become an individually rational strategy and we find that Stigler's ideas (which clearly were formulated for a world of successive market periods) have some interesting implications.

[2] One could, of course, assume that the cheat could turn away random buyers if he is in danger of exceeding the critical level of sales (though actually it would be more profitable to turn away buyers to whom he has offered a secret price cut). In that case, the model analysed in this paper would not apply in its entirety—some other mechanism would have to be found for detecting cheating. However, if, as we assume, such rejection of would-be buyers can always be observed by the other firms, or is technically not possible, then our objection continues to hold. Moreover, it seems to be consistent with Stigler's approach to assume that the number of buyers each seller gets cannot be perfectly controlled, since, if it could, the collusive agreement could specify individual firms' outputs and no possibilities of cheating would then arise.

Specifically, we consider a model of a duopoly market in which the individual firms' demands, at the collusive price, are random variables. We suppose that one firm wishes to enforce the collusive agreement on the other by choosing a critical level of the other's sales which, if exceeded, will be taken as evidence of cheating and so will induce retaliatory price competition, so as to punish the "cheat". We find that where the number of buyers is reasonably large—at least 70—and for a reasonable range of per-period interest rates, an "enforcement equilibrium" exists in which the threat of retaliatory action is enough to induce the other firm never to cheat.

It is, of course, a rather one-sided approach to cast one firm in the role of the enforcer and the other in the role of the cheat. However, *given* that enforcement is effective and no cheating takes place, the analysis is symmetrical: each firm can be thought of, in turn, as the enforcer and the potential cheat. The analysis of the paper then defines a Nash equilibrium: one firm's best reply to choice of a particular critical level and the decision not to cheat by the other, is itself not to cheat and to adopt its own optimal critical level. Moreover, the expected cost to each firm—in terms of the expected value of the loss of profit from adopting the retaliatory pricing strategy—is very small. Thus, the enforcement equilibrium, implying a stable collusive agreement, seems to be a plausible market outcome. This is in contrast to Stigler's analysis, which seemed to suggest that cheating would be widespread.

II. THE CONSTITUENT GAME

Let $t = 0, 1, \ldots$ denote the time period, and at each t, the same game will be played. There are two firms, indexed $i, j = 1, 2, i \neq j$, with homogeneous outputs and equal, constant unit costs c. The market demand function $x(p)$, with $p = \min(p_1, p_2)$, is assumed to be both certain and constant over time. Each firm chooses a price. If $p_i = p_j$, then $q_i = 1/2$ is the probability that each buyer in the market at that price will buy from i, expressing the idea that buyers are indifferent between sellers. $p_i < p_j \Rightarrow q_i = 1$, so the firm with a lower price would capture the entire market. If x_{it} is firm i's sales at t, then when $p_i = p_j = p$ at t, x_{it} is a binomial variable, that is, $x_{it} \sim B(q_i x(p), q_i q_j x(p))$, although in this paper it will be assumed that market demand x is sufficiently large that x_{it} can be regarded as a normally distributed real variable on $[0, x]$. Let $f_i(x_{it}, x)$ denote the probability density function for x_{it}, when x is the total demand which will be allocated between the firms randomly.

Given this simple model, it is straightforward to define a number of equilibrium concepts for the constituent game. Since the model is essentially one of homogeneous, symmetric price-setting duopoly, it is well known that the Nash or non-competitive equilibrium in this model implies $p_i = p_j = p^c = c$, the marginal-cost pricing or perfectly competitive outcome. If, therefore, the game was played non-competitively, at any t expected profit of firm i is $\bar{\pi}_i^c \equiv (p^c - c) q_i x(p^c) = 0$. Note that this solution is the only equilibrium having the best-reply property in a single-play of the constituent game: given any $p_j \neq c$, the p_i which maximizes i's profit $\neq p_j$, but $p_i = c$ maximizes i's profit when $p_j = c, i, j = 1, 2, i \neq j$.

The *collusive equilibrium*, of course, looks much better for the firms. Since market demand is certain and constant, at each t, the joint-profit maximizing price p^* is the same. Then, when $p_i = p^*$, expected profits in each period are $\bar{\pi}_i^* \equiv (p^* - c)q_i x^* > 0, i = 1, 2$ with $x^* = x(p^*)$.

Open defection occurs when at some t, firm i chooses a price $p_i^D = p^* - \varepsilon, \varepsilon > 0$. Since, by assumption, j has set $p_j = p^*$ at this t, i will make "defection profits" of $\pi_i^D = (p_i^D - c)x(p^D) > \bar{\pi}_i^*$, with j's resulting profit $\pi_j^D = 0$. We have $\pi_i^D > \bar{\pi}_i^*$ because, since outputs are homogeneous, ε can be arbitrarily small, and the entire market output at $p^* - \varepsilon$ must yield more profit[3] than the expected output $q_i x^*$ at p^*.

We can now introduce the concept of a *balanced temptation equilibrium* (bte).[4] Suppose i were to defect openly at some t, and j retaliated by moving to the Cournot equilibrium $p_j = p^c$ from $t+1$ onward. Such open defection would not be worthwhile to i if, given the per period interest rate r, we have:

$$(1) \qquad \pi_i^D - \bar{\pi}_i^* \leq \frac{\bar{\pi}_i^*}{r}$$

since this implies that the single period profit gain from open defection, $\pi_i^D - \bar{\pi}_i^*$, is at least offset by the value at t of the loss of profit in each future period resulting from j's retaliation, $(\bar{\pi}_i^* - \bar{\pi}_i^c)/r = \bar{\pi}_i^*/r$. Then, define:

$$(2) \qquad r_i^0 \equiv \frac{\bar{\pi}_i^*}{\pi_i^D - \bar{\pi}_i^*}, \qquad i = 1, 2$$

and the set

$$(3) \qquad \mathcal{R} = \{r \in \mathbb{R}_+ \mid r \leq \min(r_1^0, r_2^0)\}$$

Assuming both firms face the same interest rate, a bte is said to exist when this interest rate $r \in \mathcal{R}$. Although each firm might be tempted to defect openly, it pays neither to do so. Of course, in any given market, the interest rate may be too high for a bte to exist—future losses are discounted sufficiently heavily that they do not offset the immediate gain from open defection. However, we can interpret Stigler's assumption that open defection is ruled out as implying that the market is in a bte.[5]

---

[3] More precisely, given continuity of the demand function, it is always possible to find small enough ε to make this statement true for $q_i = 1/2$.

[4] The concept was introduced by Friedman [1977], though the underlying idea can be found in Luce and Raiffa [1966].

[5] In fact, this assumption is not a terribly strong one in the present model. Since ε can be very small, we can take

$$r_i^0 = \frac{\bar{\pi}_i^*}{\pi_i^D - \bar{\pi}_i^*} \approx \frac{(p^* - c)q_i x^*}{(p^* - c)x^* - (p^* - c)q_i x^*} = \frac{q_i}{1 - q_i} = 1$$

Finally, then, we come to the *cheating constituent game*. We consider first i's choice of a cheating strategy *given that j* adheres to the agreement and that no detection-retaliation mechanism is in force. Let $s_{it} \in [0, x^*]$ denote the amount of sales i acquires at time t by making secret offers of price cuts to selected buyers. Then, his expected payoff at time t is:

$$(4) \quad \bar{P}_{it}(s_{it}) = (p_i^D - c)s_{it} + (p^* - c)\int_0^{x^* - s_{it}} x_{it} f_{it}(x_{it}, x^* - s_{it}) dx_{it}$$

$$= \bar{\pi}_i^* + \{(p_i^D - c) - q_i(p^* - c)\}s_{it}$$

Thus, i's expected payoff consists of the sure profit on cheating sales *plus* the expected profit on the remaining sales he will get by chance, $x_{it} \in [0, x^* - s_{it}]$. This exceeds $\bar{\pi}_i^*$ for $s_{it} > 0$ iff

$$(5) \quad \frac{p_i^D - c}{p^* - c} > q_i = 1/2$$

In fact, $\bar{P}_{it}$ is linear and increasing in s_{it} if condition (5) is satisfied. This condition has a nice intuitive meaning. To cheat is essentially to convert a possible sale with *expected* profit $q_i(p^* - c)$ into a sure sale with profit $(p_i^D - c)$, and this is profitable as long as the latter exceeds the former—not too large a discount must be given. Since in this model p_i^D can be arbitrarily close to p^*, we assume condition (5) is always satisfied.

It then follows that i's best reply to the choice $p_j = p^*$ in any t is to set $s_{it} = x^*$, since this maximizes i's expected payoff. Now of course, we must accept that each firm realizes this, and so would *not* regard itself as having the payoff function (4) in the cheating game, since this assumes the other is not cheating. But, in this case, we are back with the conclusion that the equilibrium of this single-play game is the Nash equilibrium in prices, $p_i = p_j = c$. To see this, suppose at any t, i expects j to set $s_j^0 \in [0, x^*]$ and to offer a price $p_{jt}^D = p^* - \varepsilon^0$, $\varepsilon^0 \geq 0$ on these sales. But then, i's best response is to set $s_{it} = x^*$ at a price $p_{it}^D = p^* - \varepsilon^1$ where $\varepsilon^1 > \varepsilon^0$. But then, j's best response is to set $s_{jt} = x^*$ and price $p_{jt}^D = p^* - \varepsilon^2$ where $\varepsilon^2 > \varepsilon^1$, and so on. Essentially, even though firms are cheating, we have a non-cooperative game with prices as the strategy variables, and so we must revert to the unique Nash price equilibrium of the constituent game. The difference is that output is $x^* < x^c$, but firms still earn zero profit. In the sense, therefore, that price and profits are the same with and without cheating, the analysis of cheating in the one-shot game is essentially uninteresting.[6] Its main purpose is to allow definition of the expected payoff function in (4), and to suggest the need for some kind of enforcement mechanism. But, since such a

---

[6] The only difference is that price competition, if "secret", does not expand the market beyond x^* and so, unlike the "open" game in prices, market output does not change throughout the process of adjustment to the Nash equilibrium. There is, however, something artificial in this. Since equilibrium profits in each case are the same, it is hard to see why *open* price competition would not break out, so that we are essentially back with the open constituent game, and cheating is neither here nor there.

mechanism is necessarily intertemporal, we need to consider it in the context of the supergame, to which we now turn.

III. CHEATING IN THE SUPERGAME

Given that the constituent game is to be repeated at each t, a strategy for player i in the supergame is now a set of functions $\{\sigma_{it}(H_t^i)\}$, where $\sigma_{it}(H_t^i)$ specifies a particular choice of action for i at time t, as a function of H_t^i, the information i possesses about the entire previous history of the game. In the present case, we would have for firm i

(6) $\quad H_t^i \equiv [\{(x_{10}, x_{20}), \ldots, (x_{1t-1}, x_{2t-1})\}, \{(p_{10}, p_{20}), \ldots, (p_{1t-1}, p_{2t-1})\},$

$$\{s_{i0}, \ldots, s_{it-1}\}]$$

that is, i knows the past sequence of outputs, open price choices, and his own level of cheating in each period. He would then choose p_{it} and s_{it} in the light of H_t^i.

It would be interesting to pursue the general analysis of these supergame strategies, but in the present paper, in line with Stigler's analysis, we adopt a simpler approach. We consider the situation from the point of view of one firm, say j, which wants to *enforce* the collusive equilibrium on the other. It does this by choosing a critical level of i's sales which, if exceeded, and given that it itself does not cheat, will trigger a retaliatory strategy which takes the form of setting price at the competitive level forever. More formally, firm j is considering an enforcement strategy of the form:

$$s_{jt} = 0, \quad t = 0, 1, \ldots$$

$$p_{jt-1} = p^* \text{ and } x_{it-1} \leq \hat{x}_{it-1} \Rightarrow p_{jt} = p^*, \quad t = 1, \ldots$$

$$p_{jt-1} = p^* \text{ and } x_{it-1} > \hat{x}_{it-1} \Rightarrow p_{jt} = p^c, \quad t = 1, \ldots$$

$$p_{jt-1} = p^c \Rightarrow p_{jt} = p^c, \quad t = 2, \ldots$$

Since $p_j = p_i = p^c$ is the Nash equilibrium of the constituent game, the kind of retaliatory strategy envisaged here is very similar to that underlying Friedman's balanced temptation equilibrium. The difference, apart from the fact that firms choose prices and not outputs, is that "defection" cannot now be observed with certainty, but must be inferred from the observed output of the "defector". Each firm is thought of as casting itself in the role of j as well as i. There is a possible inconsistency here, in that when j views himself as the "enforcer", he sets $s_{jt} = 0$, $\forall t$, and so the equilibrium choice of sequence of critical levels is based on the assumption that only i cheats. But then, if each firm's choice of critical levels implies that the other firm would find cheating profitable, these critical levels could not constitute an equilibrium—each "enforcer" is also a "cheat" and so could not rationally calculate its critical levels on the assumption that it does not cheat. However, in the model of this paper, we find that the simplification involved in the assumption that the enforcer does not cheat can be sustained: we find that when j chooses his optimal critical level, i sets $s_{it} = 0$, $i, j = 1, 2, i \neq j$. Thus, when each firm adopts its optimal critical level, neither firm would cheat, and each is justified in adopting a critical level which assumes it itself does not cheat. In other words, the critical levels we derive constitute a Nash equilibrium.

Figure 1 shows the structure of the supergame. We suppose firm i faces a given sequence of critical levels $\{\hat{x}_{i0}, \hat{x}_{i1}, \ldots\} \equiv \{\hat{x}_{it}\}_0^\infty$, with $p_{j0} = p^*$. At $t = 0$, firm i may choose $s_{i0} = 0$ or $s_{i0} > 0$—the precise positive value of s_{i0} does not matter at the moment. Following a move along an initial branch, chance "makes a move" at the nodes marked C_0 and C_0^1. Let

$$F_i(\hat{x}_{it}, s_{it}) \equiv \int_0^{\hat{x}_{it} - s_{it}} f_i(x_{it}, x^* - s_{it}) \, dx_{it}, \qquad t = 0, 1, \ldots, s_{it} \geq 0,$$

denote the probability that the sales i obtains at random at t do not exceed the level $\hat{x}_{it} - s_{it}$. This is also the probability that i's *total* sales at t do not exceed the critical level $\hat{x}_{it}$. Then, if $s_{i0} = 0$, chance's move at C_0 is to send i along the upper branch with probability $F_i(\hat{x}_{i0}, 0)$, and along the lower branch (dashed line) with probability $1 - F_i(\hat{x}_{i0}, 0)$. Alternatively, if $s_{i0} > 0$, at C_0^1 chance sends i along the upper branch (dashed line) with probability $F_i(\hat{x}_{i0}, s_{i0})$, and along the lower with probability $1 - F_i(\hat{x}_{i0}, s_{i0})$. Whatever the route by which i returns to the node marked $t = 1$, the future game looks exactly the same and, moreover, is identical to that which faced i at $t = 0$. This recursive form of the supergame will be exploited in what follows. If, at C_0 or C_0^1 chance sends i to $\mathcal{N}_0$, the game is, in a sense, over. At $t = 1$ and forever after, expected profits will be zero because the game enters the "retaliation phase", the Cournot–Nash equilibrium in prices. Essentially then, i's choice of s_{i0} determines the probability with which he will be faced with the same game at $t = 1$, or, more generally, choice of s_{it} determines the probability of repeating the game at $t + 1$.

We can use Figure 1 to define the value of the game to i at $t = 0, 1, \ldots$ as a function of any sequence $\{s_{it}\}_t^\infty$, given some sequence $\{\hat{x}_{it}\}_t^\infty$. Denote this value by $\bar{V}_{it}$. Then

(7) $\qquad \bar{V}_{it} = \bar{P}_i(s_{it}) + F_i(\hat{x}_{it}, s_{it}) \bar{V}_{it+1}(1 + r)^{-1}, \qquad t = 0, 1, \ldots,$

$$s_{it} \in [0, x^*]$$

where $\bar{P}_i(s_{it})$ is defined as in (4). By successive substitution, we have:

(8) $\qquad \bar{V}_{it} = \bar{P}_i(s_{it}) + \sum_{k=t+1}^{\infty} \frac{\bar{P}_i(s_{ik})}{(1+r)^{k-t}} \prod_{\tau=t}^{k-1} F_i(\hat{x}_{i\tau}, s_{i\tau}), \qquad t = 0, 1, \ldots,$

$$s_{it} \in [0, x^*]$$

We shall refer to (7) as the *recursive form* and to (8) as the *expanded form* of $\bar{V}_{it}$. Each $\bar{V}_{it}$ is bounded above since $r > 0$, $F_i(\hat{x}_{it}, s_{it}) \leq 1$, $\forall t$, and

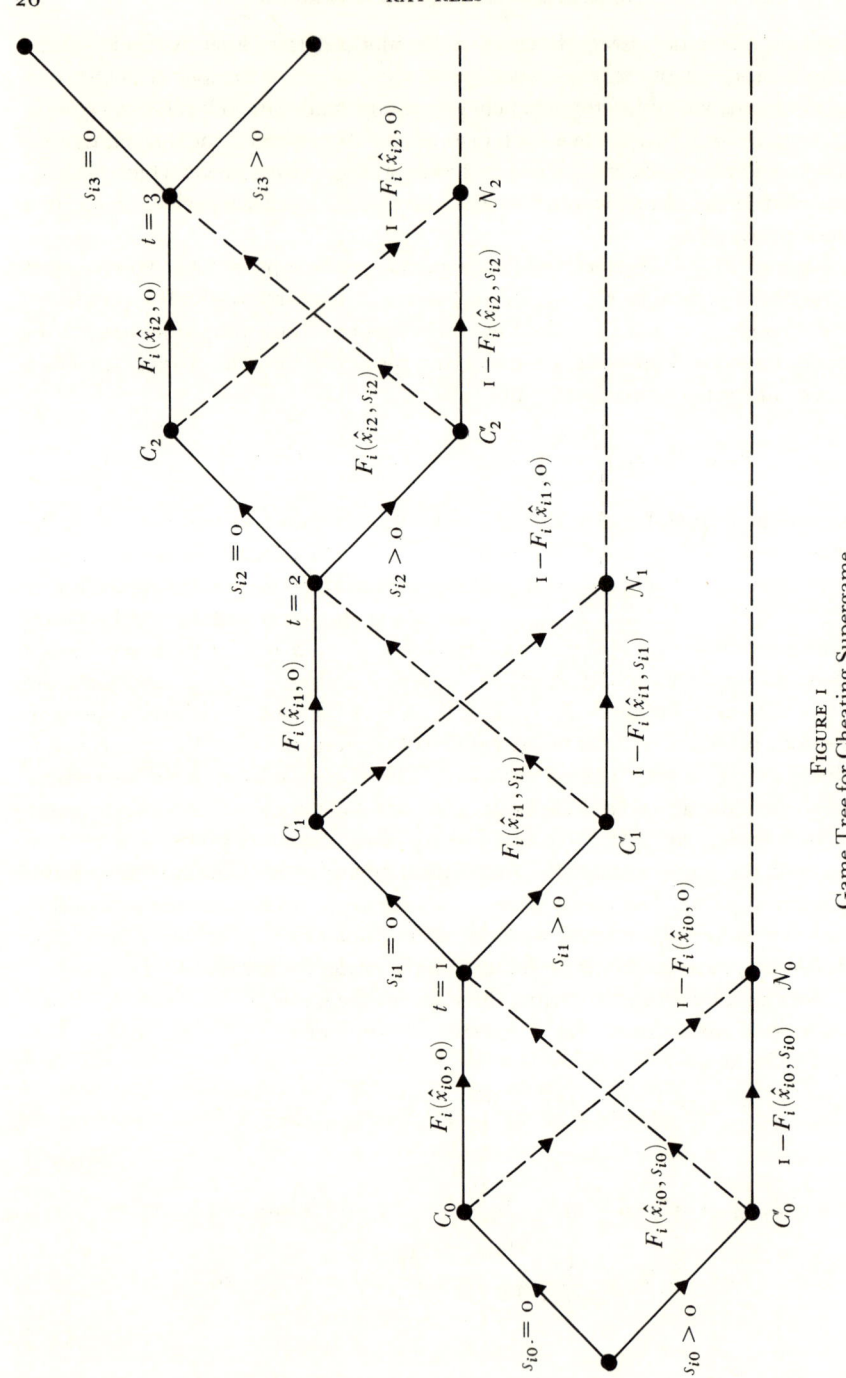

FIGURE 1
Game Tree for Cheating Supergame

$\bar{P}_{it}(s_{it}) \leqslant \bar{\pi}_i^* + \alpha_i x^*$, where $\alpha_i \equiv (p_i^D - c) - q_i(p^* - c)$. Each $\bar{V}_{it}$ is also bounded below since $\bar{P}_i(s_{it}) \geqslant \bar{\pi}_i^*$ and $F_i(\hat{x}_{it}, s_{it}) \geqslant 0$.

It seems reasonable to assume that for any sequence $\{\hat{x}_{it}\}_0^\infty$, i will choose $\{s_{it}\}_0^\infty$ in such a way as to maximize $\bar{V}_{i0}$. It can be shown by straightforward differentiation that over the relevant range, $\bar{V}_{i0}$ is strictly concave in each s_{it}, and so there is a unique sequence $\{s_{it}\}_0^\infty$ for each $\{\hat{x}_{it}\}_0^\infty$. Thus, denote

(9) $\quad \bar{V}_{i0}^* = \max_{\{s_{it}\}_0^\infty} \bar{V}_{i0} = \bar{V}_{i0}(\{s_{it}^*\}_0^\infty; \{\hat{x}_{it}\}_0^\infty)$

It follows from the fact that j knows the function $\bar{V}_{i0}$ that he can find $\{s_{it}^*\}_0^\infty$ for any $\{\hat{x}_{it}\}_0^\infty$, that is, he can predict exactly i's response to his own choice of sequence of critical levels. Thus, j's problem is not really one of "detecting" cheating, but rather of setting up an optimal incentive mechanism given the rule embodied in (9), which can be thought of as a form of *incentive constraint*.[7] The mechanism which is optimal for j is that which maximizes the value of the game to himself, subject to the incentive constraint. We can define this value at each t in recursive form as

(10) $\quad \bar{V}_{jt} = \bar{P}_j(s_{it}) + F_i(\hat{x}_{it}, s_{it})\bar{V}_{jt+1}, \qquad t = 0, 1, \ldots, \qquad s_{it} \in [0, x^*]$

where $\bar{P}_j(s_{it}) = \bar{\pi}_j^* - q_j(p^* - c)s_{it}$ is j's expected payoff at t when i cheats by $s_{it} \geqslant 0$, since $q_j(p^* - c)$ is j's expected profit on each unit i secured by cheating. The idea here is exactly that used in defining $\bar{V}_{it}$: choice by j of $\hat{x}_{it}$ and by i of s_{it} at any t determines the probability of facing exactly the same game at $t+1$, or of earning zero forever—essentially the end of the game. In expanded form, we have:

(11) $\quad \bar{V}_{jt} = \bar{P}_j(s_{it}) + \sum_{k=t+1}^{\infty} \frac{\bar{P}_j(s_{ik})}{(1+r)^k} \prod_{\tau=t}^{k-1} F_i(\hat{x}_{i\tau}, s_{i\tau}), \qquad t = 0, 1, \ldots,$
$$s_{it} \in [0, x^*]$$

The problem for j is then that of maximizing $\bar{V}_{j0}$ subject to the constraint that i will choose $\{s_{it}\}_0^\infty$ to maximize $\bar{V}_{i0}$ given any choice of $\{\hat{x}_{it}\}_0^\infty$ by j.

To simplify the analysis, we can make use of the recursive nature of the supergame. Let $\{\hat{x}_{it}^*\}_0^\infty$, $\{s_{it}^*\}_0^\infty$ denote the optimal solution sequences for j's problem. Then, the optimality principle of dynamic programming says that $\{\hat{x}_{it}^*\}_t^\infty$, $\{s_{it}^*\}_t^\infty$ must be optimal sequences for the supergame beginning at $t = 0, 1, \ldots$. Furthermore, if $\bar{V}_{it+1}^*$, $\bar{V}_{jt+1}^*$ denote these optimal values for the supergame beginning at $t+1$, then j's choice of $\hat{x}_{it}$ and (*implied*) s_{it} must solve the problem:

(12) $\quad \max_{\hat{x}_{it}, s_{it}} \bar{P}_j(s_{it}) + F_i(\hat{x}_{it}, s_{it})\bar{V}_{jt+1}^*(1+r)^{-1}$ subject to

$$\frac{\partial \bar{V}_{it}}{\partial s_{it}} = \alpha_i + \frac{\partial F_i}{\partial s_{it}}\bar{V}_{i1}^*(1+r)^{-1} \leqslant 0, \qquad s_{it}^* \geqslant 0, \qquad s_{it}^* \frac{\partial \bar{V}_{it}}{\partial s_{it}} = 0,$$
$$t = 0, 1, \ldots$$

---

[7] The problem is obviously very similar in structure to that studied in the literature on principal-agent problems. See, for example, Rees [1984].

where the constraint expresses the condition that s_{it} must maximize $\bar{V}_{it}$ for given $\hat{x}_{it}$.

We then immediately have the first proposition: sequences which are optimal solutions to (12) are in fact *constant* sequences $\{\hat{x}_i^*, \ldots\}$, $\{s_i^*, \ldots\}$. The reason is that since the supergames beginning at each t are all identical, they have the same optimal values $\bar{V}_{jt}^*$, $\bar{V}_{it}^*$. But that implies that the problem in (12) has exactly the same parameters at each t, and so must have the same solution at each t. Hence, the optimal solutions form constant sequences.

With the help of this proposition, the problem of characterizing the optimal solution to j's problem then becomes very straightforward. Since we know that the solutions are constant sequences, we can state the problem as that of finding values $\hat{x}_i$, s_i which solve the problem, expressed in the expanded form

$$(13) \quad \max_{\hat{x}_i, s_i} \bar{V}_{j0} = \bar{P}_j(s_i)\left[1 + \sum_{t=1}^{\infty}\left\{\frac{F_i(\hat{x}_i, s_i)}{1+r}\right\}^t\right] \text{ subject to}$$

$$s_i = \operatorname{argmax} \bar{V}_{i0} = P_i(s_i)\left[1 + \sum_{t=1}^{\infty}\left\{\frac{F_i(\hat{x}_i, s_i)}{1+r}\right\}^t\right], \quad s_i \in [0, x^*]$$

Since $[F_i(\hat{x}_i, s_i)]/(1+r) < 1$, the sums to infinity in (13) certainly converge and the terms in square brackets can be replaced by the term

$$(14) \quad \phi(\hat{x}_i, s_i) \equiv \left[1 - \frac{F_i(\hat{x}_i, s_i)}{1+r}\right]^{-1}$$

where ϕ can be thought of as a "risk-adjusted annuity factor". Hence, the optimal critical level $\hat{x}_i^*$ and associated cheating level s_i^* must maximize the Lagrangean function $L_j(\hat{x}_i, s_i, \lambda) = \bar{V}_{j0} - \lambda(\partial \bar{V}_{i0}/\partial s_i)$ subject to $s_i \geq 0$. These optimal values are therefore characterized by the conditions:

$$(15) \quad \frac{\partial L}{\partial s_i} = -q_i(p^* - c)\phi + \bar{P}_j\frac{\partial \phi}{\partial s_i} - \lambda^*\left\{2\alpha_i\frac{\partial \phi}{\partial s_i} + \bar{P}_i\frac{\partial^2 \phi_i}{\partial s_i^2}\right\} \leq 0, \quad s_i^* \geq 0$$

$$s_i^*\frac{\partial L}{\partial s_i} = 0$$

$$(16) \quad \frac{\partial L}{\partial \hat{x}_i} = \bar{P}_j\frac{\partial \phi}{\partial \hat{x}_i} - \lambda^*\left\{\alpha_i\frac{\partial \phi_i}{\partial \hat{x}_i} + P_i\frac{\partial^2 \phi_i}{\partial \hat{x}_i \partial s_i}\right\} = 0$$

$$(17) \quad \frac{\partial L}{\partial \lambda} = -\frac{\partial \bar{V}_{i0}}{\partial s_i} \geq 0, \quad \lambda^* \geq 0, \quad \lambda^*\frac{\partial \bar{V}_{i_0}}{\partial s_i} = 0$$

The main interest in examining these conditions is to ascertain whether $s_i^* > 0$, so that there would be positive cheating at the equilibrium. If this were the case, then the simplistic approach adopted so far is inadequate to analyse the equilibrium of the market, since firm $j = 1, 2$ could not determine its enforcement strategy on the assumption that $s_j = 0$ if it is in fact profitable for it to set $s_j > 0$, given firm i's optimal critical level. The conditions themselves, however, do not give a clear answer. It is straightforward, if tedious, to show that $\partial F_i/\partial s_i < 0$, and $\partial^2 F_i/\partial s_i^2 < 0$, from which we have that in (15), $\partial \phi_i/\partial s_i < 0$, and $\partial^2 \phi_i/\partial s_i^2 < 0$. Thus, we cannot conclude that in (15), $\partial L/\partial s_i < 0$ unambiguously—it will all depend on the relative magnitudes of all the terms in conditions (15) and (16). It does not appear possible to obtain clearcut conclusions analytically.

However, it is relatively straightforward to carry out simulations of the model, particularly given the assumption that $x^* > 70$, so the normal distribution can be used. The basic parameters of the model are x^*, the total market size, and r, the per-period interest rate. Since p_i^D can be arbitrarily close to p^*, we set $p_i^D = p^*$, the most favorable case to cheating. Combinations of cases were taken for the following parameter ranges:

$$x^* = 70, 100, 500, 1000$$

$$r = 0.05, 0.1, 0.2, 0.5$$

The range of interest rates in particular seems to encompass all reasonable possibilities, since the time-period considered in the model is unlikely to be longer than a year and could be as short as one week. The main results of the simulations[8] were then as follows:

(i) In *all* cases, $s_i^* = 0$, that is, the optimum for j involves choice of a critical level which makes no cheating optimal for i.
(ii) The critical level $\hat{x}_i^*$ lay between 2 and 3 standard deviations above $1/2x^*$, i's mean sales, with lower values for high r and low x^*.
(iii) In general, because the probability with which j would have to retaliate in any one period was very low, the expected cost of the enforcement mechanism—the difference between $\bar{V}_0^* \equiv \pi_j^* (1 + 1/r)$ and $\bar{V}_{j0}^*$, the expected present values of profits with and without the enforcement mechanism, with $s_i = s_j = 0$ in either case, was very small.

Figure 2 illustrates the typical results for a case which would tend to favor cheating, with high r and low x^* (resp. 0.5 and 70). In each part of the figure, the vertical axis shows the value of the game to one firm as a proportion of the value the game would have if there were no cheating *and* no enforcement. The upper figure shows that for given $\hat{x}_i$, $\bar{V}_{i0}$ is strictly concave in s_i. As $\hat{x}_i$ increases, the curve shifts down. The lower figure shows that the critical level is optimally set at about 2.2 standard deviations above the mean. The large majority of the other simulations had even higher critical values and higher value ratios. Thus, we conclude that in the model examined in this paper, deterrence of cheating is both cheap and fully effective, over a wide range of plausible parameter values.

Intuitively, the reason for the "no-cheating" result is that the normal distribution with $q_1 = 1/2$ has very nice properties: it is possible for the

---

[8] Copies of the Appendix setting out the simulation method and numerical results are available from the author.

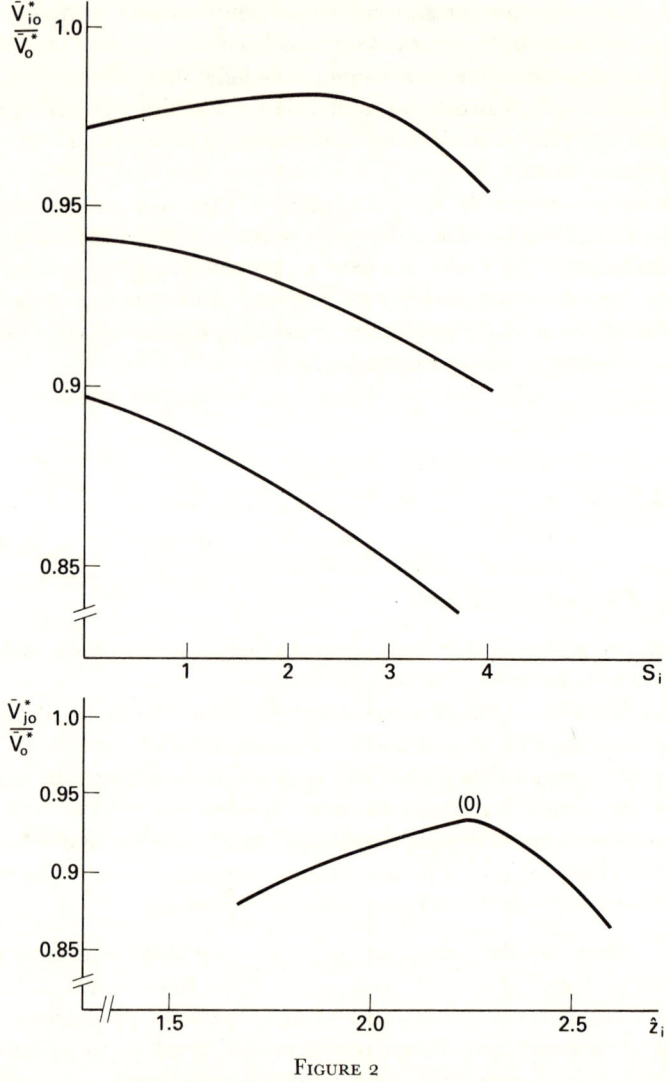

FIGURE 2
Gain from Cheating and Cost of Deterrence

enforcing firm to choose a critical level far out in the upper tail of the distribution, thus ensuring a very low probability that it will have to retaliate, but at the same time, just a little cheating so increases the probability that this retaliation will take place that the potential cheat finds it not worthwhile. Thus, the conclusion may fail to hold if the assumptions about the random process which generates firms' demands yielded a less nice distribution.

The picture of market equilibrium which emerges from this analysis is then the following: each firm adopts its optimal critical level $\hat{x}_i^*$, $i = 1, 2$, neither cheats and market price continues at p^* as long as one of the two mutually exclusive events $x_{it} > \hat{x}_i^*$, $i = 1, 2$, does *not* occur. The question then arises of the rationality, in a game-theoretic sense, of this "enforcement equilibrium". First, we have to assume that each firm communicates its choice of critical level to the other because if they had to learn these by experience, it would be too late. Then, each firm's choice of $s_i = 0$ is a best reply to the other's choice of critical level. Moreover, neither firm has an incentive to change its critical level in equilibrium because, given that the other firm would know of such a change, this would either induce cheating (if the critical level were raised) or deter cheating at higher expected cost (if the level were lowered). In either case, this reduces the value of the supergame to that firm, and so cannot be optimal. Thus, the enforcement equilibrium has the self-reinforcing "best-reply" property of a Nash equilibrium, provided communication of critical levels is permitted.

A less attractive aspect of the equilibrium is the very "grim" nature of the punishment strategy—moving to the competitive equilibrium forever. The choice of the competitive equilibrium is perfectly acceptable once we allow firms to choose prices, since this is the noncompetitive equilibrium of the constituent game. What seems objectionable is that punishment goes on forever. In fact, along the lines of a recent paper by Green and Porter [1984],[9] it would be possible to define retaliation in terms of a move to the competitive equilibrium for some finite time period. In the present model, this would reduce critical levels[10] and so increase the probability of observing competitive episodes in the market. Some preliminary simulations done for this case suggest that the basic conclusion of no cheating at the equilibrium, for the parameter values considered in this paper, continues to hold, with the duration of punishment as well as the critical level at which punishment is applied being jointly determined.[11]

IV. CONCLUSIONS

This paper takes a market in which there is symmetric, homogeneous price-setting duopoly with constant costs. The firms have reached an agreement to set

[9] The subject of Green and Porter's paper is closely related to this one, and, in a sense, that paper and this are dual to each other. Green and Porter consider two firms which choose outputs—unobservably to the other—the sum of which then determines market price *via* a stochastic market demand function. Retaliation to an observed market price below some critical level takes the form of a move to the Cournot output-equilibrium for some finite time-period. Though clearly inspired by Stigler's original paper, Green and Porter's analysis does not attempt to develop Stigler's analysis as closely as that of this paper.

[10] Note that compensation for a reduced-punishment period could not be provided by cutting price below the competitive level, thus inflicting negative rather than zero profits on the cheat, because zero production is always possible: the lowest profit either firm can inflict on the other is zero.

[11] On the other hand, some simulations with unequal probabilities q_i show that the no-cheating result ceases to hold when q_i is very small—around 0.1 and x^* is close to its lower limit of 60. There is an asymmetry, with firm j "allowing" i to cheat at the equilibrium, but i not allowing j to do so. Intuitively, this is because i is so small relative to j that it has a lot to gain from cheating and little to lose by retaliating, whereas for j, the converse applies. It is hoped to pursue the case of unequal probabilities in a further paper.

the joint-profit maximizing price and there is no incentive for open defection on the agreement. We then explore the implications of Stigler's original idea that randomness in individual firms' demands permits cheating, in the form of secret price cuts to selected buyers. To have any interest at all, the situation must be modelled as a supergame, in which each firm chooses a critical level of the other's sales, such that if this is exceeded at any time, the firm retaliates by setting price at the competitive level forever. It also chooses a level of cheating for itself in the light of the other's choice of critical level. In this model, detection of cheating as such is not a problem. Since each firm knows the other's profit function, it can predict what the other's profit-maximizing cheating level is in response to its own choice of critical level. The problem is to find the critical level which maximizes each firm's profit, given the level of cheating by the other firm induced by the critical level, that is, it is a problem in incentive design. The particular features of the supergame model are used to solve this problem in quite a simple way. The general analytical form of the solution does not appear to offer any clearcut conclusions. However, simulations over a very wide and reasonable set of parameter values show that, at the optimum, neither firm cheats, the critical levels adopted are far out on the upper tails of the respective output distributions, and the expected cost of enforcing the collusive agreement is very small. This simultaneous choice of critical level and zero cheating constitutes a Nash equilibrium in the supergame.

The results of this paper then suggest that, at least for the case where the number of buyers is large enough for each firm's sales to be normally distributed and each buyer is indifferent to which seller it buys from (that is, $q_i = 1/2$), a collusive agreement is easily enforced, with no cheating. This contrasts with the results of Stigler's original paper. On the other hand, although at any one time the probability of reversion to the competitive equilibrium is very small, in the long-run, as $t \to \infty$, it becomes virtually certain that this will take place. In this respect, it would be attractive to assume a *finite* period of retaliation, as in Green and Porter [1984], so that the market would be subject only to competitive episodes. But this, along with relaxation of some other assumptions in this paper, will have to be pursued elsewhere.

RAY REES,
Department of Economics,
University College,
P.O. Box 78,
Cardiff CF1 1XL,
U.K.

CARTEL BEHAVIOUR AND ADVERSE SELECTION

Kevin Roberts

I. INTRODUCTION

Cartels are central to any general theory of market structure. For, given the prevailing notion of rationality based upon self-interest, the rational behaviour of a group of firms should be to form together into a cartel and maximize joint profits or, more generally, act in a manner efficient to the group. If other forms of conduct, or market structures compatible with such conduct, are to be rationalizable then an exploration of why firms fail to act in this way is central.

Some constraints on firms can be imposed by a society's legal structure, broadly defined. If, as is common, collusive action by firms is deemed to be illegal, collusion may still occur but be hampered; for instance, side-payments made between firms to encourage members of a cartel to act in the group interest may be hard to disguise and in consequence may be ruled out. As well as these, what may be termed, external constraints, there are internal constraints which are part and parcel of a society's economic system. Here, one naturally thinks of the costs of communication which are often used as an argument against collusion. However, a more basic constraint is the informational structure of an economic system—in loose terms, what information about the economic system is known or can be found out by agents within the system. Assume that transfers of goods or income cannot take place between firms; then in a world of full information—all tastes, technologies and behaviour known to all—there is no need for direct communication between firms. Each firm can calculate what would be the result under costless communication and act accordingly; there is an incentive to do so because, as behaviour can be observed, firms can respond to any erring firm in exactly the same way as if there was direct communication. It is the lack of full information which makes communication between firms necessary or useful.

A lack of full information can take different forms and have different implications. For present purposes, it is desirable to distinguish between *moral hazard* and *adverse selection*. Moral hazard exists when the behaviour of other agents is less than perfectly observable whereas adverse selection arises when it is the preferences of other agents which are unobservable. Following the seminal work by Stigler [1964], the extensive literature on the problems of implementing rules for cartels has tended to equate lack of full information with moral hazard.[1] The classic example of moral hazard occurs when the demand for a firm's product is stochastic and other firms can observe only the level of demand

---

[1] See, for instance, McKinnon [1966], Osborne [1976], Scherer [1980, ch. 6], Porter [1983a] and Green and Porter [1984].

but not the price being charged. If there is a high demand for the firm's product then the other firms do not know whether the high demand is a stochastic "fluke" or the result of "secret" price-cutting. For this case, interest centres on the policing of cartel rules, i.e. to provide a disincentive to price-cutting, action must be taken against firms with high demand but, at the same time, it must be recognized that this will sometimes involve action when a firm is not erring. However, notice that as the preferences of firms are known under pure moral hazard, it is clear to all firms how much "cheating" will occur under any particular cartel rule and policing policy.

Unlike moral hazard, adverse selection has not been the subject of careful investigation in the cartel literature.[2] Both demand and cost considerations will affect a firm's preferences and a firm's information about its own demand and cost position is likely to be better, or at least different, to information possessed by other firms.[3] Thus, the reasonableness of assuming that adverse selection problems exist seems clear. However, it is the *implications* of assuming the existence of adverse selection that are relevant for judging whether it is an important feature of cartel problems. Its most basic implication can be uncovered by considering a situation without an adverse selection problem but, perhaps, where moral hazard exists. As all preferences are known to all, there is no need for direct communication for a cartel rule to be implemented—there is the initial problem of deciding what rule is to be followed but, even here, it is not completely untenable that firms can work out, in isolation, the rule that would be agreed upon if they were to meet together. This point was clearly made by Chamberlin [1929], now more than half a century ago. The implication of this is that with only moral hazard present, what can be achieved under explicit collusion by firms can also be achieved under "tacit" collusion with each firm acting in isolation and following some decentralized rule. In consequence, there has been little underpinning to arguments which suggest that tacit and explicit collusion will differ. The existence of moral hazard restricts the possibilities of what rules can be implemented but it is adverse selection which draws tacit and explicit collusion apart.

With moral hazard, the natural focus of attention is the incentive for a firm to "cheat" in the hope that its action will go undetected and, together with this, the form of cartel rules with respect to the detection and punishment of cheating, e.g. trigger strategies (see, for instance, Green and Porter [1984]). With adverse selection and no moral hazard, behaviour is observed without error so cheating, as such, has no role.[4] Instead, attention must focus on the

---

[2] Adverse selection problems are considered in Roberts [1983] and, though not labelled as such, in Simpson and Waterson [1984].

[3] The following example is considered in Roberts [1983]: By looking at a firm's published accounts, its level of costs may be observable to other firms. However, it may be impossible to disentangle marginal costs—the crucial parameter necessary to determine efficient behaviour—from this observation. The net result of this is that cartel rules tie the behaviour of firms to their level of total costs—under some conditions, mark-up pricing becomes the optimal response to the posited informational parsimony.

[4] Under pure adverse selection, there is still the problem that a firm may wish to break the cartel

fact that if the implementation of a cartel rule depends upon the use of information private to one firm, that firm must be given an incentive to correctly reveal the information.

To simplify the problems to be investigated, the consequences of adverse selection when moral hazard is *not* present will be examined. Roberts [1983] considered rules of tacit collusion under adverse selection, but explicit collusion gives a greater degree of freedom for the form of cartel rules. In particular, under explicit collusion, the cartel rule for one firm can be made sensitive to information provided by another firm. More generally, explicit collusion permits the transmission of information between firms and a lessening of the problems created by adverse selection.

The next two sections examine the implications of mutually determined behaviour and explicit information transmission. In both sections, side-payments are assumed to be ruled out by some external constraint but their potential role is considered in section 4.

II. INTERDEPENDENT BEHAVIOUR

Throughout, the problem of entry into an industry is avoided: it is assumed that there are a fixed number of firms producing goods which are substitutes for each other. For convenience, attention will concentrate on the two-firm case. Firm i is assumed to possess a profit function of the form

(1) $\quad \Pi_i = \Pi_i(q_1, q_2, \alpha_i)$

where q_1, q_2 are the outputs of firms 1 and 2 and α_i is a parameter known only to firm i—the other firm knows the functional form of the profit function and that α_i is drawn from some support A_i. However, the other firm has a Bayesian belief about α_i which is captured by a probability density function $f_i(\alpha_i)$ (with support A_i). The parameter α can affect the profit function in any way but two extreme cases of interest are

(2) $\quad$ I: $\quad \Pi_{q_j \alpha_i}$ is negligible if $i \neq j$, non-negligible if $i = j$

(3) $\quad$ II: $\quad \Pi_{q_j \alpha_i}$ is non-negligible if $i \neq j$, negligible if $i = j$

In case I, the unknown parameter relates solely to firm i's preferences with regard to its own output; for instance, this will be the case when α relates to the firm's cost structure. Case II is less plausible but captures the idea that only firm i knows how interdependent it is with the other firm. The example developed in section 3 is compatible with such an information structure.

The purpose of this section is to consider the usefulness of mutually

---

rule when, through the operation of the rule, it finds out information (about other firms) that it did not know when the rule was determined. To simplify the problems to be studied, it will be taken for granted that there exist credible punishment strategies which deter rule-breaking. Because there is no randomness, these strategies are never employed.

determined behaviour for a cartel. For this, asymmetric information of the type embodied in case I will be considered. It will also be assumed that α can take on only two values and that the profit function is of the form (where $Qd(Q)$ is assumed to be strictly concave in Q):

(4)
$$\Pi_1(q_1, q_2, \alpha) = q_1(d(q_1+q_2)+\alpha)$$
$$\Pi_2(q_1, q_2, \alpha) = q_2(d(q_1+q_2)+\alpha)$$

This corresponds to the classic Cournot case of a homogeneous good being produced under conditions of constant marginal cost, the marginal cost of a firm being in direct negative relation to α.

If interdependence is not admitted then a cartel rule for the two firms would take the form of specifying output as a function of own α. If interdependence is admitted, then a firm's output will be dependent on the α values of each firm. The simplest way of achieving this is to adopt a rule which specifies one firm's output as a function of own α and the other firm's output $(q_1(\alpha_1, q_2), q_2(\alpha_2, q_1))$. More generally, each firm can report a signal to a coordinating agency, the signal being dependent upon one's own α value, and the agency can then specify the output of each firm as a function of signals received. As specified, one can do no better than have the firms signal their α type so that it is rules of this form that will be investigated.[5] Notice, however, that recontracting is not permitted, i.e. a firm cannot change the α value reported on finding out what the other firm reported. This is closer in spirit to the situation considered in the next section.

There are two issues that need looking at. First, the above story of information transmission does not include a specification of incentives—as the α value of a firm is known only to that firm, it must have the incentive to reveal it truthfully. Second, there is the problem of objective for the cartel. With no asymmetric information problem, the two firms would face a standard co-operative bargaining problem which would be expected to entail a resolution that embodied efficiency and symmetry, e.g. the Nash bargaining solution which involves the maximization of the product of the gains of the agents as compared to some *status quo* position. What happens under asymmetric information?[6] To simplify the problem, assume that α can take on only two values, o or β, $\beta > 0$. Furthermore, if p_i is the prior probability, held by the other firm, that i is of type o, then assume that $p_i = p_j = p$—the two firms are in a symmetric position. By bargaining and attempting to secure particular outcomes, the firms may reveal more information about themselves. Transmission of information will be considered in the next section—for present purposes, assume that the stage has been reached where firms do not wish or have no credible way of transmitting more information.[7] Under symmetry, the cartel

---

[5] This is the so-called revelation principle.
[6] For an axiomatic extension of the Nash bargaining solution to asymmetric information situations, see Myerson [1984].
[7] The point here is that no more information is being transferred *before* the cartel rule is to be

rule decided upon by the two firms will be symmetric between the two firms and will specify four output levels—$q_{00}, q_{0\beta}, q_{\beta 0}, q_{\beta\beta}$—where the subscript denotes one's own type and the type of the other firm. Efficiency will have the implication that the bargaining resolution will occur at a position where the weighted sum of the expected profits for firms of each type, E_0 and E_β, is at a maximum. Thus, the rule will maximize (for some $y > 0$)

(5) $\quad E = \gamma p E_0 + (1-p) E_\beta$

where

(6) $\quad E_0 = pq_{00} d(2q_{00}) + (1-p) q_{0\beta} d(q_{0\beta} + q_{\beta 0})$

(7) $\quad E_\beta = pq_{\beta 0} [d(q_{0\beta} + q_{\beta 0}) + \beta] + (1-p) q_{\beta\beta} [d(2q_{\beta\beta}) + \beta]$

For the correct incentives to exist, a firm of each type cannot expect to gain by reporting itself to be a firm of the other type, this revelation occurring after the rule is determined. As the output of a firm produces an external diseconomy on the other firm, the rule used is likely to involve output being restricted, the level of restriction being higher for an o-type. Thus, the relevant incentive constraint will take the form that an o-type must not prefer to misreport itself as a β-type (it will be shown below that a β-type will never wish to misreport itself). This constraint is given by

(8) $\quad pq_{00} d(2q_{00}) + (1-p) q_{0\beta} d(q_{0\beta} + q_{\beta 0}) \geq pq_{\beta 0} d(q_{0\beta} + q_{\beta 0})$
$$+ (1-p) q_{\beta\beta} d(2q_{\beta\beta})$$

The chosen rule will maximize (5) subject to (8). With a multiplier $\lambda \geq 0$ for the constraint, first-order conditions are given by

(9) $\quad q_{00} \geq 0; \quad d(2q_{00}) + 2q_{00} d'(2q_{00}) \leq 0 \qquad$ (c.s.)

(10) $\quad q_{0\beta} \geq 0; \quad (1-p)(\gamma p + \lambda) [d(q_{0\beta} + q_{\beta 0}) + (q_{0\beta} + q_{\beta 0}) d'(q_{0\beta} + q_{\beta 0})]$
$$- [\lambda + (\gamma - 1) p (1-p)] q_{\beta 0} d'(q_{0\beta} + q_{\beta 0}) \leq 0 \qquad \text{(c.s.)}$$

(11) $\quad q_{\beta 0} \geq 0; \quad (1-p-\lambda) p [d(q_{0\beta} + q_{\beta 0}) + (q_{0\beta} + q_{\beta 0}) d'(q_{0\beta} + q_{\beta 0})]$
$$+ p(1-p)\beta + [\lambda + (\gamma - 1) p (1-p)] q_{0\beta} d'(q_{0\beta} + q_{\beta 0}) \leq 0 \qquad \text{(c.s.)}$$

(12) $\quad q_{\beta\beta} \geq 0; \quad (1-p-\lambda) [d(2q_{\beta\beta}) + 2q_{\beta\beta} d'(2q_{\beta\beta})] + (1-p) \beta \leq 0 \qquad$ (c.s.)

where (c.s.) denotes a complementary slackness relationship.

Unsurprisingly, the rule depends upon the weight in the maximand γ. If γ is very different from unity then the rule is biased in favour of one particular type of firm and it is unlikely that firms reaching such a bargaining outcome would not convey more information to the other firm about their type. Consider, first, the case where the incentive constraint fails to bite ($\lambda = 0$). Equations (9)–(12)

---

determined. After the cartel rule is determined, the incentives for revelation change and revelation will be a feature of the operation of the rule.

then solve to give

$$(13) \quad \begin{cases} q_{oo} = \dfrac{q_0^m}{2}, \quad q_{\beta\beta} = \dfrac{q_\beta^m}{2} \\ \gamma < 1 + \dfrac{\beta}{d(q_\beta^m)} \to q_{o\beta} = 0 \quad \text{and} \quad q_{\beta o} = q_\beta^m \end{cases}$$

where q^m is the monopolistic output that would be produced by a firm if it had sole control of the market (notice that the complementary slackness relationships in (10) and (11) are important for deriving (13)).[8] (13) shows very clearly the desirability of coordination of firms. If the objective is not biased too much in favour of o-type firms, it is desirable for production to take place by the most efficient firm so that a signal of high efficiency leads to permission to produce a higher output with the output of the other firm being cut back.

In a second-best situation where the incentive constraint bites, the solution is not so simple. Manipulation of (9)–(12) gives

(14a) $\quad q_{oo} = \dfrac{q_0^m}{2}$

(14b) $\quad q_0^m \leq q_{o\beta} + q_{\beta o} \leq 2q_{\beta\beta}$

(14c) $\quad q_{\beta\beta} \geq \dfrac{q_\beta^m}{2}$

and using this information in (8) for the case where the constraint bites gives

(14d) $\quad q_{o\beta} \leq q_{\beta o}$

Before going further, it can now be seen why the incentive constraint that a β-type firm must have no incentive to say that it is an o-type firm can be ignored in the optimization exercise. When $\lambda = 0$ and (13) holds, this incentive constraint is obviously satisfied and when λ is positive and (8) bites, $q_{\beta o} \geq q_{oo}$, $q_{\beta\beta} \geq q_{o\beta}$ and equality in (8) again ensures satisfaction of the constraint. Thus it can be ignored.

Turning to the second-best solution (14), (14a) is a standard feature of incentive problems—if both firms are willing to say that they have the low productivity then the first-best solution is implemented. Given the form of the incentive constraint, (14b) and (14c) are natural responses though it is somewhat surprising that such clear-cut results are possible. The second-best solution preserves the feature that if a firm chooses to say it is efficient (a β-type rather than an o-type) then it is permitted to produce a higher output. However, to induce the correct incentives, it is necessary to counteract the effect in the first-best outcome which leads to a reduction in the other firm's output if efficiency is reported. The second-best solution will usually involve a strictly

---

[8] If γ exceeds $1 + \beta/d(q_\beta^m)$ then the rule is sufficiently biased in favour of o-type firms for $q_{o\beta}$ to be positive and, for γ large enough, $q_{o\beta}$ will equal q_0^m and $q_{\beta o}$ will be zero.

positive $q_{0\beta}$ and a $q_{\beta 0}$ which is reduced relative to $q_{\beta\beta}$ as compared with the first-best. Thus there are two, partially offsetting, arguments for why a central coordinating agency is useful: (1) efficiency considerations suggest the desirability of a coordinated policy with the output of the other firm dropping when it is desirable to produce a higher output; (2) coordination itself acts as an incentive device and a firm can be discouraged from misreporting by ensuring that the output of the other firm rises if the firm makes a report which allows it to produce a higher output.

Finally, it is worth considering when the first-best solution is achievable. Putting (13) into (8), gives

$$(15) \quad \left(\frac{p}{p+1}\right) q_0^m d(q_0^m) \geq q_\beta^m d(q_\beta^m)$$

so that, as q_0^m maximizes $qd(q)$, (15) is satisfied when β exceeds a critical β^* (q_m^β is an increasing function of β). Thus, the incentive constraint fails to bite when the two types are sufficiently different and q_β^m is "too high" an output for a type-0 firm to wish to produce.

III. EXPLICIT INFORMATION TRANSMISSION

In the last section it was mentioned that in a cooperative bargaining set-up, the cartel rule that a group of firms would decide upon could change as a result of information about others being gleaned from the operation of the cartel rule. Knowing that this will happen affects the incentive to report or misreport information.

With evolution, one is interested in the final rule that will be implemented and this will depend upon the reporting behaviour of firms. In the last section, the form of the final rule was examined, taking for granted the uncertainty that firms possessed about each other. Here, attention will be directed to the process of movement towards a final rule. Given that the final rule to be used is not decided upon at the outset, firms now have an incentive to pretend that they are of a type with strong bargaining power. When recontracting takes place concerning the rule to be used, firms can hope that a rule will be chosen which is biased in their favour.

The bargaining power of a firm will depend upon the effect that the firm can have on other firms and the effect that other firms can have on it. In terms of private information, it is the effect that other firms can have on a particular firm which is likely to be private to that firm. This corresponds to the case II which was considered at the beginning of the last section.

As in the last section, assume that there are only two firms and that a firm can be of only two types—a dependent type (d) or an independent type (i). The profit function of an i-type is independent of the other firm's output and q^i is the profit-maximizing output for such a firm. For convenience, assume that only one other output, q^d, can be produced. A d-type firm has a profit function which depends upon both firms' outputs. Let Π_{di} be profit if it produces q^d and the other firm produces q^i. Let Π_{dd}, Π_{id}, and Π_{ii} be defined in a similar way. These profits are assumed to be of the form so that two d-type firms are in the classic "prisoners' dilemma" position:

(16) $\quad \Pi_{id} > \Pi_{dd} > \Pi_{ii} > \Pi_{di}$

As a repeated situation will be looked at, it is also convenient to assume that

(17) $\quad \Pi_{id} + \Pi_{di} \leq 2\Pi_{dd}$

This ensures that a cooperative correlated policy which moves between id and di does not dominate dd.

Given the output of the other firm, a dependent firm would prefer to produce q^i—the output chosen by an independent firm. However, with two dependent firms, a situation where both firms produce q^d is superior to one where they both produce q^i.

Each firm has to choose what output to produce in each period. This will convey information to the other firm about the likely type of the firm in question. An i-type firm will profit maximize by always producing q^i so this can be assumed to be its strategy. A d-type firm would like to produce q^i but, if it thinks that its opponent is a d-type, it may wish to encourage a situation which allows the cooperative solution to arise where both firms produce q^d.

At date t, let $P_t^1(P_t^2)$ be the prior probability held by firm 2 (1) that firm 1 (2) is of type i. A firm of type d must choose a probability p_t with which to produce output q^i. Given that this probability can be inferred by the other firm, its prior can be updated:

(18) $\quad P_{t+1}^1 = \begin{cases} 0 & \text{if } q^d \text{ produced at } t \\ \dfrac{P_t^1}{P_t^1 + p_t^1(1 - P_t^1)} & \text{otherwise} \end{cases}$

What strategy should a d-type firm follow? If it has revealed itself to be of a d-type by choosing q^d then it does not wish to allow a situation where it produces q^d and the other firm produces q^i to continue. The most appealing strategy for a d-type takes the form:

(i) if q^i chosen in the past and other firm has always chosen q^i, choose q^i with probability p_t;
(ii) if q^i chosen in the past and other firm has just chosen q^d, choose q^i with probability 0;
(iii) if q^d chosen at $r < t-1$ and other firm has chosen q^i after r, choose q^i with probability 1;
(iv) if q^d chosen at r and other firm has chosen q^d at every date after r, choose q^i with probability 0.

Thus, if a firm has not revealed itself to be a d-type, it follows some mixed strategy; if it has revealed itself then it gives the other firm one chance to allow itself to be a d-type before it reverts to q^i forever. This strategy for each firm will be a perfect equilibrium if a d-type firm finds it optimal to respond to the other firm announcing that it is a d-type by declaring itself to be a d-type.[9] Thus, if δ is the firm's discount factor, equilibrium requires

$$(19) \quad \Pi_{dd} + \frac{\delta}{1-\delta}\Pi_{dd} \geq \Pi_{id} + \frac{\delta}{1-\delta}\Pi_{ii}$$

which is the standard condition for the cooperative solution to be achievable in an infinitely repeated prisoners' dilemma problem. If both firms are of type d then, once one firm has revealed itself, the strategy produces an efficient outcome from then on for the two firms.

The probability p_t has still to be determined. The expected discounted profit for firm 1 of type d at time t, given that both firms have yet to reveal themselves, is given by

$$(20) \quad {}^iV_t^1 = (1-P_t^2)(1-p_t^2)\left[\Pi_{id} + \frac{\delta}{(1-\delta)}\Pi_{dd}\right] + (1-(1-P_t^2)(1-p_t^2))[\Pi_{ii} + \delta V_{t+1}^1]$$

if q^i is chosen and

$$(21) \quad {}^dV_t^1 = (1-P_t^2)p_t^2\left[\Pi_{di} + \frac{\delta}{(1-\delta)}\Pi_{dd}\right] + (1-P_t^2)(1-p_t^2) \times \left[\Pi_{dd} + \frac{\delta}{(1-\delta)}\Pi_{dd}\right] + P_t^2\left[\Pi_{di} + \delta\Pi_{di} + \frac{\delta^2}{(1-\delta)}\Pi_{ii}\right]$$

if q^d is chosen. V_{t+1}^1 is the expected discounted profit at $t+1$, given that an optimal policy is followed from then on. Thus

$$(22) \quad V_t^1 = p_t^1 \, {}^iV_t^1 + (1-p_t^1) \, {}^dV_t^1$$

and optimizing behaviour implies that

$$(23) \quad \begin{cases} {}^iV_t^1 > {}^dV_t^1 \Rightarrow p_t^1 = 1 \\ {}^dV_t^1 > {}^iV_t^1 \Rightarrow p_t^1 = 0 \end{cases}$$

In the non-degenerate case where p lies between zero and unity for both firms, p_t^1 and p_t^2 can be derived from the two equations

$$(24) \quad \begin{cases} {}^iV_t^1 = {}^dV_t^1 \\ {}^iV_t^2 = {}^dV_t^2 \end{cases}$$

As (20) is a difference equation, the solution to (24) will be a difference equation.

---

[9] As is common in infinitely repeated games, there are many perfect equilibria of which this is only one. Kreps et al. [1982] examine a perfect equilibrium in a repeated prisoners' dilemma game with a different type of incomplete information; there, agents with non "prisoners' dilemma" preferences have preferences biased in favour of cooperation.

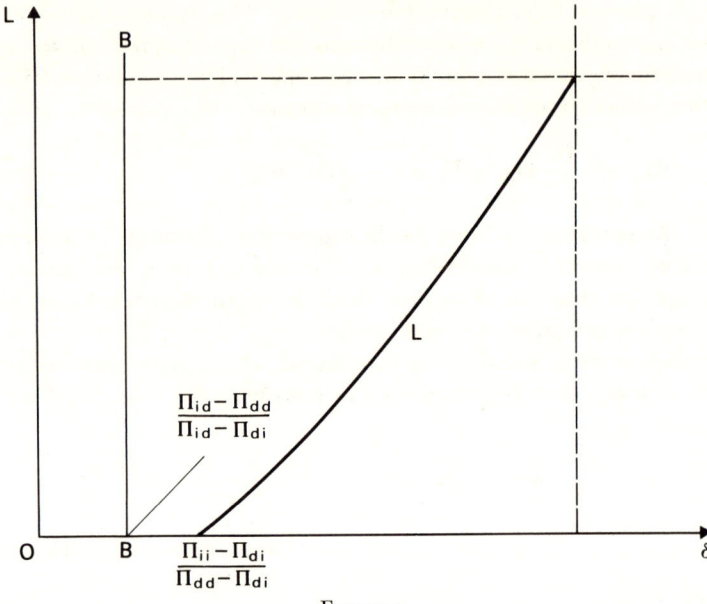

FIGURE 1

The information transfer will be complete if a firm's type is eventually known with probability one. This will be the case if P_t rises to unity so that a firm who never reveals itself is, in probabilistic terms, certain to be an i-type. The question to ask is what states of the system (P_1, P_2) have the feature that $p_1 = p_2 = 1$ so that (P_1, P_2) is not updated and no further information is transferred? If this steady state is reached, $V_{t+1} = {}^iV_t$, and (20), (21), (23) imply

$$(25) \quad P \geqslant \frac{\frac{\delta}{1-\delta}[\Pi_{dd} - \Pi_{ii}] - [\Pi_{ii} - \Pi_{di}]}{\frac{\delta^2}{1-\delta}[\Pi_{dd} - \Pi_{di}] + \delta[\Pi_{ii} - \Pi_{di}]} = L$$

where each term in square brackets is positive (from (16)). With $\delta < 1$, (25) can be satisfied with $P < 1$ so that information is not always transferred in the limit. Figure 1 shows L as a function of δ. If the discount factor δ lies below $\Pi_{ii} - \Pi_{di}/\Pi_{dd} - \Pi_{di}$ then whatever the level of initial beliefs held by the two firms, neither will ever reveal itself to be a d-type firm. The line B is defined by (19) so that collusion cannot be sustained at lower values of δ. As shown, it is possible for δ to be high enough for collusion to be sustained but too low for information transfer, which would engender profitable collusion, to take place. Whatever the value of δ below unity, if both firms have the belief that it is very likely that the other firm is of type i then, again, no information transfer will take place.

In this model, the cost to a firm of revealing itself to be a d-type is a loss of profit for two periods. However, if a d-type is in a poor bargaining position because of its dependence on the other firm, the model could be easily amended to allow for the fact that a firm may suffer permanently from revelation. If a d-type firm gains from being thought an i-type after the other firm has revealed itself, revelation only occurs in the model because both firms can gain if they both reveal themselves to be d-types at the same time. The strategy probabilities p for both firms will either be low or unity—after some time, the probabilities "jump" to unity and no revelation can occur thereafter.[10]

What is interesting about this story is that though it is useful to have information transfer when asymmetric information is present, the incentive structure may be such that full revelation never occurs. What is suggested is that firms have an incentive to present themselves in a way so that they appear to have a strong bargaining position and as one of the most obvious ways of being in a strong bargaining position is to be unaffected by other firms' actions, collusive equilibria will, in probabilistic terms, be shifted towards what would happen under limited interdependence in a world of full information. These inefficient equilibria are cooperative equilibria but have features of non-cooperative equilibria; for instance, if other firms can observe the local behaviour of the own demand curve that a firm faces—other firms' outputs being held constant—then to convince these other firms of its independence from them, a Cournot strategy becomes optimal.[11] Thus, non-cooperative equilibria can be viewed as "poor" cooperative equilibria that arise when information fails to be transferred between firms.

IV. SIDE-PAYMENTS

Thus far, it has been assumed that side-payments between firms cannot be made. The most obvious role that they have is to increase the set of opportunities available to a group of firms. The sharing out of benefits can be divorced from production decisions so that, in a world of full information, an efficient co-operative bargaining solution will always involve the maximization of joint profits together with a sharing rule dependent upon the exact form of the bargaining solution. But in a world of asymmetric information, side-payments also have the role of an incentive device—if the share out depends upon what a firm reports then incentives for misrepresentation are affected by the share out.

To see how side-payments can be used as an incentive device, consider again the model of section 2. Side payments which do not favour one of the firms in an arbitrary way will affect the objective only through the effect on incentives. In the model assume that the coordinating agency tries to implement the

[10] Other equilibria are also possible. For instance, revelation may only occur at odd dates but not at even dates.

[11] The form that the equilibrium takes depends on what other firms observe. If other firms observe the slope of the demand curve with other prices constant then independence is exhibited by adopting Bertrand strategies.

first-best rule given by (13) and specifies a transfer t to be paid by a firm announcing itself to be a β-type if the other firm announces itself to be an o-type. Putting down the appropriate incentive constraints, a firm will always wish to reveal itself correctly (whatever the other firm announces)[12] if

(26)
$$\begin{cases} \dfrac{q_0^m}{2} d(q_0^m) \geqslant q_\beta^m d(q_\beta^m) - t \\[6pt] t \geqslant \dfrac{q_\beta^m}{2} d(q_\beta^m) \\[6pt] q_\beta^m d(q_\beta^m) + \beta q_\beta^m - t \geqslant \dfrac{q_0^m}{2} d(q_0^m) + \beta \dfrac{q_0^m}{2} \\[6pt] \dfrac{q_\beta^m}{2} d(q_\beta^m) + \dfrac{\beta q_\beta^m}{2} \geqslant t \end{cases}$$

As q_0^m and q_β^m are the profit-maximizing outputs for monopolistic firms of types o and β respectively, it is clear that (26) is satisfied by

(27) $\qquad t = \dfrac{q_\beta^m}{2} d(q_\beta^m)$

The present problem is very similar to an auction scheme. Attainment of the first-best requires that production should be undertaken by the most efficient firm and this can be ensured by allowing the firms to bid for the right to produce. (27) is the amount an o-type firm would be willing to bid to be allowed to produce when the other firm is of type β. Thus with such a transfer, the coordinating agency is similar in operation to a second price auction where the highest bidder wins but only pays the second highest price. As is well known (Vickrey [1961]), this auction mechanism has the property that truthful revelation is the dominant strategy so it is unsurprising that (27) ensures satisfaction of (26).

When a firm is called upon to report its type before it can observe what the other firm reports, and no recontracting is possible—the set-up of section 2—it is clear that by making side-payments sensitive to what a firm reports, one could hope to be able to provide appropriate incentives without requiring the cartel rule implemented by the coordinating agency to be used as an incentive device.[13] But when bargaining can take place after a firm has obtained information about another firm, the usefulness of side-payments is less certain. The problem here is that side-payments are within the domain of what is bargained over and can no longer be specifically formulated to cope with the problem of incentives. To take the example of the last section, in the steady state

---

[12] Truth will be, in this case, a dominant strategy.
[13] For a general analysis of the implementation of rules when agents have beliefs about the preferences of other agents and side-payments are possible, see d'Aspremont and Gerard-Varet [1979].

with no further revelation of information, side-payments will be determined through a bargaining process that takes place between firms uncertain of the type to which the other firm belongs. The side-payment will depend upon the state of the system (P^1, P^2) and though the firms may decide upon a particular side-payment to induce more information transmission, they may not be able to commit themselves to a particular side-payment structure in the future as this will be the outcome of the negotiation process at that time—side-payments can be used to enlarge the set of opportunities available under the bargaining process but there may be little role for side-payments as an incentive device.

KEVIN ROBERTS
Department of Economics,
University of Warwick,
Coventry CV4 7AL,
U.K.

ON THE INCIDENCE AND DURATION OF PRICE WARS*

Robert H. Porter

I. INTRODUCTION

THE PURPOSE of this paper is to test some theoretical predictions about the incidence and duration of price wars, when these price wars are viewed as an enforcement device to maintain a cooperative or tacitly collusive agreement in an uncertain environment. The theoretical model of Green and Porter [1984] and Porter [1983a] predicts that price wars should be triggered by unanticipated demand fluctuations, and that they will be more frequent the greater the number of firms in the industry, or the greater the degree of market concentration. Correspondingly, the optimal duration of price wars is also affected by the number of firms.

The tests employ weekly time series data on the Joint Executive Committee railroad cartel (henceforth referred to as the JEC) from 1880 to 1886. Porter [1983b] and Lee and Porter [1984] previously used this data in order to identify periods in which price wars occurred, and to test whether pricing behavior in cooperative periods was consistent with predictions of the theoretical model. The present paper will look more closely at the price wars themselves, in order to test another set of predictions about their incidence and duration.

Section 2 summarizes the theoretical model in more detail, with emphasis on markets with price-setting firms. The models in Green and Porter [1984] and Porter [1983a] consider quantity-setting firms, but the railroads in the JEC chose prices, not quantities. The distinction has some bearing on the econometric work, but the basic ideas from the theory still apply.

There is a brief description of the JEC and the data set in section 3. Empirical results are covered in section 4, and section 5 contains some concluding comments.

II. NONCOOPERATIVE COLLUSION UNDER UNCERTAINTY

Consider an industry analogous to that originally studied by Stigler [1964]. A number of price-setting firms produce a good of relatively homogeneous quality in a market that is immune from entry. Individual firms cannot monitor the prices chosen by their competitors, so that any tacitly collusive scheme must face the problem of detecting and deterring deviations from the agreement.

---

* I have benefited from the research assistance of Cristina Mazon and the financial support of a Sloan Foundation Grant to the University of Minnesota Economics Department. I am also indebted to Tom Ulen, who made this data set available to me, and to Paul Geroski for helpful comments.

The static noncooperative outcome is that associated with Bertrand, with firms pricing at marginal cost. Any scheme by the firms to jointly raise their prices would benefit them all, assuming that their cost and demand functions are well behaved (for example, marginal costs not declining too rapidly). However, any single firm would profit from a unilateral price cut which attracted enough customers away from its competitors. Thus the collusive price vector is not an equilibrium point in a one-shot market game. It pays to defect. (For more detail, see Friedman [1983].)

Suppose, however, that the firms operate in this market in perpetuity and that there is no exogenous source of uncertainty. As Friedman [1983] and Telser [1972] show, it is then possible to support the collusive price vector as a noncooperative equilibrium of this repeated game by "trigger strategies", as long as future profits are not discounted too heavily. Absent uncertainty, detection of cheating is straightforward. Firms know what market shares they should get if they all adhere to the agreed-upon price vector, and any discrepancy between actual and anticipated shares (in particular, any shortfall) occurs only when some rival has surreptitiously lowered its price.

In this context, trigger strategies are quite simple. Firms choose prices according to the following rules:

(1) As long as no firm has ever defected from the agreement, firms continue to price at collusive levels.
(2) If at any point someone cheats on the agreement, firms permanently revert to noncooperative price levels, i.e., price at marginal cost.

Any firm contemplating a secret price cut would face a tradeoff. It could increase its short-run profits by earning more than it would at the agreed-upon prices, but it would then permanently sacrifice the present discounted value of the difference between collusive and competitive profits, beginning with the next period. Here periods are determined by the length of time it takes rivals to learn of the decrease in their market share and the additional time it takes them to cut their prices in response. Spence [1978] refers to these as the observation and response lags, respectively, and their sum as the reaction lag. As long as the firm does not discount its future profit stream too heavily, the threatened future retaliation will be sufficient to dissuade it from deviating.

The rate at which firms discount profits will depend on a number of factors, as enumerated by Telser [1972]. The longer the reaction lag, the longer the relevant time period, and so the more future profits are discounted. In addition, the firms will discount both according to their subjective rate of time preference (perhaps the market rate of interest), and according to their beliefs about the expected duration of the market. The expected length of the market game could be finite, perhaps because either government regulation or nationalization is possible, and yet the game can appropriately be modelled as one of infinite duration whenever there is some chance of its not ending. Suppose, for example, that the probability of the game ending in any period is described by a geometric distribution. That is, there is a constant probability p that the game will end in any period, given that it has lasted that long. Then, if r is the subjective rate of time preference, firms will use a discount factor of $\beta = (1-p)/(1+r)$. A dollar next period is worth β dollars today, where $0 < \beta < 1$.

As long as β is large enough, the agreement will be noncooperatively viable, since it does not pay to defect when every other firm cooperates. Thus we require that both p and r be relatively small. Note that the threatened punishment is a credible threat, because firms revert to static noncooperative prices. By definition, if every other firm reverts to that level, any single firm maximizes its profits by doing so as well. Note also that the critical level of the discount factor depends on the cooperative price vector chosen. If β is smaller than the level necessary to support prices which maximize joint profits (perfectly collusive prices) as a noncooperative equilibrium with simple trigger strategies, it may still be possible to support prices greater than competitive prices but less than perfectly collusive prices by a simple trigger mechanism. It is easy to show that the closer prices are to perfectly collusive levels, the greater the critical level of β, as the short run gains from cheating increase with prices more rapidly than does the difference between cooperative and competitive profits. The closer cooperative prices are to competitive levels, the smaller the critical value of β.

Now suppose that there is an exogenous source of demand uncertainty, so that market shares are a random function of prices. Firms are then faced with an inference problem. For any firm, a smaller market share than had been anticipated could be the result of cheating by a competitor, or an adverse demand shock. If competitors' prices are not directly observable, uncertainty about the source of market share movements cannot be resolved. Nevertheless, it is still possible for firms to tacitly raise prices above marginal cost and create incentives to adhere to the collusive prices, provided that there is not too much exogenous demand variability, and if future profits are not discounted too heavily.

Consider the following amendment of simple trigger strategies. Rather than having price wars triggered by any deviation from anticipated market shares, let the required deviation be some percentage of the total industry output. For example, sum the absolute value (or the square) of the individual discrepancies, and if this sum exceeds a given fraction of total demand (or demand squared), start a price war. Alternatively, suppose that some firm acts as a price leader. Then reversions to competitive prices would be triggered if the market share of the price leader falls enough below its allotted share. In both of these cases, price wars are triggered by large deviations of actual from allocated market shares, an event caused either by actual cheating or by an atypical interfirm demand pattern. Actual cheating by some firm would increase the likelihood of these deviations being large, and so be more likely to trigger a price war. According to Ulen [1983], the JEC monitored these deviations in order to detect cheating. In addition, rather than have a permanent reversion to competitive prices, suppose that the price war is of finite length. This is a more "forgiving" punishment, which takes into account the fact that price wars could be triggered by random events, and not by actual cheating.

Whether this scheme will be stable, i.e. whether it pays to defect, depends on a number of factors. Any firm considering a secret price cut again faces a tradeoff. As before, there are short run profits to be had. However, by cutting price, the firm increases the probability that a price war will occur, and so decreases the expected discounted value of future profits. If the cartel is to be stable, the costs of cheating—the increased probability of foregone future earnings—must exceed the short run benefits for any price cut. Thus we again require that firms' discount factors be sufficiently close to one.

Now suppose that prices in cooperative periods, the trigger mechanism, and the price war length are chosen optimally, that is to maximize total industry expected discounted profits subject to the constraint that no firm benefits by deviating from cooperative prices. (This is the problem studied by Porter [1983a] for quantity-setting firms.) This could be accomplished either by an explicit mutual agreement, or by firms following the strategy of an industry leader. In either case, firms are pursuing their own interests in charging cooperative prices and so have no incentive to secretly cut prices.

One conclusion which emerges is that, when there is uncertainty, the prices charged in cooperative periods will not be as high as those which would maximize joint profits in a single period. In equilibrium, the marginal gains from cheating in cooperative periods must be exactly offset by the marginal losses implicit in the increased probability of a reversion to competitive behavior. The gains from cheating increase as prices in cooperative periods increase towards perfectly collusive levels, so expected losses must be increased by decreasing the market share deviations necessary to trigger a price war, or by increasing the length of reversionary episodes. Expected discounted industry profits will be maximized at price levels between competitive and perfectly collusive levels. Furthermore, the greater the number of symmetric firms or the greater the degree of demand uncertainty, the closer the cooperative price is to competitive levels. If there are too many firms, or if demand uncertainty is too large, the only equilibrium is that of competitive prices.

It is important to note that in equilibrium, the incentive structure is designed to guarantee that firms do not deviate from agreed-upon-prices in cooperative periods, but that price wars will still occur as random demand shocks will occasionally induce large discrepancies between allotted and actual market shares. Rational firms will realize that, in equilibrium, this occurs only when demand shocks are unusually asymmetric, and never because of individual firm deviations. Nevertheless, rational firms will revert to competitive prices for the prescribed number of periods, precisely because the enforcement mechanism must be employed on these occasions if firms are to have the correct incentives in cooperative periods. If they do not believe that the enforcement mechanism will be employed, they will then have an incentive to cheat on the agreement. Thus observed price wars will always be preceded by a period with an unexpectedly large deviation of actual from allotted market shares.

It is difficult to predict how the frequency and duration of competitive reversions will be affected by changes in market structure without specifying how the joint distribution of market share shocks is affected. However, Stigler's [1964] intuition that collusion is more difficult the greater the number of firms seems reasonable, so that the frequency of reversions might be expected to increase with the number of firms. This intuition is borne out in the simple environment studied by Porter [1983a]. However, no simple comparative statics result is available for the duration of price wars. When duration is selected optimally, there are several conflicting considerations. As the number of firms increases, so does the incentive to free ride on the gains from cooperation, and so the penalty to cheating must increase. For essentially this reason, the expected frequency of reversions will increase. However, the cartel may want to employ shorter, and so more forgiving, punishments when reversions occur, in order to partially offset the increased fraction of time spent at competitive prices. In the case of the JEC, this second effect appears to have predominated.

In the following sections we examine the JEC to see whether these theoretical predictions are correct.

III. THE JOINT EXECUTIVE COMMITTEE

This section contains a brief description of the JEC, with emphasis on the period to 1880 to 1886. A more complete account is contained in Ulen [1983], and the references cited there.

The JEC was a cartel formed by the railroads which controlled eastbound freight shipments from Chicago to the Atlantic seaboard in the 1880s. The agreement was publicly acknowledged, as it preceded the passage of the Sherman Act (1890) and the formation of the Interstate Commerce Commission (1887).

The assumption that a homogeneous good was sold seems to have been approximately satisfied. Through shipments of grain accounted for 73% of all dead freight tonnage handled by the JEC. The railroads also carried flour and provisions, but the prices charged for transporting these commodities were tied to the grain rate. While different railroads shipped grain to different port cities, most of the wheat handled by the cartel was subsequently exported overseas, and the rates charged by different firms adjusted to compensate for differences in ocean shipping rates.

The JEC cartel agreement took the form of market share allotments rather than absolute amounts of quantity shipped. Firms set their rates individually, and the JEC office took weekly accounts so that each railroad could see the total amount transported. Total demand was quite variable, and the actual market share of any particular firm depended on both the prices charged by all the firms and unpredictable stochastic forces. Thus, the problem faced by the members of the JEC seems to be comparable to that posed in the preceding section.

In their model, Green and Porter [1984] explicitly rule out the possibility of entry into the market. In the case of the JEC, entry occurred twice between 1880 and 1886. It appears that the cartel passively accepted the entrants, allocated them market shares, and thereby allowed the collusive agreement to continue. The reason for this is undoubtedly that when a firm entered the rail freight industry in this period, it faced a "no-exit" constraint. To put it briefly, bankrupt railroads were relieved by the courts of most of their fixed costs and instructed to cut prices to increase business. Therefore, it would not be rational for a railroad cartel to engage in predatory pricing practices in response to entry. Of course, entry may have increased the frequency of future price wars as the collusive agreement became more difficult to maintain.

Lake steamers and sailships were the principal source of competition for the railroads, and at no point did they enter into an agreement with the JEC. The opening and closing of the Great Lakes to navigation therefore resulted in semi-annual fluctuations in demand for the JEC. These predictable fluctuations should not have disrupted industry conduct, according to the theory.

A principal function of the JEC was weekly information gathering and dissemination to member firms. This can be viewed as an effort to reduce the observation lag mentioned in the previous section. As a result, the following data is available from week 1 in 1880 to week 16 in 1886:

Q, total quantity of grain shipped; in tons (times 10^{-5})
L, dummy variable; 1 if Great Lakes were open to navigation, 0 otherwise
W, regime classification indicator; 1 if colluding reported by *Railway Review*, 0 otherwise
I, estimated regime classification indicator; 1 if colluding predicted by Lee and Porter [1984], 0 otherwise
H, Herfindahl index of allotted market shares
SSD, sum of squared deviations of actual from allotted market shares.

The data set employed is weekly time series, a frequency which is probably close to the actual reaction lag of the firms in the JEC, so that temporal aggregation bias is not likely to be a problem here.

A price variable is also available, but it is somewhat suspect. The JEC polled member firms and provided an index of prices charged. This index may not reflect secret price cuts, since there is a moral hazard problem in reporting actual prices. Therefore, any price war that was precipitated by secret price cuts may have been recorded with a lag. In this case, I, the estimated dummy variable which indicates when the cartel was successfully maintaining high prices, may also record cartel breakdowns with a lag. For each week t, I_t is the maximum likelihood estimator of whether a price war was occurring, given the observed price, quantity and the exogenous variables listed above. It is also assumed that the reported adherence series, W, is correct some fraction of the time, and so its value is accounted for. The calculation of I is done according to Bayes' rule. Typically, I_t predicts that price wars occurred in period t when prices are unaccountably low, and so is inaccurate if the price series is subject to measurement error. As a result, both I and W, the incidence of competitive episodes reported by the trade press at the time, will be employed as indicators of cartel adherence. Whether I or W is more accurate will depend on the relative accuracy of the price series and the reports of cartel success. Note also that, while the price series is suspect, the existence of this sort of imperfect information structure is necessary if an enforcement mechanism involving reversions to competitive behavior, or price wars, is to be witnessed. It is of crucial importance that firms monitor some variable (in this case their own market share) which only imperfectly reflects the actions of other firms. Here firms knew the prices they charged their own customers, but the reported price index would not be of much use in determining whether other firms were secretly cutting prices.

The Herfindahl index, H, is computed using the allotted market shares of JEC firms. These varied following entry, and because allocations were revised periodically to satisfy internal conflicts. I use H rather than the number of firms as an explanatory variable in order to see whether these reallocations reflected changes in the degree of competition. Of course, the reallocations subsequent to entry had a more dramatic effect on the Herfindahl index.

The L variable documents when the JEC faced its main source of competition. It would be preferable if the prices charged by lake steamers, or some other index of whether lake steamers were successfully colluding, had been used in the econometric work, but such data are not available.

There are five distinct periods in the sample, separated by either entry, additions to existing networks, or the temporary departure of the Chicago and Atlantic from the JEC (due to a dispute with a non-JEC railroad (the Erie) which provided it with access to the eastern seaboard). From week 1 through week 28 in 1880, three firms were members. The Grand Trunk then entered. In week 10 of 1883, the New York Central added another line to its network. In week 26 in 1883, the Chicago and Atlantic entered, and then in week 12 of 1886, through the end of the sample (week 16 of 1886), it departed due to its dispute with the Erie. The second and fourth of these episodes encompass the greater portion of the sample (281 of 328 sample points), and all reversionary periods occurred during these intervals, according to I. A very brief reversion began in week 17 of 1883, according to W. I therefore will run my regressions for both the full sample and these two subsamples separately to test for evidence of structural change.

I now turn to the econometric results, as well as a heuristic description of the pattern of price wars in this sample.

IV. EMPIRICAL RESULTS

Before discussing the econometric results, we examine the pattern of cooperation in the JEC in the 1880–86 sample, employing both W, the series reported at the time by trade publications and newspapers, and I, the series estimated by maximum likelihood methods from price movements by Lee and Porter [1984]. I consider two subsets of the sample. During period 1, from week 28 in 1880 to week 10 in 1883, there were four active firms in the market. In period 2, from week 26 in 1883 to week 11 in 1886, there were five firms. The former period lasted 139 weeks and the latter 142 weeks.

According to the contemporaneous press reports, as captured by W, there were three price wars in period 1 and seven in period 2. In period 1, their average duration was 14 weeks. As a result, 30.2% of the weeks in the period involved relatively competitive behavior by the firms. The probability of a price war beginning in any particular week, given that the preceding week was cooperative, was 0.0395. When the number of firms increased in period 2, the seven price wars had an average duration of 11.6 weeks. The increase in the frequency of competitive reversions was greater than the fall in their duration, and so 57% of the weeks in this period witnessed competitive behavior. The probability of a price war beginning increased to 0.1167.

The estimated adherence series, I, reflects a similar pattern, although fewer weeks are labelled as reversionary and their pattern differs somewhat. According to I, there was one 37 week long price war in period 1, and seven reversions

TABLE I
DETERMINANTS OF W_t (GIVEN $W_{t-1} = 1$)*

Independent Variable	1. Full Sample	2. Period 1	3. Period 2
Constant	−2.25 (1.67)	15.89 (16.58)	−6.12 (15.35)
L_{t-1}	0.331 (0.349)	0.767 (0.636)	0.387 (0.477)
Q_{t-1}	1.38 (1.86)	2.91 (4.17)	2.43 (2.56)
H_{t-1}	9.79 (4.52)	−42.38 (47.31)	22.01 (52.00)
SSD_{t-1}	3.26 (6.22)	7.73 (11.62)	0.81 (9.37)
N	201	94	62
$-2 \log L$	7.30	2.05	1.69

* Estimated standard errors are in parentheses. N is the number of observations. The statistic $-2 \log L$ is twice the difference between the log likelihood function and that when all parameters but the constant are set equal to zero. Under the null hypothesis of no explanatory power, it has a chi-squared distribution with 4 degrees of freedom.

TABLE II
DETERMINANTS OF I_t (GIVEN $I_{t-1} = 1$)*

Independent Variable	1. Full Sample	2. Period 2
Constant	−1.72 (2.12)	−0.62 (9.32)
L_{t-1}	−0.286 (0.386)	0.093 (0.442)
Q_{t-1}	−3.55 (1.84)	0.25 (2.43)
H_{t-1}	15.13 (6.82)	7.56 (31.36)
SSD_{t-1}	−6.77 (6.19)	−9.52 (7.40)
N	232	85
$-2 \log L$	12.86	1.99

* Estimated standard errors are in parentheses. The statistic $-2 \log L$ is calculated as in Table I, with the same distribution under the null hypothesis.

in period 2, which were on average 8.1 weeks long. The percentage of weeks involving competitive behavior was 26.6% in period 1 and 40.1% in the second period. The probability of a price war being triggered increased from 0.0099 to 0.0833 when the additional firm entered.

Both I and W indicate that, as the number of firms increased, the frequency of price wars increased as their duration fell. The net effect was a less stable cartel, as a greater percentage of weeks were accounted for by periods of reversionary conduct. In addition, the estimates of Porter [1983b] and Lee and Porter [1984] indicate that, *ceteris paribus*, prices were 9–10% lower in the second period. One goal of the econometric work of this section is to determine whether the JEC was less successful in maintaining cooperative prices in the second period because of the entry of an additional firm, as the theoretical model would predict, or because of some other developments. The lower prices in the second period are consistent with the theory of noncooperative collusion under uncertainty.

The econometric work estimates the determinants of both the frequency and the duration of price wars, for the full sample and for periods 1 and 2 separately. (The Herfindahl index of allotted shares varied within the two subsamples because of occasional renegotiations, as mentioned in the previous section, and so can be employed as an additional explanatory variable.) Tables I and II display the results of a probit regression of whether or not a price war begins, conditional on the preceding period witnessing cooperative behavior, for each of the three possible samples. (Tables I and II employ W and I as the dependent variable, respectively. In the latter case, there was only one price war in period 1, so that a separate regression cannot be run.) Thus the periods selected are those in which the previous period was cooperative. The regression is designed to determine which variables cause price wars to begin. (See Ulen [1983] for a similar logit regression of cooperation versus noncooperation in which all the sample points are used.)

The results reported in Table I are discouraging. The regressions for the cartel adherence series reported by the press do indicate that the frequency of reversion increased when the number of firms increased. (H has a positive and significant coefficient for the full sample.) No other variable has significant explanatory power, however. In the case of L, this conforms with the theory, since predictable demand disturbances should not influence cartel stability. The statistic $-2 \log L$, which is a likelihood ratio test statistic for the hypothesis that the independent variables do not explain variations in W (see Maddala [1983]), lead one to accept the hypothesis of no explanatory power, except for the full sample, where changes in H affected price war incidence. Within periods 1 and 2, changes in H associated with changes in allotted market shares had no effect. Here H may simply be a proxy for some unspecified difference between the two periods. Total eastbound grain shipments were similar in these two periods (see Porter [1983b, Table 6]), however, and so the effect of entry is the most likely difference.

The results in Table II conform more closely with the theory of section 2. Again H has a significant coefficient for the full sample, although not for period 2, and L is not significant. At a 90% confidence level, SSD is now significant and has the right sign in both samples. In addition, Q is significant for the full sample. Curiously, its coefficient indicates that price wars were more likely to begin the larger the quantity sold in the previous period. Perhaps large values of Q were associated with greater incentives to cheat. In any event, the regressions show that the incidence of price wars increased as the number of firms increased, and as the sum of squared deviations of actual from allotted market shares increased, consistent with the theory.

Tables III and IV show the results of regressions with the duration of price wars as the dependent variable, for the full sample and for period 2. (There were not enough price wars in period 1 to do a separate regression for it.) The duration variables of Tables III and IV are obtained from W and I, respectively. $\hat{W}$ and $\hat{I}$ are predicted values of W and I in the first period of the price war, given by the appropriate probit equation in Table I or II. The other explanatory variables are also computed using their values at these dates.

In the models of Green and Porter [1984] and Porter [1983a], it was assumed that the price war length was fixed, although the optimal duration could vary with the number of active firms. This restriction was imposed for reasons of computational tractability. More generally, one might expect that the length of the price war could depend on the factors which triggered it. Therefore, both $\hat{W}$ (or $\hat{I}$) and SSD were employed as regressors, in order to

TABLE III
DETERMINANTS OF PRICE WAR LENGTH*

Independent Variable	1. Full Sample	2. Period 2
Constant	3.32 (6.96)	−191.3 (115.2)
$\hat{W}$	—	249.5 (137.8)
L	—	−30.11 (12.25)
SSD	277.6 (203.0)	—
R^2	0.172	0.603
N	11	7
F	1.87	3.04

* W is used to calculate price war length. Estimated standard errors are in parentheses.

TABLE IV
DETERMINANTS OF PRICE WAR LENGTH*

Independent Variable	1. Full Sample	2. Period 2
Constant	−121.7 (23.8)	12.33 (3.00)
L	−7.71 (3.89)	−7.33 (3.96)
H	455.6 (80.4)	—
R^2	0.865	0.406
N	8	7
F	19.28	3.42

* I is used to calculate price war length. Estimated standard errors are in parentheses.

determine whether the duration of price wars was positively correlated with the predicted probability of its occurring or the size of the discrepancy between actual and allotted market shares, respectively. If this was the case, then a firm contemplating defection would risk losing future profits, both because of an increase in the probability of a price war, and because of an increase in expected duration should one occur. Once a price war has begun, it is assumed that its length is determined solely by the factors which triggered it, and not by firms' behavior during the price war. If other firms behave competitively, each has no incentive to alter its behavior, and so to affect the duration of the reversion.

The results reported in Tables III and IV represent the best fits available in each case. Since degrees of freedom are limited, insignificant variables have been dropped. Both tables indicate that price wars were longer when the lakes were closed. While this predictable shift in demand does not appear to have influenced the likelihood of reversions to competitive behavior, their expected duration increased 6 to 8 weeks, according to the equations in Table IV. For the reported cartel adherence series W, reported in Table III, the length of a price war is positively correlated with the predicted probability of its occurring, $\hat{W}$, or with SSD, the sum of squared deviations of actual from allotted market shares. In the case of I, the estimated adherence series, price wars were significantly shorter when the number of firms increased (and so H fell). Thus the conjectures of the preceding paragraph, and those of section 2, are substantiated by the empirical results, at least to some extent. Note, however, that only the full sample results of Table IV can be viewed with confidence, according to the F-statistics. Also, because degrees of freedom are limited, these results are merely suggestive.

V. SUMMARY

The operation of the JEC appears to conform with the theoretical model of Stigler [1964], Green and Porter [1984] and Porter [1983a]. As the number of active firms increased from four to five, collusion became more difficult to enforce. As estimated by Porter [1983b], prices in cooperative periods were approximately 10% lower when there were five firms, *ceteris paribus*, presumably to reduce the short run gains from cheating. Furthermore, as documented in the previous section, the percentage of time spent in reversions to relatively competitive pricing behavior increased from 26.6% to 40.1%, according to the estimated incidence series of Lee and Porter [1984], or from 30.2% to 57% according to contemporaneous press reports. While the average duration of price wars decreased, there was a dramatic increase in the frequency of their incidence.

ROBERT H. PORTER,
Department of Economics,
State University of New York at Stony Brook,
Stony Brook, NY 11794,
U.S.A.

THE GAINS FROM MERGER OR COLLUSION IN PRODUCT-DIFFERENTIATED INDUSTRIES*

JONATHAN B. BAKER AND TIMOTHY F. BRESNAHAN

I. INTRODUCTION

A MERGER in an industry with differentiated products increases the market power of the merging firms to the extent that their products are close substitutes and that other firms produce only more distant substitutes.[1] Such a merger makes the residual demand curve of each partner steeper, by shifting each in the direction of the industry demand curve.[2] The extent of this increase in market power depends upon the own-elasticity of demand for each merging firm's product, as well as the cross-elasticity of demand for each with all other firms' products. As a result, evaluating the effect of a merger between two firms with $n-2$ other competitors would seem to require the estimation of at least n^2 parameters (all of the price elasticities of demand), a formidable task.

That extremely difficult estimation task is unnecessary, however. The necessary information is contained in the slopes of the two single-firm (residual) demand curves before the merger, and the extent to which the merged firm will face a steeper demand curve. For example, suppose a merger between two U.S. brewing firms, say Pabst and Anheuser–Busch, were proposed. It is not particularly important to determine whether it is competition from Miller or competition from Stroh (or from Heileman, or . . .) which puts the most effective brake on Anheuser–Busch's pricing. Only the total effect of these other firms and the particular effect of competition from Pabst are of interest.

This paper proposes econometric procedures for estimating the demand system that merger partners will face, based only on pre-merger data. The key to the procedures is that the effects of all other firms in the industry are summed together. Formally, we start with a model of an n-firm product-differentiated industry. Manipulation of the model removes the prices and quantities of all but two firms. This reduces the dimensionality of the problem to manageable size; rather than an n-firm demand system, we estimate a two-firm residual demand system. In this way the technique extends our econometric method for

---

* We would like to thank Paul Geroski and an anonymous referee for comments on an earlier draft. Acknowledged is grant support from the Sloan Foundation to the Department of Economics at Stanford University.

[1] This definition of the increase in market power from a merger ignores possible changes in industry conduct resulting from the change in industry structure. If the merger raises the likelihood of collusion (Stigler [1964]), the definition underestimates the change in market power. If the merger induces entry by new firms or competitive product introductions by existing firms, the definition overestimates the change in market power.

[2] Our definition of the residual demand curve is distinct from, but closely related to, Chamberlin's [1933] dd'. We make the distinction precise in Note 6 below.

evaluating single-firm demand elasticities in product-differentiated industries (Baker and Bresnahan [1984]).

Throughout, we do not distinguish a merger between two firms from a bilateral collusive arrangement between them. We use the language "the increase in market power from a merger" but could equally well use the phrase "the gains from a bilateral collusive arrangement between these two firms".

We apply our technique to three U.S. brewing firms: Anheuser–Busch (A–B), Pabst and Coors. Since U.S. brewing is quite concentrated, and since all of these firms are large,[3] a merger between any two of the three would likely be challenged under current U.S. antitrust guidelines. The question of bilateral collusion is therefore more interesting. Our estimates show that neither of the two smaller firms, Pabst and Coors, would have a significant increase in market power from bilateral collusion, although A–B would gain substantially from colluding with either of the other two.

II. TWO FIRMS IN A PRODUCT-DIFFERENTIATED INDUSTRY

This section derives the residual demand curve facing two firms in a product-differentiated industry. The residual demand curve is the relationship between those two firms' prices and quantities, taking the reactions of all other firms into account. This is a natural generalization of the residual demand curve facing a single firm: the relationship between its price and quantity, taking other firms' reactions into account. In product-differentiated industries, it is natural to suppose that there will be a (private) gain to merger, because the merged firm will face a steeper residual demand curve.[4]

A simple location model of product differentiation can illustrate these ideas. Suppose stores are distributed along a road as in Figure 1(a). The road goes on forever, but we show only the four firms at locations ℓ_1, ℓ_2, ℓ_3 and ℓ_4. Each initially charges the price P_0. Customers need to travel to the stores; their costs per mile are given by the slopes of the delivered-price lines. Customer c_{12} is just indifferent between going to store 1 or 2, but everyone located to the right of c_{12} would rather buy at store 2 than store 1. Suppose that competition in the industry takes the Bertrand (price) form, and that the stores are spaced such that the reaction functions have slope $+\frac{1}{3}$. That is, every store would respond to a price increase by either of its neighbors with a price increase $\frac{1}{3}$ as large.

To define the residual demand curve facing firm 2, suppose that firm 2's costs increased, leading it to increase its price to P_1. After all other stores have reached equilibrium, both of firm 2's neighbors will have increased their prices by slightly over $\frac{1}{3}$ as much.[5] Figure 1(b) shows that firm 2 will lose customers to both stores 1 and 3. The slope of firm 2's residual demand curve can be

---

[3] In 1983, Anheuser–Busch had a 32.9 percent national market share (in unit sales), Coors 7.5 percent, and Pabst 7.0 percent.
[4] This presumption is typically false in homogeneous-product industries. See Salant et al. [1983].
[5] It is slightly over $\frac{1}{3}$ because store 3's increase leads to an increase by 4, which feeds back to 3, and so on.

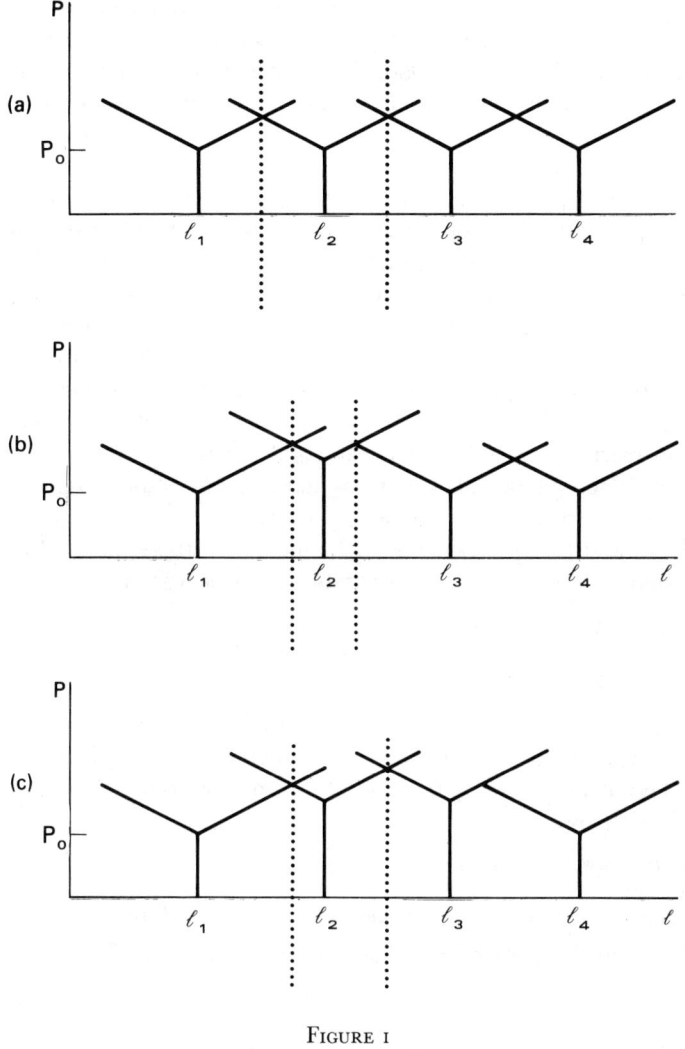

FIGURE I
Spatial Example

calculated by the amount of sales it loses for a given price increase.[6] As the figure is drawn, the slope of residual demand for firm 3 is identical to that for firm 2, since the firms are symmetric to one another.

Alternatively, stores 2 and 3 might be merged into a single firm. Since its two stores are identical, this firm would set a single price. Figure 1(c) shows what

[6] The slope of the residual demand curve is different from the slope of Chamberlin's dd'. The latter would be defined in our spatial-Bertrand context keeping other firms' prices constant. The residual demand curve lets other firms adjust. It is possible to estimate the slope of dd' as well as a residual demand: see, for example, Bresnahan [1981].

would happen if the merged firm raised price. Now, customers switch from store 2 to store 1 *but not to store* 3. Similarly, store 3 loses customers to store 4 but not to store 2. As a result, each store loses only half as many customers as it would have acting independently. The residual demand elasticity for the merged firm is only half that of the pre-merged firms, a considerable increase in market power.

Any real-world product-differentiated industry is likely to be much more complicated than this example. If there are n firms with different products in the industry, one might expect a price increase by any one firm to lead some customers to switch to most or all of the other $n-1$ firms. The situation is unlikely to be symmetric; some particular firms' products will have greater cross-elasticities of demand than others. Further, the assumption of price (Bertrand) competition in our example might be incorrect; firms might exhibit Cournot or other forms of behavior. It therefore seems that calculating the increase in market power due to a real-world merger involves an extremely difficult econometric task. All of the own- and cross-elasticities of demand must be estimated and the nature of competitive interaction must be determined.

Let firms 1 and 2 propose a merger in an industry with $n-2$ other firms. The inverse demand curves for the merger partners may be written

(1) $\quad P_1 = h_1(Q_1, Q_2, \underset{\sim}{Q}, Y; \eta_1)$

(2) $\quad P_2 = h_2(Q_1, Q_2, \underset{\sim}{Q}, Y; \eta_2)$

Here $\underset{\sim}{Q}$ is an $(n-2)$ vector of quantities produced by all other firms, Y denotes a vector of exogenous variables which shift demand, and η_i is a parameter vector. The remaining $(n-2)$ demand curves in this industry may be written compactly as follows:

(3) $\quad \underset{\sim}{P} = \underset{\sim}{h}(Q_1, Q_2, \underset{\sim}{Q}, Y; \eta)$

Note that estimation of (1), (2) and (3) can be very difficult. Denoting the elasticity of h_i with respect to Q_j as η_{ij}, (1), (2) and (3) might be approximated as

(1') $\quad p_1 = \eta_{10} + \eta_{11} q_1 + \eta_{21} q_2 + \sum_{j=3}^{\eta} \eta_{j1} q_j + \langle \eta_{1Y}, Y \rangle$,

(2') $\quad p_2 = \eta_{20} + \eta_{12} q_1 + \eta_{22} q_2 + \sum_{j=3}^{\eta} \eta_{j2} q_j + \langle \eta_{2Y}, Y \rangle$,

(3') $\quad p_i = \eta_{i0} + \eta_{1i} q_1 + \eta_{2i} q_2 + \sum_{j=3}^{\eta} \eta_{ji} q_j + \langle \eta_{iY}, Y \rangle, \quad i = 3, \ldots, n$

where $q_i = \log(Q_i)$, $p_i = \log(P_i)$ and $\langle \cdot, \cdot \rangle$ is the inner product of two vectors. There are n^2 elasticities of demand η_{ij}, even before considering the exogenous-variable elasticities, η_{iY}. Unless some further structure can be put on (1'), (2') and (3'), for example, by grouping firms into market segments, direct estimation will be very difficult if not impossible.[7]

Next we specify the behavior of the $(n-2)$ non-merging firms. It can be cooperative or non-cooperative, and if non-cooperative it can be Cournot, Bertrand, or some other oligopoly equilibrium. Each firm will satisfy a first-order condition equating marginal cost with *perceived* marginal revenue. For the non-merging firms, perceived marginal revenue, which differs across oligopoly solution concepts, is written as follows:

(4) $\quad \underset{\sim}{MR} = \underset{\sim}{P} + \underset{\sim}{g}(Q_1, Q_2, \underset{\sim}{Q}, Y; \eta) \underset{\sim}{Q}$

In equation (4), $\underset{\sim}{g}$ is a vector of slopes of the demand curves $\underset{\sim}{h}$ perceived by each of the $(n-2)$ non-merging firms.

Although (4) is written as if quantity were the choice variable of the oligopolists, appropriate choice of $g(\cdot)$ can make (4) correspond to any behavioral rule, including equilibria in which firms choose prices.

The vector of marginal costs for the $(n-2)$ non-merging firms depends on output $\underset{\sim}{Q}$, factor prices W, and parameters $\underset{\sim}{\beta}$,

(5) $\quad \underset{\sim}{MC} = \underset{\sim}{MC}(\underset{\sim}{Q}, W, \underset{\sim}{\beta})$

Thus the first-order conditions describing the behavior of the non-merging firms take the following form[8]

(6) $\quad \underset{\sim}{MC}(\underset{\sim}{Q}, W; \underset{\sim}{\beta}) = \underset{\sim}{P} + \underset{\sim}{g}(Q_1, Q_2, \underset{\sim}{Q}, Y; \eta) \underset{\sim}{Q}$

Solving the $2(n-2)$ equations in the vector relations (6) and (3) for the vector $\underset{\sim}{Q}$, we derive

(7) $\quad \underset{\sim}{Q} = \underset{\sim}{E}(Q_1, Q_2, Y, W; \eta, \underset{\sim}{\beta})$

A different equation $\underset{\sim}{E}_j$ corresponds to each of the $(n-2)$ outputs of non-merging firms. We denote the elasticities of $\underset{\sim}{E}_j$ with respect to Q_i ($i = 1, 2$) as ε_{ji}; this is the elasticity of firm j's reaction function (to firm i).

Equation (7) defines a partial reduced form for the $(n-2)$ non-merging firm outputs; it defines equilibrium $\underset{\sim}{Q}$, given Q_1 and Q_2. Substituting equation (7) into demand curves (1) and (2) for the merger partners, we derive *partial residual demand curves* for those two firms:

(8) $\quad P_1 = h_1(Q_1, Q_2, \underset{\sim}{E}(Q_1, Q_2, Y, W; \eta, \underset{\sim}{\beta}); Y; \eta_1)$

$\quad\quad = r_1(Q_1, Q_2, Y, W; \eta_1, \eta, \underset{\sim}{\beta})$

(9) $\quad P_2 = r_2(Q_1, Q_2, Y, W; \eta_2, \eta, \underset{\sim}{\beta})$

---

[7] For methods which use such further structure, see Bresnahan [1980], Cowling and Cubbin [1972], and Joskow [1983], all applied to the Automobile industry.

[8] Note that (6) are supply relations, functions of both $\underset{\sim}{P}$ and $\underset{\sim}{Q}$. They are the analog of the supply function $P = MC(Q)$ in the theory of perfect competition.

We estimate equations (8) and (9), the partial residual demand system applicable to firms 1 and 2. They are *residual* demand curves because the actions of firms 3 to n have been taken into account. They are *partial* residual demand curves because, for each firm, the potential merger partner's action remains to be specified. Note that this approach includes as a special case the possibility of perfect competition. If P_1 and P_2 are completely explained by Y and W, so that Q_1 and Q_2 have coefficients of zero in (8) and (9), then firms 1 and 2 have no power over price, even acting jointly.

In our empirical work, we approximate (8) and (9) with log–log functional forms

(10) $\quad p_1 = \eta_{10} + \eta_{11}^{PR} q_1 + \eta_{21}^{PR} q_2 + \Gamma_1 y + \Delta_1 w + v_1$

(11) $\quad p_2 = \eta_{20} + \eta_{12}^{PR} q_1 + \eta_{22}^{PR} q_2 + \Gamma_2 y + \Delta_2 w + v_2$

The interpretation of the parameters η^{PR} may be obtained by logarithmically differentiating (8) and (9). This yields

(12) $\quad \eta_{11}^{PR} = \eta_{11} + \sum_{j=3} \eta_{j1} \varepsilon_{j1}$

(13) $\quad \eta_{21}^{PR} = \eta_{21} + \sum_{j=3} \eta_{j2} \varepsilon_{j2}$

(14) $\quad \eta_{12}^{PR} = \eta_{12} + \sum_{j=3} \eta_{j1} \varepsilon_{j1}$

(15) $\quad \eta_{22}^{PR} = \eta_{22} + \sum_{j=3} \eta_{j2} \varepsilon_{j2}$

Thus the partial residual demand elasticities η_{ij}^{PR} depend both on the structural demand elasticities η_{ij} and on the reaction function elasticities ε_{ij}. By estimating only the parameters η_{ij}^{PR}, we obtain only a subset of the information about the industry. For example in (12), we cannot separate the effects of firms 3 through n; only the total effect enters the equation.

Calculation of post-merger market power from the partial residual demand curve is straightforward. Suppose that the merged firm will decrease Q_1 and Q_2 in the same proportion to exploit its increased market power.[9] Then a decrease of both Q_1 and Q_2 of one percent will raise P_1 by $\eta_{11}^{PR} + \eta_{21}^{PR}$ and will raise P_2 by $\eta_{22}^{PR} + \eta_{12}^{PR}$.

Pre-merger (current) market power depends on the residual demand curve facing each of firms 1 and 2 acting alone. Since the formal derivation closely follows that of the partial residual demand curve, we present it in Appendix I and just give the main ideas here. The residual demand curve facing firm 1 will take the form

(16) $\quad P_1 = R_1(Q_1, Y, W, \eta_1, \eta, \beta)$

---

[9] The merged firm may not find it optimal to decrease Q_1 and Q_2 in the same proportion to exploit its market power. See Orr and MacAvoy [1964] for analysis of when proportional-quantity rules are jointly profit maximizing for two firms.

This is exactly the same as (8), except firm 2 has been "equilibrated out" along with firms 3 to n. The elasticity of P_1 with respect to Q_1 defined by (16) is η_1^R, the residual demand elasticity for firm 1.

Suppose instead of solving the $2(n-2)$ equations (3) and (4) for $Q_3, \ldots, Q_n$, we expanded them by one demand curve (2) and a first-order condition for firm 2. Then we would have $2(n-1)$ equations for $Q_2, \ldots, Q_n$. We solve for the $(n-1)$ outputs as functions of Q_1:

$$(17) \quad \begin{pmatrix} Q_2 \\ \vdots \\ Q_n \end{pmatrix} = \underset{\sim}{E}(Q_1, Y, W; \underset{\sim}{\eta}, \underset{\sim}{\beta})$$

where (17) differs from (7) because Q_2 is on the left, not right. Let the elasticity of Q_i with respect to Q_1 in (16) be ξ_{i1}. Note that there is no obvious relationship between the *partial* residual demand elasticity η_{11}^{PR} and the residual demand elasticity η_1^R, since they are defined by different conceptual experiments. In the partial residual demand system, firm 2's output is held fixed along with firm 1's. In the residual demand curve, firm 2's output is solved out along with all of the other $n-2$ firms.

$\underset{\sim}{E}(\cdot)$ is the vector of outputs of all firms except firm 1. The elasticity of firm 1's residual demand curve is

$$(18) \quad \eta_1^R = \eta_{11} + \eta_{21}\xi_{21} + \sum_{j=3} \eta_{j1}\xi_{j1}$$

We could similarly define a residual demand curve for firm 2. It would have elasticity

$$(19) \quad \eta_2^R = \eta_{22} + \eta_{12}\xi_{12} + \sum_{j=3} \eta_{j2}\xi_{j2}$$

To summarize, the difference between the residual demand curve facing a single firm and the partial residual demand curve facing two firms is this: the price discipline that each of the two firms exerts on the other is isolated. When we estimate the residual demand curve for firm 1, the slope depends (in part) on how firm 1's customers defect to firm 2. When we estimate the partial residual demand curve, we can perform the conceptual experiment of raising both firms' prices together.[10]

Calculation of the exact, quantitative increase in market power as a result of the merger rests on the assumption that the elasticity of demand does not change along the demand curve. Estimates based on pre-merger historical data cannot reveal the elasticity of demand at the hypothetical post-merger point. What they can do is measure the extent to which the merger will change

---

[10] In a product differentiated industry, residual demand elasticities correspond directly to a firm's markup of price over marginal cost. For an explanation, and a discussion of other circumstances in which the markup is related to residual demand elasticities, see Baker and Bresnahan [1984, section B].

price-quantity incentives. If the demand curve grows steeper as a result of the merger, we can be sure that the merged firm will have an incentive to raise price from the pre-merger level. But we cannot be sure how far; if for some (unlikely) reason the demand curve rapidly flattens at quantities slightly below those observed in the market, the merger will have little effect.

III. THREE BREWERS

In this section, we empirically investigate the extent to which existing competition from other firms' products limits market power in the U.S. brewing industry. Three hypothetical mergers are considered: between Anheuser–Busch (A–B), the largest firm in the national market, and Pabst, another important producer of "premium" beer; between A–B and Coors, the largest firm in the Western states; and between Pabst and Coors.[11] After a discussion of the structure of the industry,[12] we estimate residual demand curves for each of the three firms, and partial residual demand curves for each of the three pairs of firms.

The brewing industry is highly concentrated. In 1983, the last year of our sample, the two-firm (A–B and Miller) concentration ratio was over 50 percent. Four more firms (Pabst, Coors, Heileman and Schlitz) had market shares between seven and thirteen percent. There is also considerable evidence of product differentiation. An FTC study[13] shows substantial long-term trends in the relative prices of different kinds of beer ("popular", "premium", etc.) indicating they must be imperfect substitutes in demand. Similarly, the correlations over time among the prices charged by our three firms suggest they are selling distinct products. Table I reports correlation coefficients for the log of the real price of each firm's primary brand in mid-summer in Northern California, over the period 1962–83.

Data limitations prevent straightforward extension of our techniques to Miller, Heileman or Stroh–Schlitz. Each of these firms has acquired a rival or been acquired. Miller and Heileman have both been closely held within our sample period. Thus firm-specific data on these firms cannot be assembled from published sources.

Given the concentration and the product differentiation present in the industry, it is natural to ask whether there are gains to collusion or merger. If we find that coordinated pricing between two firms would substantially increase their market power, we can draw two conclusions. First, a merger between them would worsen industry conduct, and would therefore worsen performance if it did not yield cost savings. Second, the firms are not now

---

[11] None of these hypothetical mergers is likely to occur without antitrust challenge. For a history of brewing mergers and their antitrust treatment, see Ornstein [1981].

[12] Elzinga [1982] presents a detailed review of brewing industry history. The demand for beer has been discussed by Greer ([1971], [1981]), Hogarty and Elzinga [1972], Kelton and Kelton [1982], and McConnel [1968]. Product differentiation issues are discussed in Greer [1981].

[13] Keithahn [1978].

TABLE I
CORRELATIONS AMONG PRICES[a]

	P_{A-B}	P_{Coors}	
P_{A-B}	1.0	0.83	0.93
P_{Coors}		1.0	0.61
P_{Pabst}			1.0

[a] Log of real prices. See Appendix II for description of price data.

pursuing completely colluding pricing policies, which follows directly from the nature of our estimates. If a coordinated pricing policy *would* yield a steeper demand curve than the firm *does* face, we can conclude that a completely coordinated pricing policy is not now being used.

Several long-term trends in the brewing industry's environment and structure affect the specification of residual demand curves for our 1962–83 sample period. First is the question of what variables to include in the equation. The derivation of (8) and (9) shows that variables shifting the cost curves of other firms in the industry must be included, as must variables that shift the demand curve for any brand. The second issue is whether the residual demand system is stable over time.

Regarding the question of cost-side variables, w, we first include two indexes of factor prices. One is short-run average variable cost (SRAVC) for the industry, defined to include labor, agricultural inputs, and energy inputs.[14] The other is a price of capital series (PK). A third variable is suggested by the increasing exploitation of scale economies over time (Elzinga [1982]). If marginal costs are falling because of exploitation of scale economies, then it is important to capture this effect econometrically. Our variable is the average plant size (APS) in the industry, defined to be industry-wide capacity divided by the number of operating plants. The fourth variable is suggested not by long-term trends but by the cyclicality of the demand for beer. If firms $3, \ldots, n$ have excess capacity, then their marginal costs are likely to be lower. We capture this with the variable EKTI, defined as $\mathrm{EKTI} = \Sigma_{j=3}^{n}(K_j - Q_j)$, excess capacity of the other $n-2$ firms.

On the demand side, economic and marketing studies suggest the inclusion of several economic demographic variables.[15] We include *per capita* disposable income (PCDI), firm advertising expenditures, the percentage of the drinking-age population under 45 years old, and the percentage of drinking-age women who ever drink beer. Of these, only PCDI ever approaches significance in our regressions. It is therefore the only demand variable reported below. We suspect the insignificance arises because most demographic variables move very slowly.

On the question of structural stability, there are two important considerations. One is the increasing concentration of the industry over our sample

[14] See Appendix II for precise definitions of all variables.
[15] Hatten and Schendal [1977]; Ellison and Uhl [1964].

period. Two-thirds of the firms in the industry in 1962 exited before 1983; over the same period, the five firm concentration ratio rose from 35 percent to 84 percent. Thus we allow for the possibility that residual demand curves are getting steeper over time by interacting both their slopes and intercepts with a variable which increases by one each year, TIME. The second issue of structural change is the introduction of the heavily advertised "LITE" brand beer by Miller.[16] Other firms responded with the introduction of their own "light" beers. We take account of the effect of this structural change on residual demand by introducing a dummy variable LITE that takes in the value of 1 beginning in 1975. This dummy variable is allowed to shift both the residual demand elasticity and the intercept of the residual demand curve.

Our procedure for estimating these residual demand elasticities regresses both P_1 and P_2 on the two quantities Q_1 and Q_2, demand shift variables Y, and industry-wide cost variables W. In double-log form, we estimate:

(20) $\quad p_1 = \eta_{10} + \eta_{11}^{PR} q_1 + \eta_{21}^{PR} q_2 + \Gamma_1 y + \Delta_1 w + v_1$

(21) $\quad p_2 = \eta_{20} + \eta_{12}^{PR} q_1 + \eta_{22}^{PR} q_2 + \Gamma_2 y + \Delta_2 w + v_2$

The primary econometric problem that must be solved to estimate (20) and (21) is the simultaneity of these equations with as yet unspecified supply relations for the two merging firms. The solution to this problem will also prove that equations (20) and (21) are econometrically identified. The supply relations are derived from equating marginal revenue with marginal cost:

(22) $\quad MC_1(Q_1, W, W_1; \beta_1) = P_1 + Q_1 t_1(Q_1, Q_2, Y, W; \eta_1, \eta, \underline{\beta})$

(23) $\quad MC_2(Q_2, W, W_1; \beta_2) = P_2 + Q_2 t_2(Q_1, Q_2, Y, W; \eta_2, \eta, \underline{\beta})$

Equilibrium in the industry at issue is defined by the simultaneous determination of the two partial residual demand curves (8) and (9) with the two supply relations (22) and (23). As is evident, identification of the parameters of the residual demand curve requires the presence of the firm-individuated cost variables W_1 and W_2. We therefore estimate (20) and (21) by employing firm-specific cost variables as instruments for quantities q_1 and q_2.[17] In addition, to conserve degrees of freedom, we impose a cross-equation restriction that the different industry-wide prices W enter proportionately for both firms. Finally we estimate partial residual demand curves jointly for the two merging

---

[16] Miller acquired the rights to Meister Brau Lite beer in 1972, which had been unsuccessfully marketed as a diet beer for women by a small Chicago brewery. Miller's innovation was in the nationwide marketing of light beer. Light beers, now made by many firms, are lower in alcohol and calories than premium beers. In estimating demand curves from time series data, we implicitly assume that no unobserved changes in product quality or reputation occur. The one exception to this is the obvious change in the relative attractiveness of different brands after the invention of light beer, which we treat by introducing a dummy variable in the residual demand curve of each firm.

[17] In our earlier paper, we showed that even if we lack such instruments, the estimation of single firm residual demand elasticities will be biased in the conservative direction of disproving market power. Baker and Bresnahan [1984].

TABLE II
PARTIAL RESIDUAL DEMAND CURVES FOR A–B AND COORS

Dependent:	P_{ab}	P_{cs}
Independent		
Constant	1.97	3.67
	(1.71)	(0.92)
q_{ab}	−0.466	0.036
	(−1.94)	(5.35)
q_{cs}	0.093	−0.661
	(5.6)	(−1.76)
SRAVC	0.148	0.699
	(0.75)	(1.17)
APS	−0.009	−0.452
	(−1.10)	—
PK	0.057	0.272
	(2.93)	—
EKTI	0.00019	0.00094
	(2.2)	—
LITE	0.610	
	(2.18)	
q_{ab}*LITE	−0.219	
	(−2.88)	
q_{cs}*LITE	0.043	
	—	
TIME		0.0849
		(1.57)
PCDI	0.404	−0.012
	(0.824)	(−0.007)

partners by three-stage least-squares, a procedure which takes advantages of information available from the correlation of errors in those equations.[18]

Substantial experimentation with the specification produced some simplifications. First, advertising and the demographics were never significant. Thus "Y" in (20) and (21) consists only of PCDL. Second, only the slope and intercept of A–B's residual demand equation are changed by the LITE dummy; this change in industry structure appears to have had little effect on the other two firms. Finally, the TIME coefficient appears to enter the intercept of each of the Pabst and Coors equations, but not to affect the slope of any residual demand curve. The following tables report only the estimates for specifications after these simplifications have been imposed.[19]

---

[18] If we begin with all of the structured equations of the model (1′), (2′), (3′) and (4) linear in the logs with additive error, then (10) and (11) will have additive error, but v_1 and v_2 will be correlated. Thus three-stage least-squares will increase the power of our estimators.

[19] Baker and Bresnahan [1984] reports on the specification tests in considerably greater detail.

Table II reports the partial residual demand curve for A–B and Coors. Most of the coefficients have the expected signs: a decrease in either firm's quantity would raise its own price and lower that of the other firm. If factor prices were higher (SRAVC or PK), the residual (inverse) demand curve would shift up, as one expects. Similarly an increase in APS (and the resulting lowering of industry-wide costs) shifts the residual demand curve down. The coefficient of excess capacity is of the incorrect sign but small. The demand elasticities appear to be substantial: a one-percent quantity decrease by A–B would lower its price by 0.466 percent, and raise Coors price by 0.093 percent—these price effects take into account the reactions of all firms but Coors. A–B's partial residual demand curve is somewhat flatter when the LITE dummy is turned on. Taking into account the competitive responses of all other firms, A–B plus Coors would have only about half as much control over P_{ab} when LITE = 1.

The results for the partial residual demand curve for A–B and Pabst (Table III) are similar in some respects. The coefficients again have mostly the ex-

TABLE III
PARTIAL RESIDUAL DEMAND CURVES FOR A–B AND PABST

Dependent:	P_{ab}	P_{pb}
Independent		
Constant	1.50	3.92
	(8.42)	(1.57)
q_{ab}	−0.523	−0.011
	(−3.27)	(0.58)
q_{pb}	0.185	−0.035
	(1.82)	(0.077)
SRAVC	0.133	0.096
	(1.22)	(2.44)
APS	−0.193	−0.139
	(−1.6)	—
PK	0.072	0.028
	(2.40)	—
EKTI	0.0015	0.0012
	(2.68)	—
LITE	0.805	
	(0.81)	
q_{ab}*LITE	−0.67	
	(−4.1)	
q_{pb}*LITE	0.016	
	—	
TIME		−0.01
		(−1.7)
PCDI	0.249	−0.11
	(4.33)	(−0.13)

TABLE IV
PARTIAL RESIDUAL DEMAND CURVES FOR PABST AND COORS

Dependent:	P_{pb}	P_{cs}
Independent		
Constant	3.96	3.34
	(12.6)	(2.20)
q_{cs}	0.16	−0.648
	(0.312)	(−2.61)
q_{pb}	−0.006	−0.028
	(−0.16)	(−1.18)
SRAVC	0.105	0.225
	(1.71)	(1.44)
APS	−0.197	−0.422
	(−1.39)	—
PK	0.042	0.090
	(1.66)	—
EKTI	0.00033	0.00071
	(0.503)	—
TIME	−0.011	0.041
	(−1.42)	(1.39)
PCDI	−0.218	0.991
	(−1.76)	(1.37)

pected sign. A–B's demand curve is again downward-sloping in own-quantity and increasing in Pabst's quantity. The LITE effect is again to substantially flatten A–B's demand curve. The Pabst equation, however, shows very little market power for the firm.

The results for Pabst and Coors (Table IV) are consistent with what one would expect from the first two tables. Pabst has no market power, even with the cooperation of Coors. The Coors partial residual demand curve is again quite steep.

To use the information in Tables II–IV to evaluate mergers or collusion, we need to estimate the residual demand curves for each of the three firms. This is reported in Table V. The estimates show that Coors, acting alone, has a steep demand curve. Pabst, acting alone, has very little power over price. A–B's market power appears to vary over time, because of the effects of LITE.

Table VI summarizes the coefficients needed to evaluate the gains from a merger or collusion. The first section reports η_{11}^R for each firm, the inverse demand elasticity when all other firms act independently. The second section reports $\eta_{11}^{PR} + \eta_{12}^{PR}$, the inverse demand elasticity if two firms moved their quantities proportionately. Looking first at the A–B/Coors merger, we observe that the A–B demand curve would be steeper after a merger with Coors. In the 1967–74 period the A–B demand elasticity grows slightly as a result of the merger (−0.373 vs. −0.313), while it grows substantially after the "LITE"

TABLE V
Residual Demand Curves For All Three Brewers

Dependent:	P_{ab}	P_{cs}	P_{pb}
Independent			
Constant	2.625	2.85	3.53
	(7.77)	(3.73)	(12.00)
q_{ab}	−0.313		
	(−5.99)		
q_{cs}		−0.633	
		(1.82)	
q_{pb}			−0.028
			(−0.961)
SRAVC	0.094	0.326	0.086
	(1.811)	(2.33)	(1.81)
APS	−0.079	−0.277	−0.073
	(−1.15)	—	—
PK	0.025	0.082	0.024
	(1.31)	—	—
EKTI	0.0023	0.008	0.0023
	(0.54)	—	—
LITE	0.629		
	(0.918)		
q_{ab}*LITE	−0.311		
	(9.07)		
TIME		0.042	−0.011
		(2.91)	(−2.57)
PCDI	0.115	0.537	−0.026
	(0.775)	(1.50)	(−0.19)

TABLE VI
Gains to Merger or Collusion

I. Residual Demand Elasticities: η^R_{11}
  Coors: −0.633 (−10.07)
  Pabst: −0.028 (−0.961)
  A−B, 1962−74: −0.313 (−5.99)
  A−B, 1975−83: −0.002 (−0.014)

II. Post-Merger Demand Elasticities: $\eta^{PR}_{11} + \eta^{PR}_{12}$
  Merger of A−B and Coors:
  Coors: −0.625 (−7.81)
  A−B, 1962−74: −0.373 (−3.45)
  A−B, 1975−83: −0.176 (−2.57)
  Merger of A−B and Pabst:
  Pabst: +0.024 (+0.14)
  A−B, 1962−74: −0.338 (−6.28)
  A−B, 1975−83: −0.151 (−2.14)
  Merger of Pabst and Coors:
  Coors: −0.676 (1.97)
  Pabst: +0.01 (0.103)

dummy is turned on (-0.176 vs. -0.002). Hence, as expected, a merger with Coors would substantially increase A–B's market power. The Coors demand curve, by contrast, grows slightly less steep as a result of the merger. We conclude from this insignificant change that Coors' market power would be unaffected by merger with A–B.

The merger of A–B and Pabst would be similar. The Pabst demand curve moves from being small, negative, and insignificantly-sloped, to being small, positive, and insignificantly-sloped. Just as Pabst is a price-taker now, so would the merged A–B/Pabst firm be a price-taker in its Pabst product line. The A–B demand curve, however, again grows steeper by a small amount before the introduction of "LITE" and by a large amount after it.[20] The Pabst/Coors merger does not substantially enhance the market power of either product; though the Coors elasticity grows slightly; this occurs because Pabst and Coors appear to be *complements* in demand.

All three sets of estimates show an increase in the slope of the demand curve only for A–B. We can determine the importance of this increase by a simple calculation. Suppose a merger increased the inverse demand elasticity for Budweiser, A–B's flagship product, by 0.05. This is conservative: except for the merger with Pabst in the pre-1975 period, all of our estimates show a larger increase. An increase of 0.05 means that the price–cost margin for Budweiser would increase by five percent of cost. A conservative estimate A–B marginal cost is $50/barrel. In 1983, A–B sold 42 million barrels of this brand. Thus collusion or a merger with a smaller firm would yield additional monopoly profits of at least $105 million per year.

IV. CONCLUSION

Our estimates show that collusion or a merger between A–B and either Pabst or Coors would lead to a substantial increase in market power for A–B. No merger among any two of the three firms yields any increase in market power for the other two brands.[21] We draw a strong and a weak conclusion about the nature of competition in brewing.

Our strong conclusion is that these three brewers are not colluding in price, even though there is substantial market power in the industry. The evidence for the absence of complete collusion is compelling; a change from the pricing rules firms now use to coordinated pricing would yield very large increases in profits. Market power such as we measure can exist even without collusion in a product-differentiated industry.

[20] The Pabst/A–B merger suggests that our convention of assuming proportional decreases in post-merger quantities may be too conservative. Since the post-merger Pabst demand curve remains flat, but decreases in Pabst sales shift the A–B demand curve out, the merged firm would find it profit-maximizing to decrease Pabst quantity much more sharply than A–B.

[21] This statement presumes that the merger will not increase the probability of collusion on an industry-wide basis. In general, we would expect mergers between larger firms to have a greater effect on the probability of collusion. Thus we think our assessment of A–B's gains to merger is conservative.

Our weak conclusion concerns the competitive role of the producers, such as Coors and Pabst, with market shares in the 5–15 percent range. These firms seem to provide an important brake on the pricing power of the market leader, A–B. This conclusion is weak because data limitations prevent extension of the analysis to other firms. First, we do not know whether our results about Coors and Pabst also apply to the other "second tier" firms; Schlitz, Stroh, and Heileman. We conjecture that we would also find substantial anti-competitive effects of bilateral collusion (or merger) between any of these and A–B. Second, the conclusion is weak because we can say nothing about the role of Miller, the second-largest producer.

JONATHAN B. BAKER AND TIMOTHY F. BRESNAHAN,
Department of Economics,
Encina Hall,
Stanford University,
Stanford,
California,
U.S.A.

APPENDIX I*

The (inverse) demand function for firm 1, the firm of interest, is

(A.1) $P_1 = P^1(Q_1, \underset{\sim}{Q}, Y, \eta^1)$

Here P_1 and Q_1 are price and quantity for firm 1's product, $\underset{\sim}{Q}$ is a vector of quantities for other firm's products, Y are exogenous variables entering the demand system, and η^1 are parameters. Q_i is a typical element of $\underset{\sim}{Q}$. $\underset{\sim}{Q}$ includes Q_2, as well as $Q_3, \ldots, Q_n$.

The model also includes (inverse) demand equations for $\underset{\sim}{Q}$, the vector of quantities of all other relevant products, including 2.

(A.2) $P_i = P^i(\underset{\sim}{Q}, Q_1, Y, \eta^i), \qquad i = 2, \ldots, n$

$\underset{\sim}{P}$ is a vector composed of the P_i.

The third element of the model is the supply behavior of all the firms i. Their supply relations are written in the form marginal cost equals marginal revenue:

(A.3) $MC^i(Q_i, W, \beta^i) = MR^i(\underset{\sim}{Q}, Q_1, Y, \eta^i), \qquad i = 2, \ldots, n$

The first step in deriving the single-firm residual demand is to solve the equations (2) and (3) simultaneously for the vectors $\underset{\sim}{Q}$ and $\underset{\sim}{P}$.

(A.4) $\underset{\sim}{Q} = \underset{\sim}{E}(Q_1, Y, W; \eta, \beta)$

The elasticity of Q_i with respect to Q_1 in this partial-reduced form is denoted ξ_{i1}:

$$\xi_{i1} = \frac{\partial \ell n E^i}{\partial \ell n Q_1}$$

---

* A complete development of this appendix can be found in Baker and Bresnahan [1984].

GAINS FROM MERGER OR COLLUSION 75

The residual demand curve facing firm 1 is derived by substituting $\underset{\sim}{E}(\cdot)$ into (A.1):

(A.5) $\quad P_1 = P^1(Q_1, \underset{\sim}{E}(Q_1, Y, W, \eta, \beta), Y, \eta^1)$

Substituting out the redundancies, we have:

(A.6) $\quad P_1 = R(Q_1, Y, W, \eta, \beta)$

where the notation $R(\cdot)$ means (inverse) residual demand. The arguments of the residual demand curve are threefold; own quantity, structural demand variables, and other firm's cost variables.

Note that the elasticity of residual demand depends on all the ordinary demand elasticities and on the elasticities of other firms' reactions, ξ_{i1}:

(A.7) $\quad \eta_1^R = \eta_{11} + \sum_i \eta_{i1} \xi_{i1}$

where η_1^R is (inverse) residual demand elasticity, and η_{i1} is the own- or cross- (inverse) demand elasticity in the usual sense.

APPENDIX II

This appendix describes the sources for the variables employed in our study.

Price and Quantity

Nationwide production figures are available from trade publications, such as the yearly *Modern Brewery Age Blue Book* and *Brewers Almanac*. Q in our regressions is annual production of the flagship brand. *Per capita* adjustments were made using the U.S. population over age 18. Prices were transformed into real terms by dividing by GNP deflator. Flagship brand prices are reported in issues of the *Beverage Industry News of Northern California* until 1978. After 1978, newspaper advertisements are used.

Factor Prices (Cost Variables)

Time series on four factors of production were assumed to apply industry-wide: labor, materials, variable capital, and advertising. The price of labor is the average hourly wage of brewing production workers collected by the Bureau of Labor Statistics, reprinted annually in *Brewers Almanac*. The price of variable capital is the user-cost measure from Hazilla and Kopp [1983] for food and beverage industries, and updated by us through the end of the sample period.

Two variants of the materials price series were used. The first uses data on the prices and quantities of a list of specific inputs: malt, corn, rice, hops, cans, bottles, and power. The second divides cost of materials for brewers, as reported in *Brewers Almanac*, by quantity of beer manufactured in barrels. The quantities consumed of all specific inputs are found in *Brewers Almanac*, except power. *MBA Blue Book* reports expenditures on power. The price series for the specific inputs are from *Producer Prices and Prices Indexes*. In real terms, the two materials price series are correlated at 0.99. The advertising price series is computed as an index of media prices; brewing industry weights are from *Leading National Advertisers*.

Demand Variables

Population and income variables are taken from Census and other Commerce Department Sources.

Instruments

Brewer capacity, by plant, is reported in *Beer Marketer's Insights*. This is the basis of both K and APS. The Colorado manufacturing wage rate series is from the *Statistical Abstract of the United States*.

Other Variables

Advertising variables, include each firm's expenditures on advertising, as reported in *Brewers Almanac*. These variables are normalized either by sales, or by the industry price of advertising as described above and a population index.

PREYING FOR TIME

DAVID EASLEY, ROBERT T. MASSON AND ROBERT J. REYNOLDS*

I. INTRODUCTION

THE RECENT antitrust policy literature which seeks to define predatory pricing contains a flood of proposals which have "pervasively transformed an entire body of law".[1] One theme of this literature is that a readily anticipatable standard should be established, so that firms will not fear being sued for normal competitive responses; another is that, since predation is presumed to be rare, the standard should be lax so as to minimize the possibility of stifling competition in the overwhelming majority of more competitive markets.

Perhaps the most striking feature of these arguments is the omission of any analysis of predatory behavior when business firms are sophisticated and "rational". McGee [1980, pp. 295–6], for example, points out that predation only pays if the present discounted value of future high prices exceeds the costs of suffering today's low prices. But if this is so for the monopolist, then why not for the competitor?

"It only *seems* paradoxical, therefore, that if a victim were sure this is a predatory campaign, rather than normal competition..., he would *surely* want to stick it out."

The argument that predation generally costs a predator more than it costs the prey (and other arguments) led McGee to conclude that predation is non-existent or rare, and that the best standard against predation would be no standard at all [p. 317].

To resolve whether some antitrust rule would work as desired requires analysis of an equilibrium with predation assuming that businessmen are reasonably intelligent. McGee points the way in qualifying his statements. His businessman is said to be "sure" the low price is not due to normal competition. This requires certainty: i.e., the businessman always knows exactly when a price is "predatory" versus when it is simply "competitive". If the process were so simple that businessmen could always be "sure", the difference between predation and competition should also be readily demonstrable to courts. But

---

* We are grateful to numerous individuals—Lucinda Lewis and Paul Geroski, in particular. We owe a special debt to the late Richard B. Heflebower. His interpretations of some chain store behavior sowed the seeds that led to this paper. The initial work was funded in part by the United States Department of Justice and later work by the National Science Foundation (grant numbers SES-8112237 and ISI-8120315). The views presented are those of the authors.

[1] Brodley and Hay [1981, p. 740]. Brodley and Hay review much of this literature as does McGee [1980]. Some other contributors are Areeda and Turner [1975], [1976], Baumol [1979], Greer [1979], Joskow and Klevorick [1979], Ordover and Willig [1981], Posner [1976], Schmalensee [1979], and Scherer [1976a], [1976b].

if businesses cannot always distinguish the precise point at which prices cease being "normally competitive", then predation may be both profitable and hard to detect by businessmen, courts or academic economists.

This paper develops a model of predatory pricing using the tools of incomplete information games. When the problem is seen as one of incomplete information, the standard reasons for saying predation is rare are not compelling. Further the lack of proof of predation is an unreliable empirical indicator of its prevalence. The model is designed to facilitate analysis of the efficiency of the various proposed antitrust rules when predation is rational. The result is that most of the rules may not prevent all instances of predation. For example the precise standard "Price must not fall below average variable costs" (Areeda and Turner [1975], [1976]), may in some cases serve as an instruction manual on how to avoid liability when preying.

II. AN INCOMPLETE INFORMATION GAME

II.1 *Entry with Imperfect Information*

The model is developed to analyse entry dynamics when the incumbent firm is a multimarket monopolist. An entrant who experiences a negative entry value in one market will analyse its cause prior to entry into another of the monopolist's markets. For example, if the entrant decides that the incumbent's production was more efficient than it had anticipated, it should consider whether the monopolist's other markets use the same or similar production processes and revise future anticipations accordingly. If negative entry value in one market slows or deters entry to other markets, the multimarket monopolist has an incentive to assure that an entrant is met with a negative entry value. This is true even if the Nash response of the monopolist, if it were only a single market monopolist, would yield positive entry value. Thus, if the cost of driving the entrant's value negative in one or a few markets is exceeded by the margin protected by forestalling entry into other markets, the multimarket monopolist has an incentive to "prey"—as long as this behavior actually inhibits entry.

From the monopolist's point of view, the success of this strategy depends upon keeping its identity hidden from potential entrants. If it were generally known that the single market Nash response would yield a positive entry value, entrants would rapidly enter the markets, predation would then be unprofitable, so a threat to prey would not be carried out. The dynamics of entrants' expectations and the monopolist's responses is critical. If an entrant knows, or believes, that predatory responses will never occur, it will conclude that a negative entry value resulted from inaccurate estimation of real competitive factors and will halt entry after a single episode: the expectation that predation will never occur makes it quite profitable. On the other hand, if entrants expected that all markets would be profitable absent predation they would be undeterred by initially negative entry values: the unprofitability of predation in that case would mean it would never occur. Where there is imperfect information, entrants are not able to definitively attribute negative entry values to either misestimation or predation, and so some predation is liable to occur.

Two other models also analyse predation using incomplete information games. These models (Milgrom and Roberts [1982a] and Kreps and Wilson [1982b]) significantly restrict the strategies available to the players. In each period a new market appears. They require that predation, once it has begun *in any market* must continue in that market, so formally they have a series of one shot games. Since giving up is not permitted, predation, once started, is automatically credible for any market. The classical question (cf. Telser [1966], McGee [1980]), "How long can it pay to prey?" is swept aside.[2] This paper presents a model in which all prices are endogenous in all periods so that a richer strategy space appears: (a) entrants may now enter new markets to force a rise in profits in previously entered markets; (b) some monopolists may decide to prey only to gain extra time, with full knowledge that the predation will not preclude eventual entry of all of their markets. This adds three elements to the analysis: (1) the duration of predation in each market is endogenous; (2) entrants' abilities to cause predation to cease are modeled; (3) the anti-competitive potential of a type of predation which is ineffective in the longrun is also demonstrated. Each of these elements is important for antitrust analysis.

II.2 *The Model*

The model will be developed as a dynamic game with "imperfect but complete information". In each period several potential entrants consider entry into the markets of an incumbent monopolist. The monopolist in turn selects market parameters (e.g., prices, rebates, advertising...) for each market at each time. Information is "imperfect" in the sense that the potential entrants do not know all the competitive aspects of the monopolist's markets. Despite the fact that entrants do not have a perfect description of the monopolist they face, they have "complete information" about the types of monopolists they may be facing.[3] More specifically, they know that the monopolist is one of H possible monopolists and they know the probability that it is any individual type of monopolist. The formal game theoretic model structure and proofs are detailed in the Appendix.

(i) *Predatory Acts*

A definition of predatory behavior is a prerequisite to further analysis. For the purposes of this paper, predation will be defined as:

The selection of strategy in any *entered market* which does not maximize present value in that market when it is considered in isolation, but which

---

[2] In terms of Figure 1 their firms only play on the diagonal of each matrix. Once a monopolist reveals it will not prey, additional markets can only be entered at a rate of one per period. Further, unlike strategy (b), any predator which does not prey in an additional entered market has "failed".

[3] If predation is rational with complete information, it may be rational with incomplete information. See, for example, Rosenthal [1981].

is selected for the purpose of *slowing or stopping* future entry of *equally efficient* firms.

It is at times convenient to think of this "strategy" as a low price. Unlike "limit pricing", predatory pricing is only used *in response* to entry. These acts serve to slow or stop entry and need not require elimination of an entrant. They are knowingly selected in a fashion that does not maximize the monopolist's present value in each market separately. They occur where the Nash equilibrium for each market in isolation would lead to a positive entry value and involve the monopolist sacrificing profits in order to create a negative entry value. Further, the potential for a positive entry value demonstrates that the result does not simply reflect competitive overcrowding. The equal efficiency assumption (which is not essential) assures that the results do not simply reflect superior efficiency on the part of the incumbent firm.[4]

(ii) *Basic Structure of the Model*

There are J potential entrants indexed by $j = 1, \ldots, J$. They observe a monopolist which is operating in m identical markets indexed by $i = 1, \ldots, m$. From their knowledge about technology, demand, prices, and other observable characteristics the potential entrants know that the monopolist must be one of only H possible monopolists, indexed by $h = 1, \ldots, H$. They further know that of these H possible types, only for a "type 1" monopolist would these markets be "inherently competitive" (markets for which the form of the non-predatory post-entry Nash equilibrium for a single market monopolist would yield a negative present value to any of the potential entrants). They know that the other possible types of monopolists, $h = 2, \ldots, H$, all operate in "beneficial markets" (ones for which single market Nash reactions would lead to positive entry values for any entrant).

The monopolist's type is indistinguishable pre-entry. Even the post-entry results do not necessarily reveal the monopolist's type. If entry leads to profits which indicate that the entry has a positive present value, then the monopolist will have revealed itself to be a beneficial type, i.e., not of type 1. But the converse is not true. If entry leads to the level of profits which would be expected from entering a market of a type 1 monopolist, this is not a reliable indicator that the monopolist is actually a type 1 monopolist. It could instead be a beneficial monopolist feigning the reactions of a type 1 monopolist. If this occurs, a type $h > 1$ monopolist may be said to "play as a type $h = 1$ monopolist" or more simply, this may be called a "predatory response" (if the entrant is as efficient as the monopolist). Type $h > 1$ has an incentive to play as a type 1 only if, by doing so, it can slow or stop entry.

The problem of not knowing whether a non-remunerative entry episode

---

[4] As Brodley and Hay [1981] point out, successful entry of somewhat less efficient firms may raise welfare. Our standard is intended to be a non-controversial sufficient condition for predation. It allows the incumbents' fixed sunk entry costs, valued at either original cost or replacement value, to be as high as, or higher than, those of entrants.

occurs from a type 1 playing as a type 1 (competition) or a type $h > 1$ playing as a type 1 (predation) demonstrates how imperfect information creates the potential for strategic behavior. It is assumed that entrants have complete information about the distribution of possible monopolist types in two respects. Prior to any entry all potential entrants know exactly the probability that the monopolist is of each type. After entry, by observing monopolist behavior, entrants accurately revise their prior probabilities.

A simple numerical example can illustrate model dynamics. For notational ease the markets are modeled as having static demand. As a consequence, the flow profits for any market, divided by the interest rate, r, are the present value of flow profits for that market unless competitive conditions change. The monopolists' flow profits are assumed to be ΠM in any unentered market. Predation by any $h > 1$ yields monopolist flow profits of ΠP. To simplify notation, without altering qualitative results, heterogeneity is introduced in only one parameter. This parameter is Πh, the flow profits monopolist h would receive were it to react to entry by playing its Nash present value maximizing strategy for the market. It follows that $\Pi h < \Pi M$, and for $h > 1$, $\Pi h > \Pi P$.

There is little cost in the richness of qualitative results from introducing heterogeneity for the J potential entrants through only one parameter—fixed sunk entry costs. The entry costs of entrant j are f_j. Again for notational ease there are only two entrant types, entrant 1 and all others, defined by $f_1 < f_2 = f_3 = \ldots = f_J$. If an entrant enters a market of a type 1 monopolist it receives "competitive" flow profits of πC. These do not induce exit, $\pi C \geqslant 0$, but are non-remunerative in the present value sense that $\pi C/r - f_j < 0$ for all of the J potential entrants. Similarly, if an entrant meets a predatory response it receives flow profits of πC because a predatory monopolist must act so as to be indistinguishable from a type 1 monopolist. If the monopolist is of type $h > 1$ and "plays as itself" (e.g., plays to receive Πh), then entrant flow profits are πB. These are "beneficial" in the present value sense: $\pi B/r - f_j > 0$ for all of the J potential entrants.

For predation to be optimal J must be greater than 1, but the simplest case mathematically, $J > m$, is selected. Also the presence of entrant adjustment costs leads to the most interesting equilibria. This is incorporated using a simple adjustment cost rule: each entrant can enter only one market in any period.[5] Finally, no market can profitably absorb infinite entry. The simplest convention is to assume that no market can accommodate more than one entrant. Then to avoid the complications of modeling mistaken multiple entry, the extensive form of the game in each time period permits potential entrant J to go first, $J-1$ goes second, and so on until entrant 1 chooses whether to enter. After all entry decisions are made, the monopolist responds for that time period.

[5] With no adjustment costs the game collapses. For an airline to be certain not to face predation it must enter every city pair of every competitor in each entered market simultaneously. This might require entering on a single day virtually all U.S., European, Pacific, etc., city pairs. Leaving aside evidence of adjustment costs one should note that most entry is sequential. This fact should be instructive in terms of interpreting litigated predation cases as well.

(iii) *A Simple Example*

Suppose there are only three markets ($m = 3$),[6] that there are only three monopolist types ($H = 3$), and that the monopolist is drawn from a sample composed of 49 type 1 monopolists, 50 type 2 monopolists, and a single type 3 monopolist. Direct solutions for equilibria are difficult, even for simple examples, but some equilibria can be constructed by working backwards. First, assume a behavior rule for each monopolist type and then derive optimal entrant reactions, "best replies". Second, assume an entry behavior rule and derive the best reply for each monopolist type. If the model parameters are selected such that: (a) the entrants' best replies are identical to the behavior rule assumed in solving for the monopolists' best replies; and (b) the monopolists' best replies are the behavior rules assumed in solving for the entrants' best replies, then a full game Nash equilibrium has been derived.

The first step is to analyse optimal entry. Suppose any of the 50 type 2 monopolists would always prey if only one market were entered, but would always play as type 2 if two or more markets were entered. Suppose that the type 3 monopolist's rule is to prey if one or two markets are entered but not if all three are entered. What is the optimal entrant response? One potential solution involves entrant J entering market 1 in period 1. Since $(J-1)$ is identical to J, then $(J-1)$ would enter market 2 in period 1, and similarly $(J-2)$ would enter market 3. The outcome of the first stage of the game would entail steady state flow profits of $(\Pi 1, \pi C)$ with probability 0.49; $(\Pi 2, \pi B)$ with probability 0.50; and $(\Pi 3, \pi B)$ with probability 0.01. Thus if J would enter there would be a flood of entry in stage 1. Neither predation nor sequential entry would be observed. Alternatively, if not even entrant 1 is willing to enter in period 1, no entry ever occurs. Again neither predation nor sequential entry would be observed.

One interesting case for predation occurs if there are entrant parameters which yield the following entry sequence:

Time 1: Entrant 1 enters market 1.
Time 2: Entrant 1 enters market 2.
Time 3: If πB has occurred in markets 1 and 2 then entrant J enters market 3,
and
if πC has occurred in markets 1 and 2 there is no further entry.
Time 4–anon: No entry, the profit steady state is that of period 3.

Such parameters exist. The extremely low probability of type 3 monopoly relative to type 2 monopoly makes this intuitively clear. All that is needed is:

---

[6] Predation is more likely to occur as m is increased, but it can occur with only three markets. Easley, Masson and Reynolds [1981] demonstrate this result in a decision theoretic version of this model. As m increases, the monopolist's value of markets protected goes up for any level of entry. But the entrant's breakeven point, assuming πB would be revealed upon its last entry, is unaltered.

(1) entrants $2,\ldots,J$ do not find roughly even odds of πB to be attractive; (2) entrant 1 finds even odds to be attractive if it requires entering two markets sequentially; but (3) having entered 2 markets without observing πB, entrant 1 would not find entry of a third market to be attractive if the probability of πB were only 0.02 ($=0.01/(0.49+0.01)$), the conditional probability that the monopolist is of type 3 if it has not played to yield πB in markets 1 and 2.

The technical statements of conditions (1)–(3) above are:

(1) $\quad [0.49\pi C/r + 0.51\pi B/r] - f_j < 0, \quad j > 1;$

(2) $\quad \{\pi C - f_1\} + \{[2(0.5\pi C/r + 0.5\pi B/r) - f_1]/(1+r)\} > 0;$

(3) $\quad \{3(0.98\pi C/r + 0.02\pi B/r) - f_1\} - \{2\pi C/r\} < 0.$

Conditions (1)–(3) are readily seen to be compatible (e.g., if $\pi C = 0$; $\pi B = 0.1$; $r = 0.1$; $J \geqslant 4$; $0.06 < f_1 < 0.3$; and $1 > f_2 = f_3 = f_4 > 0.51$, these conditions are met). This leads the entrants' best replies to be the behavior pattern described above in the sequence from time 1 to 4–anon.

There are parameters for a type 2 monopolist such that its reaction to the above entry behavior rule would be to prey in response to a period 1 entry, but to not prey in response to the second entry. There are also parameters such that a type 3 monopolist would prey in response to entry in both periods if it knew that by so doing its third market would not be entered. To demonstrate this it is useful to give the sequencing a visual representation in matrix form. The monopolist's flow profits can be represented for each of its three markets by the rows of the matrix; the columns represent time 1, time 2, etc. Since the profit steady state is reached after the last play in time 3, the additional infinite sequence of columns which replicate the time 3 profit outcomes can be suppressed. Using the entry rule above and recalling that if any monopolist $h > 1$ selects a response with profits of Πh, then any remaining unentered markets will be entered, matrices (a) and (b) in Figure 1 show the profit sequences underlying a necessary condition for a type 2 monopolist to prey in the first time period. The only difference between matrices (a) and (b) are the "starred" profit levels in (b), elements (1, 1) and (3, 2). By foregoing period 1 profits in market 1, monopolist 2 gains by retarding entry into market 3 by one period. This condition is that profits from preying only one time exceed those from no predation.

(4) $\quad (\Pi 2 - \Pi P) < (\Pi M - \Pi 2)/(1+r)$

Further, monopolist 2 must not find it profitable to prey in period 2. A sufficient condition for this is that predation in the second period would not be remunerative even if it would stop all entry. This condition can be visualized by contrasting matrix (b) with (c): The difference is in those elements which are "starred" in matrix (c) (and for the continuing values of the third column elements in periods 4–anon). The condition for ceasing predation is found by the difference in present values between matrix (c) and (b). This difference is

Matrix (a)
No Predation

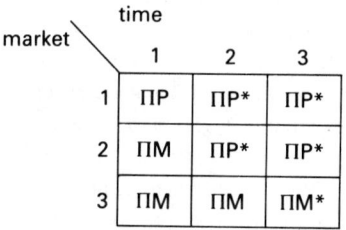

Matrix (b)
Preying Only Once

Matrix (c)
Preying Twice—
Stopping All Entry

FIGURE 1

composed of ΠP rather than $\Pi 2$ in two markets in perpetuity, and then starting one period later, ΠM rather than $\Pi 2$ in a third market in perpetuity. Rearranging terms this is:

(5) $\quad 2(\Pi 2 - \Pi P)/r > (\Pi M - \Pi 2)/r(1+r)$

Conditions (4) and (5) are consistent. By multiplying by r, the type 2 monopolist follows the conjectured strategy if

$$2(\Pi 2 - \Pi P) > (\Pi M - \Pi 2)/(1+r) > (\Pi 2 - \Pi P)$$

In order for a type 3 monopolist to behave as posited it must satisfy a condition similar to condition (4):

(6) $\quad (\Pi 3 - \Pi P) < (\Pi M - \Pi 3)/(1+r)$

Furthermore, it is necessary that it satisfy a condition which is the inverse of condition (5):

(7) $\quad 2(\Pi 3 - \Pi P)/r < (\Pi M - \Pi 3)/r(1+r)$

These conditions can be obtained by substituting Π_3 for Π_2 in matrices (a), (b) and (c). These are met for any parameters for which

$$(\Pi M - \Pi_3)/(1+r) > 2(\Pi_3 - \Pi P)$$

The type 3 monopolist has more to lose from a duopoly game ($\Pi_3 < \Pi_2$) than does the type 2. Generally, the more competitive is the non-predatory outcome, the greater the incentive to prey.

These conditions are sufficient for demonstrating the existence of an equilibrium with predation in the example. No monopolist can improve its profits given the entry decision rules and no entrant can improve its expected value given the monopolists' decision rules. In many discussions of predatory pricing the assumption is made that a predator's goal is either to eliminate a firm or attain submission (agreement or merger). Although the model can be used to illustrate these types of predation, the examples above demonstrate the existence of two other predatory strategies.[7]

The first strategy, used by monopolist 3, looks like classical "deep-pockets" predation, but it is not. The monopolist preys in some markets in perpetuity to protect others in perpetuity. In "deep-pockets" predation firms are alleged to use earnings from profitable markets to finance predation in others. That is certainly not the causality underlying this example. In fact the predatory markets may yield non-negative cash flows ($\Pi P \geq 0$). Thus, a "long purse" (see [Telser 1966]) is not required for predation to have anticompetitive effects in some markets in perpetuity.

The second strategy, used by the type 2 monopolist, involves the use of predation only to slow entry; it recognizes that it will subsequently cease its predation and face complete entry of its markets. Despite this fact, it can attain a greater present value by preying and retarding the rate of growth of competition. The fact that eventual entry is not stopped does not mean that predatory behavior has not occurred or that it has been unsuccessful. Profits can be made from slowing the inevitable.

Both of these strategies work despite the fact that potential entrants know these strategies and do their best to counteract them. For example, suppose that entrant one uses sequential entry to call the bluff. It continues to enter until it knows that accommodation is sufficiently unlikely that it is no longer profitable to enter. When it ceases to enter it knows that if it faces a predator it could force accommodation by yet further entry, and it knows it may be facing a predator. Despite this sophisticated entrant behavior, the model demonstrates that successful predation may stifle competition without either eliminating competitors or even stopping (some) competitors from entering!

---

[7] Another interesting equilibrium pattern is not demonstrated. Suppose that if there had been only monopolists $1, \ldots, (H-1)$ that no entrant would have entered, but since type H was possible, entrant 1 did enter. It is possible that once behavior reveals that the opponent is not of type H, the entrant will continue to enter. This is because it has already invested the sunk costs in some markets and it may pay at the margin to try to force the monopolist to yield πB in these, and new, markets.

(iv) *Equilibria*

For any parameters the model generates a steady state within a finite horizon (see the Appendix).[8] It is useful to note that entrants, $j > 1$, will enter at only one stage of any game. This will be either the first period or after a monopolist $h > 1$ plays as an $h > 1$ (see the Appendix).

It follows that there are equilibria of three generic types:

(1) *Instantaneous Entry:* The probability of a type 1 monopolist is so low that all markets are entered in the first period.

(2) *Zero Entry:* This has two subcases: (a) *Benign:* The probability of a type 1 monopolist is so great that even a type 1 entrant who expects no predation would not enter; (b) *Latent Deterrence:* Only a type 1 entrant would enter if all $h > 1$ monopolists would play their true types; it does not enter, however, in light of probabilities that type $h > 1$ monopolists would prey and it would be excessively costly to enter sufficient markets to force some of them to cease to prey.

(3) *Sequential Entry:* This may involve pure or mixed strategy equilibria. There are three subcases: (a) *Competition:* The monopolist is of type 1. The type 1 entrant enters some markets and then ceases entry; (b) *Predation in Perpetuity:* The type 1 entrant enters only some markets, the monopolist is of type $h > 1$, but plays as type 1. The monopolist gains by initially slowing entry to only one market per period and then by halting all entry after that; (c) *Predation to Slow Competition:* The monopolist is of type $h > 1$, but plays as type 1 for some time. It later responds to entry by playing its own type and having all of its remaining unentered markets entered in the next period. Slowing competitive entry benefits the monopolist despite the fact that it knows it may not ("will not" in pure strategies) deter eventual entry to all of its markets.

One characteristic of sequential entry equilibria is worth stressing. Given the model structure, observed sequential entry of two or more markets can mean only one thing: there is a positive probability that the monopolist is a predator. The only possibilities are that πB is observed initially and a flood of entry precludes sequential entry or that πC is observed. Continued entry to the latter set of markets is only optimal if there is some chance that πC will be revised to πB. If πC may be revised to πB then this means that one possible reason πC is being observed is that the incumbent firm is a predator.

III. POLICY ISSUES

Since 1975 there has been "...a virtual explosion in the legal and economic literature dealing with predatory pricing [which] has rapidly and pervasively

---

[8] A monopolist may be willing to prey longer if this would stop all future entry, than if it could only slow entry. When such a gap occurs the equilibrium may involve mixed strategies (within this gap). These equilibria are discussed more fully in Easley, Masson and Reynolds [1984] and a pure strategy decision theoretic solution is presented in Easley, Masson and Reynolds [1981].

transformed an entire body of [U.S. Antitrust] law, and within the briefest period of time" (Brodley and Hay [1981, p. 740]). The economic literature underlying this revolution has generally attempted to define predation without formally analysing its rationality. However, knowing when predation might work—the credibility issue—is an important step in knowing how and when to expect it. This issue is discussed in the policy literature, but its importance is not fully recognized. A closer examination of the role of imperfect/incomplete information in predatory pricing reveals fundamental infirmities in the current policy debate.

III.1. *Criteria for Policy Analysis*

The various proposals for predatory pricing rules have, either implicitly or explicitly generally contained the following points. First, some economic definition of predation is formulated. These vary by author depending upon numerous factors such as whether "fairness" is considered to be relevant. Next, a judicial definition is offered: How should courts define predation given the imperfect information that will be faced by courts? The policy goal can be seen as a rule which weighs the costs against the benefits from deterring or stopping predators. The costs are: (1) Enforcement costs; (2) Costs of type 1 errors (punishing the innocent); (3) Costs of type 2 errors (acquitting or not even detecting the guilty); (4) Costs from firms using alternative strategies to achieve the same ends; (5) Costs due to non-predatory firms acting to avoid being mistaken for predators. The potential for both benefits and costs from any rule against predation is highly dependent upon the incidence of predation. If predation is extremely rare, then costs (2) and (5) may easily outweigh the benefits. If it is very common (3) and (4) may be the primary costs, and the relative benefits from deterrence may be great.

III.2. *The Incidence of Predation*

Economists who opine that predation is rare have little evidence to go on.[9] Predators are unlikely to admit to predation lest they lose their bluff or get prosecuted. Only if it does not expect to be detected will a monopolist prey.

---

[9] If economists could definitively detect predation then; (1) it might not pay to prey if potential entrants could hire economists, and (2) predators could be easily brought to justice.
  Koller [1971] examines the results of 123 cases since 1890. Only 26 out of 95 convictions have complete records. To be categorized as predatory by Koller an episode must pass three tests. The third test is that a competitor must be eliminated or merged or that there be "improved market discipline". The predators demonstrated in this model would never violate this criterion. Koller finds 5 total cases of predation by his standards.
  It is noteworthy that many filed Sherman Act cases involve a multi-geographic market firm allegedly preying in a subset of markets, and many of the remaining cases involve a firm with several related products allegedly preying for only some of these products. Defendants and others argue that many allegedly threatening statements are the rhetoric of tough competition, but if threat-like statements come from type 1's they should also come from type $h > 1$. Finally, as noted above, markets more predisposed to competitive results are, *ceteris paribus*, more predisposed to predation.

Furthermore, predators will not wish to maintain evidence (e.g., incriminating memos) where it can be discovered. Although unambiguously incriminating evidence sometimes emerges, these firms have every incentive to settle the case out of court, leaving only the atypically ambiguous cases to go to court and become publicly reported. These cases are the bulk of the available evidence on the incidence of predation.[10] It would thus seem risky to assume that predation is rare, and hence that costs (3) and (4) may be high.

III.3. *The Model and Proposed Antitrust Rules*

At the risk of oversimplifying numerous and varied analyses in the policy literature, the literature can be viewed as based upon the case of a single market industry with high entry barriers and long entry lags. Therefore, if an entrant can be swiftly eliminated, a monopolist may enjoy a long period of elevated profits. The role of conjectures in these discussions is generally implicit or simplistic. Multimarket considerations are then tacked on as an after-thought (cf. Brodley and Hay [1981, pp. 789–790] or McGee [1980, p. 326]).

Although the model presented here has no pretense of encompassing all possible types of predation, it demonstrates that previous analyses leave out many potentially important aspects of the problem. In contrast to one common view, predation need not imply economic murder (the elimination of an entrant) or coercion (to force conspiracy or merger upon an entrant). By simply making life tough for entrants the monopolist may intimidate future entry. By the same token, large entry barriers need not be present for predation to be an optimal strategy.[11] Indeed relatively low entry barriers and the threat of rapid mass entry may motivate a monopolist to artificially manufacture an additional entry deterrent through predation.

The new proposed "economic rules" against predation have had a profound effect upon legal decisions in the last decade. It is accordingly useful to see how these rules stack up against this model in which predation is in fact a rational strategy with sophisticated players. Several of the new rules propose "bright-line" standards, which describe precisely what is predatory and, by exclusion,

---

[10] Of course additional circularity is added because if a particular predatory price does not fit the current legal precedent the case will probably not be filed. Conversely, the Robinson–Patman Act requires only the showing of injury, not predation, so there is a danger that loose use of judicial language could misbrand other cases.

[11] What courts have traditionally called monopoly is not needed either. Suppose every city has the same non-conspiring 4 grocery stores (A–D) located in a ring around the central city. An entrant entering near A (e.g., between A and B) might experience predation for precisely the reasons incorporated above, or because A (and/or B) attempt to induce it to try entering near C in the next city. If the entrant suspects all monopolists (A–D) are of the same type it may continue to enter A's markets to attempt to force a shift to πB. If A may differ from B–D (e.g., product differentiation may lead to differences in perceived or actual cross elasticities of demand, or firm cost structures may differ) it may shift to entering near C. For this type of spatial oligopoly neither entry barriers nor large city market shares are required for predation to be effective. Finally, as discussed above, markets more prone to competitive results will, *ceteris paribus*, be more prone to predation.

what is not. Stripped to their essentials, the existing proposals can be summarized as follows.[12] "The courts should find it illegal for a dominant firm to..." (1) "Set price below average variable costs"; or (2) "Set price below marginal costs"; or (3) "Eliminate a competitor by..."; or (4) "Increase price following exit"; or (5) "Set price below average costs with intent to..." or (6) "Increase output when experiencing entry".

One advantage of the "bright-line" approaches is that they let firms know exactly what they are not permitted to do, so that the fear of violating the law "by mistake" does not have a chilling effect on all activity. By the same token, a list of interdicted activities tells firms exactly what competition-stifling tactics they are permitted to employ. The parameters of the model in section II above were selected to demonstrate this. None of the predators described there could be held in violation of standards (1)–(4). Prices are not below AVC or MC and exit is not induced.[13] Nor need they necessarily violate (5) using accounting costs. Measuring costs correctly (e.g., replacement value, learning effects) reduces the rule's precision (see Brodley and Hay [1981]). Also, depending upon technological and demand factors (some of which may be manipulated prior to entry) there is no logical necessity for the modeled firms to violate standard (6). Ironically, for the modeled firms, some bright-lines may constitute the instruction manual on how to prey with impunity.

Scherer [1976a], [1976b], Brodley and Hay [1981], and Schmalensee [1979] suggest using a Rule of Reason approach. Litigation may be more costly with this approach, but the unseen portion of the evidentiary iceberg, documents or admissions of intent,[14] often come from the wider scope of inquiry. Many of the cases brought under the Sherman Act involve slashing prices by large margins (not infrequently by 50%). It seems doubtful that many firms are inhibited from socially desirable competitive price cuts due to fear of Sherman Act litigation.[15] The burden of proof is high, the number of cases filed as a proportion of price cuts is no doubt minuscule. But, to the extent that there is a small chilling effect, the by-product is that even non-predatory firms may be forced to keep pre-entry prices more closely aligned with costs in order to avoid the appearance of predation if there is entry.[16] Thus if fear of litigation

[12] These standards are for predatory pricing. It is notable that most cases involve allegations of complementary coercion as well (e.g., bribing suppliers, threatening buyers). Standards (1)–(6) are simplified from their originals. They are respectively from: (1) Areeda and Turner [1975]; (2) Posner [1976]; (3) Ordover and Willig [1981]; (4) Baumol [1979]; (5) Greer [1979]; (6) Williamson [1977]. Joskow and Klevorick [1979] use a combination of (1), (4) and (5).

[13] If (4) did not require an exit, the rule would lower an entrant's incentive to enter a potential predator's markets because it could not achieve πB in its infra-marginal markets for a quasi-permanent time period.

[14] Good documentary evidence is seldom made public because when it is available the case is typically settled before trial.

[15] The Robinson–Patman Act does not require a showing of predation. Any effect it has on pricing should not be attributed to a predation standard.

[16] Contestable market theory depends upon an incumbent not being able to respond to match the entry price for a finite period of time. If sunk costs are non-zero this time period expands. Although this limits the applicability of contestability to a general curiosum (cf. Schwartz and Reynolds [1983]), its basic elements might come into play if firms feared litigation if they cut prices in response to entry.

has any effect at all upon non-predators, whether this leads to on average higher or lower prices, is itself an open question.

DAVID EASLEY,
ROBERT T. MASSON,
Department of Economics,
Uris Hall,
Cornell University,
Ithaca,
New York 14853,
U.S.A.

ROBERT J. REYNOLDS,
ICF, Inc.,
1850K St., N.W.,
Washington D.C. 20006,
U.S.A.

APPENDIX: STRATEGIC PLAY AND EQUILIBRIUM

The model has a "sequential equilibrium" as defined by Kreps and Wilson [1982b]. All players know that the monopolist's markets are ordered in an entry sequence of $1, 2, \ldots m$. At stage "0" of the game, nature selects the monopolist. The probability of type h is p_h, where $\Sigma_{h=1}^{H} p_h = 1$. These and all other parameters are in the entrants' stage 1 information set. At stage 1, entrant J has the first move, an entry decision (on market 1). Then entrant $J-1$ moves. It can infer J's move from the model structure. If it infers that J entered 1, it decides whether to enter 2; if it infers J did not enter, its decision is on market 1. This sequence of, in effect, simultaneous moves continues until 1 has moved. Then the monopolist selects its move given the information set derived from knowing its type and knowing all entry moves. (A type $h > 1$ will clearly play only 1 or its own type in equilibrium.) The stage 2 entrant information set includes all parameters and the revealed knowledge of all moves in stage 1. The game is then infinitely repeated.

Sequential equilibria exist for finite games. The game can be made finite by imposing a finite duration on the markets. Alternatively, suppose that once entry ceases there will be no future entry (certainly no new information would be generated if the monopolist changes its play only in response to entry). In this case the model has at most m stages before reaching a steady state which defines terminus values, for a finite game.

The information of entrant j is represented as a partition, Γ^j, of the nodes of the game tree at which j must move. At time t the possible nodes are denoted S_t^j and the partition is Γ_t^j with its elements the information sets I_t^j. These indicate which monopolist(s) entrant j may be playing at time t. A monopolist's information set at any time is the individual node associated with its identity. The set of possible nodes for a monopolist at t is denoted S_t^m, and this is partitioned into individual nodes, s_t, the information sets for the monopolist at time t.

A strategy for entrant j is a sequence of functions $g^j = \{g_t^j\}_{t=1}^{m}$, where the function $g_t^j : \Gamma_t^j \to \{x \in R_+^m : \Sigma_{i=1}^{m} x_i \leq 1\}$ assigns a probability to entering each market as a function of entrant j's information at stage t. A strategy for monopolist h is also a sequence of functions $G^h = \{G_t^h\}_{t=1}^{m}$. The monopolist's possible information sets are S_t^h, so $G_t^h : S_t^h \to \{x \in R_+^H : \Sigma_{h=1}^{H} x_h = 1\}$ assigns the probabilities the monopolist will play as any type h in $\{1, \ldots, H\}$ in any entered market. (A type 1 must play as type 1, so $G_t^1(s_t) = (1, 0, \ldots, 0)$ for all t.) A monopolist of type $h > 1$ may assign positive probabilities to any play, but optimal behavior leads to zero probabilities always being assigned to all but the first and h^{th} element of the vector.

Let $g \equiv \{g^1, \ldots, g^J; G^1, \ldots, G^H\}$ describe the vector of entrants' and monopolists' strategies. Nature selects the monopolist's type using probabilities $(p_1, p_2, \ldots, p_H)$. This probability vector and any strategy vector g induces a probability p^g on the nodes of the game. The probability of reaching any node s is denoted $p^g(s)$ and the probability of reaching any set of nodes, for example I^j, is denoted $p^g(I^j)$.

Define $\mu^j(s)$ as the probability j assigns to being at node $s \in I^j$ if it arrives at information set $I^j \in \Gamma^j$. (Note $\mu^j(s)$ is implicitly conditioned upon I^j.) For any strategy vector, g, and expectation, μ^j, entrant j can assign probabilities to the terminal nodes, conditional upon any information set during the play of the game. Define $\rho^{\mu^j, g}(s \mid I^j)$ as the conditional probability entrant j assigns to terminal node s given the information set I^j. Then expected payouts are $E^{\mu^j,g}[\cdot \mid I^j]$. (For the monopolist, expected payouts are $E[\cdot \mid s]$ for any node.) Let $\mu = (\mu^1, \ldots, \mu^J)$ be the vector of entrants' expectations.

Then (μ^*, g^*) is a *Sequential Equilibrium* if three conditions are met.

(i) For all $j \in \{1, \ldots, J\}$ and $I^j \in \Gamma^j$,

$$E^{\mu^{*j}, g^*}[\pi^j(s) \mid I^j] \geq E^{\mu^{*j}, g}[\pi^j(s) \mid I^j] \text{ where}$$

$g \equiv (g^{*1}, \ldots, g^j, \ldots, g^{*J}; G^{*1}, \ldots, G^{*H})$, for all strategies g^j.

(ii) For all $\bar{s} \in S^h$ and all $h \in \{1, \ldots, H\}$

$$E^{g^*}[\Pi^h(s) \mid \bar{s}] \geq E^g[\Pi^h(s) \mid \bar{s}] \text{ where}$$

$g \equiv (g^{*1}, \ldots, g^{*J}; G^{*1}, \ldots, G^h, \ldots, G^{*H})$, for all strategies G^h.

(iii) There exists a sequence (μ_n, g_n) with $\lim_{n \to \infty}(\mu_n, g_n) = (\mu^*, g^*)$ such that for each n:

(a) $1 \gg g_n^j(I^j) \gg 0$ for all $I^j \in \Gamma^j$,
(b) $G_n^h(s) \gg 0$ for all s for each $h \in \{2, \ldots, H\}$ and
(c) $\mu_n^j(s) = p^{g_n}(s)/p^{g_n}(I^j)$ for any $s \in I^j$, for all $I^j \in \Gamma^j$, and all j.

Conditions (i) and (ii) are simply that all entrants and the monopolist maximize expected profits given the equilibrium strategies of all other players. Condition (iii) is the "consistency condition". One heuristic interpretation is that (a) and (b) force positive probabilities on all possible outcomes. Condition (c) requires that expectations be derived from Bayes rule where applicable. The positive probabilities in (a) and (b) allow for expectations to be defined when attaining information sets which are logically possible, but off any equilibrium path. The limit assures that this assignment rule accurately presents expectations along any equilibrium path.

With these definitions, Proposition 1 follows directly from Kreps and Wilson's Proposition 1:

Proposition 1. The extensive form game of section II and this Appendix has at least one sequential equilibrium.

The model generates at most two truly strategic players, entrant 1 and the monopolist, if the monopolist is of type $h > 1$. This vastly simplifies constructing examples like those in the text.

The intuition is simple, if any $j > 1$ is willing to enter at stage 1; then all are willing at stage 1, so the game ends. Further, unless πB is observed in some later stage, entrants $j > 1$ have only "bad news", so they will not enter. Hence types $j > 1$ can be treated as "exogenous", entering all unentered markets only at stage 1 or at the stage after observing πB. Proposition 2 demonstrates these two entry equilibria for $j > 1$ in sections (i) and (ii) respectively.

Define: p_1 as the initial probability of a type 1 monopolist; $h(I_t^j)$ as the monopolist type played in stage $t-1$ (which entrant j observes at stage t); $n(I_t^j)$ as the number of markets entered at information set I_t^j; and $\|g_t^j\|$ as the norm of g_t^j. (Note that $\|g_t^j\| = 1$

only if j chooses to enter some market with probability one and $\|g_t^j\| = 0$ if j chooses not to enter.)

Proposition 2. There exists an equilibrium where:

(i) *If $(p_1 \pi C + (1-p_1)\pi B)/r \geq f_2$ then:*

$\|g_1^j\| = \{1, \text{ if } j \in \{\mathcal{J}, \ldots, \mathcal{J}-m\}; 0, \text{ otherwise}\}$ *and*

$\|g_t^j\| = 0 \text{ for all } t > 1, \text{ for all } j.$

(ii) *If $(p_1 \pi C + (1-p_1)\pi B)/r < f_2$ then for all $j > 1$ and all t:*

$\|g_t^j\| = \{1, \text{ if } h(I_t^j) > 1 \text{ and } j > \mathcal{J} - (m - n(I_t^j)); 0 \text{ otherwise}\}.$

Proof

(i) If $(p_1 \pi C + (1-p_1)\pi B)/r \geq f_j$ for all j then entry is profitable if there will be no predation (if $h > 1$ yields πB). From Proposition 1, condition (ii), if all m markets are entered h will play its true type. Entrants $\mathcal{J}, \ldots, \mathcal{J}-m$ will enter sequentially, as for any $j' > \mathcal{J} - m$ to delay for one period would lead to pre-emption by the entry of $\mathcal{J} - m - 1$.

(ii) If $(p_1 \pi C + (1-p_1)\pi B)/r < f_j$ for $j > 1$ then the optimal stage 1 strategy for $j > 1$ is $\|g_1^j\| = 0$. This results because j's payoff from entry, even with the most favorable strategies for its opponents, is negative. Thus no entrant $j > 1$ will enter in stage 1.

At any information set I_t^j, j will enter ($\|g_t^j\| = 1$) if there is an unentered market, that is, $j > \mathcal{J} - (m - n(I_t^j))$ and if $\mu(s) = 1$ for any node $s \in I_t^j$ on a branch of the tree following a selection by nature of $h > 1$ (that is, if Πh is played and πB received). This strategy is optimal for the same reason as in (i) above.

At any information set I_t^j, $j > 1$ will not enter ($\|g_t^j\| = 0$) if $h(I_t^j) = 1$ because $\Sigma \mu(s) \leq (1-p_1)$ for $I_t^j \subset I = \{s : s \text{ is on a branch following selection by nature of } h > 1\}$.

PATENT RACES AND THE PERSISTENCE OF MONOPOLY*

CHRISTOPHER HARRIS AND JOHN VICKERS

I. INTRODUCTION

PATENT RACES are important determinants of market structure. For a new firm, a patent can be an entry ticket into the market. For an incumbent firm already in the market, patents for related technologies can ensure that no new firm enters. In this spirit recent work has explored the implications of patenting for the persistence of monopoly (see, for example, Dasgupta [1982], Gilbert [1981], Gilbert and Newbery [1982]). Much attention has been given to "pre-emptive patenting"—the strategic acquisition of patents by an incumbent firm solely to prevent potential rivals from entering the market.

In this context it is important to distinguish between two kinds of patent race. A *standard race* is a competition in which a prize is awarded to the first player to reach the finishing line. An *asymmetrical race* is a competition in which one player loses something of value if one of his rivals reaches the finishing line (he is content if nobody wins), but a prize is won by the first of the other players to reach the finishing line, if any of them does so. A patent race in which an incumbent firm's sole concern is to prevent potential rivals from entering his market is an asymmetrical race and not a standard race.

The distinction between the two kinds of race can be captured only in models with a sufficiently rich dynamic structure. This, and other, advantages of a properly dynamic model are explained in section II. A model of an asymmetrical race with two firms is presented in section III. In this model the "challenger" wins a prize, and the "incumbent" loses a prize, if the challenger is first to reach the finishing line. It is shown that the challenger is often automatically deterred from making any effort to win the race, because the strategic interactions between the players are such that the incumbent would outdo any reasonable effort made by the challenger in order to stop the challenger being first to reach the finishing line. Then the incumbent has no need to make any effort in the race in order to maintain his existing monopoly. The reason is that the incumbent—unlike the challenger—does not need to go all the way to the finishing line to achieve his objective. On the other hand, it may be true—depending on the parameters describing the firms—that the challenger wins the patent, proceeding to the finishing line just as if he were the only contender for the patent. Of particular interest is the case in which the firms are identical

---

* We are very grateful to Jim Mirrlees, John Sutton and an anonymous referee for their helpful comments and suggestions.

except for the incumbent/challenger asymmetry. It turns out that the incumbent generally has strategic supremacy here: the challenger is automatically deterred from actively pursuing the patent.

In section IV we briefly set out a variant upon our (1985) model of a standard race, which we compare with the model of an asymmetrical race of section III. The comparison illustrates generally the strategic advantages of wanting one's rival *not* to win, rather than wanting to win oneself.

In section V we solve an explicit example to obtain a clear picture of the solutions to the standard and asymmetrical races—and the differences between them. In order to do this neatly, we look at the models in the limit as the intervals between the rivals' actions and reactions become shorter. This limiting case may also be of independent interest.

The concluding section discusses the implications of our results for the theory of the persistence of monopoly.

II. THE ECONOMICS OF PATENT RACES

Patent Races as Bidding Games

It has been suggested that the essence of a patent race among fully informed competitors can be distilled by analysing bidding games: see Dasgupta [1982, p. 30] and Gilbert and Newbery [1982, p. 517]. In their simple models, each of two players makes an irrecoverable bid (his R & D expenditure) for an indivisible prize (the patent), which the players may value differently. This highest bidder wins the prize. It turns out that the prize is won by the player most keen to win it, since he is prepared to pay the most for it.

It is often supposed that one player is an incumbent monopolist, currently supplying a product with which the future invention would compete. If his rival does not win the patent, then his monopoly persists. But if the challenger does win the new patent, he will enter the market and compete with the current incumbent. It is reasonable to assume that the firms' joint profits in this latter case are lower than the incumbent's profits if he retains his monopoly position. Hence it is argued that the incumbent has more incentive than the challenger to win the patent, and so will "pre-empt" the patent.[1]

Our criticism of the structure of this simple model is that it neglects important features of strategic interaction between players during the course of the race. In the simple model each player has just one bid, which would be appropriate only if the competitors made unconditional, once-and-for-all commitments of effort at the outset of the race. In fact there is action and reaction between the rivals as the race progresses. A competitor makes a series of decisions during the race, each one in the light of the moves made by his

---

[1] For a critical discussion of Gilbert and Newbery [1982] see Reinganum [1983] and the debate between Reinganum, Salant and Gilbert and Newbery in the *American Economic Review*, March 1984, Vol. 74, pp. 238–53.

rivals and with a view to influencing the moves that they make in their turn.[2]

In an attempt to capture these considerations we develop the structure of the simple model. In our framework, each player makes a series of bids, each one of which is made in the light of the bids made previously. The players take turns to bid: thus there are opportunities for action and reaction. The richer structure enables one to analyse questions that could not previously be handled. For example, we can make precise the idea that a player would give up in the race once his rival was far enough ahead; we can see why this might be so; and we can see what exactly it is to be "far enough ahead" in this sense. Moreover, the richer structure permits one to distinguish between a standard race and an asymmetrical race.

Two Kinds of Patent Race

We discuss the distinction between the two kinds of race in terms of a two-firm example which is related to the models in the following sections. In a standard race it is true of each firm that its profits increase if it obtains the patent, but that if it loses the race it forgoes only its R & D expenditures. An asymmetrical race is different. Let A be the name of a challenger to an incumbent firm B. A's payoff is as in the standard race above. But B's profits fall if A wins the patent. So if B loses the race to A, he loses not only his R & D expenditures, but also suffers a fall in profits. If A does not win the race, B avoids this latter loss, irrespective of whether he actually wins the patent himself.

To summarise: (i) in a standard race, both A and B want to win the prize; but (ii) in an asymmetrical race, A (the challenger) wants to win the prize, but B's (the incumbent's) concern is that his rival should not win the prize.

There are cases intermediate between these two types of race. For example, B might strictly prefer to have the patent than not have it, although he would rather that no one have it than his rival have it. In this paper we shall not discuss such hybrid cases. Our main concern is with "pure" asymmetrical races, in which the incumbent's sole motive is to prevent his rival from winning. Because we are concerned with the question of the persistence of monopoly, this is the natural focus of attention.

III. A MODEL OF AN ASYMMETRICAL RACE

Two players, A and B, compete for a single indivisible prize. Initially A and B are at distances x_0 and y_0 from a "finishing line". Progress by A towards the finishing line depends on his irrecoverable R & D efforts, called "bids". Thus a bid of z moves him a distance $w_A(z)$ closer to the finishing line. We assume

---

[2] In independent work, Fudenberg *et al.* [1983, section 4] have also presented a model that attempts to capture these features of strategic interaction through time. For a discussion of the relationship between that paper and our work, see Harris and Vickers [1985].

that w_A is continuous, increasing and that it exhibits increasing returns to scale for low effort levels. We assume also that $w_A(0) = 0$.[3]

We make exactly the same assumptions about B and his "progress" function w_B. It is not assumed that the w functions are necessarily identical, since we wish to allow for the possibility that the players are not equally efficient at R & D. Players bid alternately: first A, then B, then A again, and so on. We denote the sequence of bids by: $a_1, b_1, a_2, b_2, \ldots$. The prize is awarded to the first player to reach the finishing line.

If player A wins the prize his payoff is $V_A - \Sigma a_i$. If he does not win the prize his payoff is $-\Sigma a_i$. Player B's payoffs are as follows. If A wins the prize, B's payoff is $-V_B - \Sigma b_i$. If A does not win the prize, B's payoff is $-\Sigma b_i$, whether or not B wins the prize himself. Thus we think of A as a challenger to an incumbent monopolist B.

For simplicity of exposition we adopt the convention that, if player A is indifferent between winning the prize with a net payoff of zero and not winning the prize, he will choose to win the prize. And if B is indifferent between thwarting A's victory and not doing so, then he will do so. It will be clear that these conventions do not significantly affect the analysis.

Players are perfectly informed of one another's bids, and condition their choices on this information. Thus a player's strategy specifies what bid he would make contingent upon any possible history of bids. Since we want to rule out the making of threats that are not credible, Selten's [1965] notion of perfect equilibrium is the natural solution concept. While the arguments that follow are intuitive, the underlying solution concept is perfect equilibrium.

The game is most conveniently analysed by partitioning the space of pairs of distances from the finishing line in terms of two sequences of critical distances: $\{C_n\}$ for A and $\{E_n\}$ for B. (See Figure 1.)

The sequence $\{C_n\}$ is defined purely in relation to A. First, $C_0 = 0$. Then if C_{n-1} has been defined for some $n \geq 1$, C_n is the maximum distance from the finishing line that A can profitably cover if he is subject to moving to within C_{n-1} of the finishing line with his first bid. More formally:

Definition 1. $C_0 = 0$. For $n \geq 1$, C_n is the maximum x such that there exists a sequence $a_1, a_2, \ldots, a_r$ of non-negative bids such that

$$\sum_{i=1}^{r} w_A(a_i) \geq x$$

$$w_A(a_1) \geq x - C_{n-1}$$

$$V_A \geq \sum_{i=1}^{r} a_i$$

To gain another perspective on $\{C_n\}$, let us define $\Omega_A(x)$ as the value to A of

---

[3] These assumptions on w_A are similar to those models about the hazard function in the literature on R&D under uncertainty: see for example Kamien and Schwartz [1982, p. 181].

a "free run" from distance x.[4] That is to say, $\Omega_A(x)$ is the payoff that A would get if he started a distance x from the finishing line and faced no rivalry from B. Then he would face the one-player decision problem of finding the optimal path to the line. Now, if $C_{n+1} > C_n$, we have

(1) $\quad C_n - C_{n-1} = w_A(\Omega_A(C_{n-1}))$

The RHS of (1) is the distance that A would travel if he bid the full value to him of a "free run" from C_{n-1}. It is simple to show that Ω_A is strictly decreasing if it is strictly positive. Hence $C_{n+1} - C_n < C_n - C_{n-1}$ so long as $\Omega_A(C_{n-1}) > 0$.

The sequence $\{E_n\}$ is defined purely in relation to B.

Definition 2. $E_n = nw_B(V_B)$.

Thus $E_n - E_{n-1} = w_B(V_B)$. That is, increments in the $\{E_n\}$ sequence are all equal to $w_B(V_B)$, which is the distance that B would travel if he bid the maximum amount he would pay to prevent A from winning. Note that while $E_n - E_{n-1}$ is exactly equal to $w_B(V_B)$, $C_n - C_{n-1}$ is strictly less than $w_A(V_A)$ for all $n > 1$. This is because $C_n - C_{n-1}$ also reflects the cost of getting from C_{n-1} to the finishing line. If the firms are identical except for the incumbent/challenger asymmetry, that is $V_A = V_B$ and $w_A = w_B$, then $E_n > C_n$ for $n > 1$. Moreover, the ratio E_n/C_n increases with n.

Figure 1 shows the partition of the space of pairs of distances from the finishing line.

If A is within C_n of the finishing line for some n, but B is more than E_n away from it, then we say that (x,y) lies in A's *safety zone*. If B is within E_n of the line, but A is more than C_n from it, then (x,y) lies in B's safety zone. If $C_{n-1} < x \leq C_n$ and $E_{n-1} < y \leq E_n$ for some n, then we say that (x,y) lies in a *trigger zone*. The final, uninteresting, possibility is that $x > C_n$ for all n, in which case A could not profitably reach the line, even without rivalry from B.

The following proposition states what happens in the race.

Proposition 1. Suppose that the players' strategies are in equilibrium:

(i) *If (x,y) lies in player A's safety zone then A wins the prize. His bids are those he would make in the absence of rivalry from B. B always bids zero.*

(ii) *If (x,y) lies in B's safety zone both players always bid zero and no one wins the prize.*

(iii) *If (x,y) lies in a trigger zone and it is A's move then A wins the prize. His bids are those he would make if, in isolation, he were subject only to reaching his safety zone with his first bid. B always bids zero.*

(iv) *If (x,y) lies in a trigger zone and it is B's move then no one wins the prize. B moves immediately to the boundary of his safety zone and both players bid zero thereafter.*

[4] Appendix A contains a more formal discussion of $\Omega_A(x)$, including a proof that equation (1) holds.

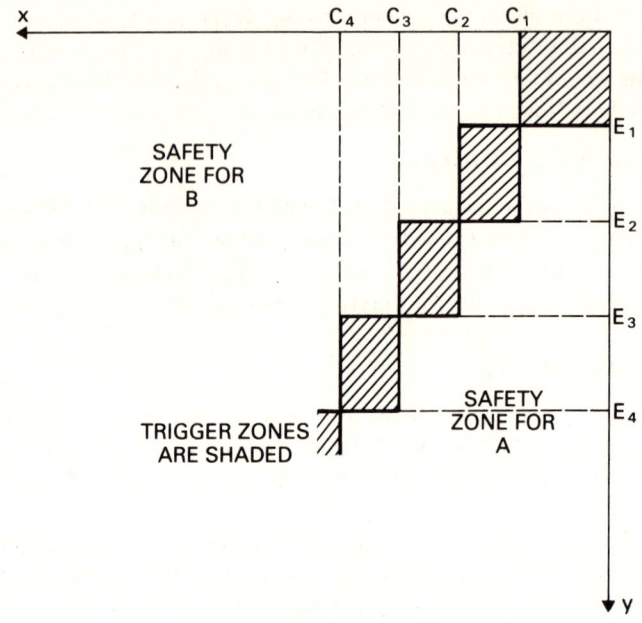

FIGURE I
The Partition of the Space of Distances from the Finishing Line
in the Asymmetrical Race

Proof. The proof is by induction. In Figure 2, consider the first trigger zone, T_1, and the first parts of A's and B's safety zones, denoted by A_1 and B_1.

If it is A's turn to bid in $T_1 = \{(x,y) \mid 0 < x \leqslant C_1 \text{ and } 0 < y \leqslant E_1\}$ then A wins the prize. Otherwise his payoff is at best zero, whereas he obtains a positive payoff by moving directly to the finishing line. Moreover, A moves immediately to the line. For otherwise it would become B's turn to move in T_1, in which case A would not win since B would do better to move to the line himself and prevent A's victory than to allow it. Finally, if it is B's turn to move in T_1 he moves immediately to the line. If he did not, it would become A's turn to move in T_1 in which case A would win: then B would get at most $-V_B$ which is worse than moving immediately to the line himself. Thus we have shown that whoever's turn it is to move in T_1 moves immediately to the line.

Next we show that A is safe in $A_1 = \{(x,y) \mid 0 < x \leqslant C_1 \text{ and } y > E_1\}$. It can never be optimal for B to finish in one move from any point in A_1. For to do so would cost him more than V_B, whereas $-V_B$ is the worst payoff that B can get if he does nothing. Nor can it be optimal for B to move into T_1 from A_1. For if he did so, A would finish immediately, and B's payoff would be $-V_B$ less the cost of his move. This is again worse than bidding zero always. Since B never moves out of A_1, A's behaviour is unaffected by B, and his bids are those he would make if he acted in isolation. Since B cannot affect A's behaviour he always bids zero.

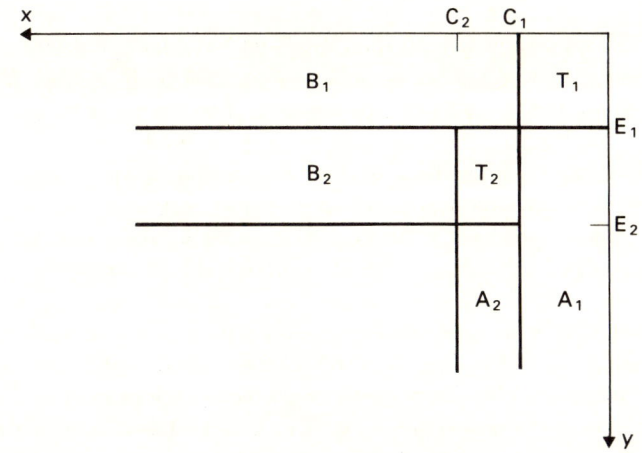

FIGURE 2

Furthermore B is safe in $B_1 = \{(x,y) \mid x > C_1 \text{ and } 0 < y \leq E_1\}$. For it is not optimal for A to finish in one move from any point in B_1, or for him to move from B_1 into T_1. In either case his payoff would be negative, whereas complete inaction yields a payoff of zero. Hence A never moves out of B_1. Indeed, he never moves at all, and B faces no effective rivalry. B therefore bids zero, and achieves a payoff of zero, the best payoff he can possibly obtain.

If it is A's turn to bid in $T_2 = \{(x,y) \mid C_1 < x \leq C_2 \text{ and } E_1 < y \leq E_2\}$ then A wins. If he did not win, his payoff would be at most zero, whereas he can obtain a positive payoff by moving directly to A_1. Moreover, A moves out of T_2 immediately. For if he did not, B would be motivated to pre-empt A by moving directly to B_1 where B is safe. By pre-empting A in this way, B's payoff would exceed $-V_B$, since he can reach B_1 at a cost less than V_B. This would be better for B than allowing A to win. Moreover, if it is B's turn to bid in T_2, he moves immediately to B_1. For otherwise A would win, by the previous argument. Thus we have shown that whoever is to move from T_2 moves immediately to his safety zone, A_1 or B_1 as the case may be.

Next we show that A is safe in $A_2 = \{(x,y) \mid C_1 < x \leq C_2 \text{ and } y > E_2\}$. It cannot be optimal for B to move from A_2 to B_1, since this would cost more than V_B. Nor can it be optimal for B to move from A_2 to T_2, since A would then win, which is worse for B than doing nothing. Therefore A faces no effective rivalry and proceeds as if in isolation. B always bids zero.

Finally we show that B is safe in $B_2 = \{(x,y) \mid x > C_2 \text{ and } E_1 < y \leq E_2\}$. It is not optimal for A to move from B_2 to A_1, since this would cost more than V_B. Nor is it optimal for A to move from B_2 to T_2 since B would then move to his safety zone B_1. Therefore A bids zero, since he cannot win the prize. And B secures his maximum possible payoff by bidding zero himself.

These arguments can be iterated. Thus the proof is complete.

Q.E.D.

Several remarks are in order. In the incumbent's (that is B's) safety zone the "race" is at a standstill. Even if the challenger (A) could profitably reach the finishing line if he were alone, he makes no attempt to do so since B credibly threatens to outdo any such attempt and beat A to the line. Of course B need never carry out this threat, and he makes no effort at all, since A is completely stymied. If the race begins with B to move from within a trigger zone, he makes an immediate dash to safety after which no player makes any further effort. In A's safety zone, A proceeds at his own pace to the finishing line, because if B attempted to thwart A's victory then A would foil B's attempt by increasing his efforts.

Note that the location of the trigger and safety zones depends upon the players' valuations of the prize (i.e. the V's) and upon their efficiency at R & D (i.e. the w functions). Not surprisingly, C_n increases the more that A wants to win the prize and the more efficient he is at R & D. Likewise E_n increases the more that B wants to avoid A winning, and the more efficient he is.

The size of the incumbent's safety zone is striking. Increments in the $\{C_n\}$ sequence (that is $C_n - C_{n-1}$) decrease and ultimately vanish, and the $\{C_n\}$ sequence is bounded above. The increments of the $\{E_n\}$ sequence, however, are constant.

It follows from this that A might be deterred from challenging the incumbent even though the incumbent was further from the line, less efficient at R & D, and less concerned to stop A's victory than A was to achieve it. This result stands in contrast to the theme of much of the literature on pre-emptive patenting and the persistence of monopoly.

The intuition behind our result is that the incumbent does not need to go all the way to the finishing line to prevent the rival from winning the prize. Once the incumbent has reached his safety zone, he has achieved his objective and makes no further effort. The rival, however, has to proceed all the way to the finishing line to attain his objective of winning the prize. The effect of this is that the incumbent's safety zone is relatively large. This point is illustrated by an example at the end of section V.

IV. A MODEL OF A STANDARD RACE

We now describe a model of standard race, which we will compare, in the following section, with that of the asymmetrical race. The model is adapted from that in Harris and Vickers [1985], to which it is closely related. In that paper we assumed that players discounted the future, whereas here we assume that they do not. This change is necessary in order to obtain direct comparability with the asymmetrical race of section III.

We have assumed that players do not discount the future in the asymmetrical race in order to render its analysis tractable. With discounting, the effort that the incumbent is prepared to make to stop his rival depends in part upon when the rival would win. This complexity is avoided if discounting is not introduced. However, in order to guarantee the existence of the C_n, and so the existence of equilibrium, in the absence of discounting, the additional assumption that the w functions exhibit increasing returns to scale for low effort levels is needed.

Our description of the standard race will be brief. A more detailed and rigorous analysis is available in our earlier paper.

The Model

The only differences between the model in this section and that in the previous section is the specification of B's payoffs. In the asymmetrical race, B lost V_B if A won the prize. Here, in the standard race, B gains V_B if he wins the prize. Thus B's payoff is now $V_B - \Sigma b_i$ if he wins the prize, and $-\Sigma b_i$ if he does not win the prize. Otherwise the model remains the same: the w functions and the structure of moves are as explained at the beginning of the previous section.

Once again, the key to analysing the game is to partition the space of pairs of distances from the finishing line in terms of two sequences of critical distances: $\{C_n\}$ for A and $\{D_n\}$ for B. The $\{C_n\}$ sequence is given by Definition 1 above. The $\{D_n\}$ sequence is defined exactly as the $\{C_n\}$ sequence:

Definition 3. $D_0 = 0$. For $n \geq 1$, D_n is the maximum y such that there exists a sequence $b_1, b_2, \ldots, b_r$ of non-negative bids such that

$$\sum_{i=1}^{r} w_B(b_i) \geq y$$

$$w_B(b_1) \geq y - D_{n-1}$$

$$V_B \geq \sum_{i=1}^{r} b_i$$

Using the sequences $\{C_n\}$ and $\{D_n\}$ we can characterise the outcome of the standard race in a fashion similar to that used to analyse the asymmetrical race in the previous section.

Figure 3 shows the partition of the space of distances from the finishing line. Once again we employ the terminology of safety zones and trigger zones. The following proposition states what happens in the race.

Proposition 2. Suppose that players' strategies are in equilibrium.

(i) *If (x, y) lies in player A's (B's) safety zone then A (B) wins the prize. His bids are those he would make in the absence of rivalry from B (A). B (A) always bids zero.*

(ii) *If (x, y) lies in a trigger zone, and it is A's (B's) move, then A (B) wins the prize. His bids are those he would make if, in isolation, he were subject only to reaching his safety zone with his first bid. B (A) always bids zero.*

(iii) *If, for all n, $x > C_n$ and $y > D_n$ then both players always bid zero.*

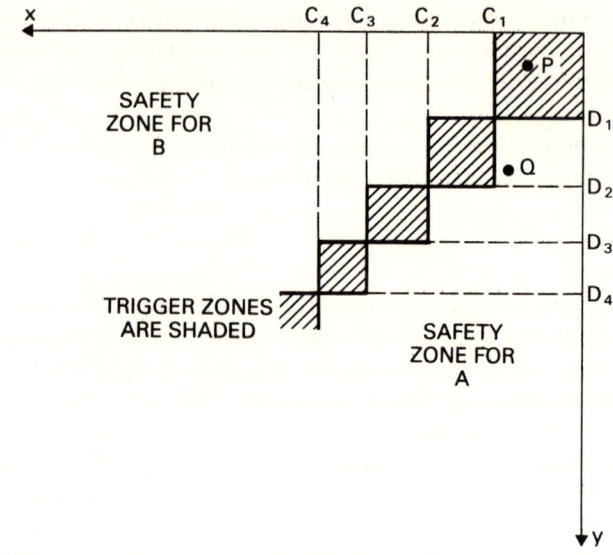

FIGURE 3
The Partition of the Space of Distances from the Finishing Line in the Standard Race

This result can be seen as follows. If (x,y) lies in the first trigger zone, such as point P in Figure 3, and if it is A to move, then A must win. For he can profitably pre-empt any attempt by B to win, simply by winning in one move. Moreover, A must win immediately, in one move. For if he did not, it would become B's move from within the first trigger zone, in which case B would win, by the previous argument. This contradiction shows that whoever's turn it is to move from within the first trigger zone must win the prize immediately.

Next consider a point such as Q, where $x \leq C_1$, but $y > D_1$. From here, B cannot win. For if he did so his path to the finishing line would involve him either (i) jumping over the first trigger zone; or (ii) passing through it. By the definition of D_1, (i) is unprofitable, and we have already established that A would win if B moved into the first trigger zone. So B cannot win in either case, and therefore he bids zero always. Thus A faces no effective rivalry from B, and his bids are those he would make if he were in isolation. That is, A is "safe". Similarly, B is safe if $y \leq D_1$ and $x > C_1$.

The second trigger zone, and the parts of the safety zone adjacent to it, can be analysed in much the same way as the first; and so on, inductively. Thus equilibrium takes the form described in the Proposition and illustrated in Figure 3.

V. AN EXAMPLE

In this section we present an explicit example of our models of standard and asymmetrical races. To do this neatly, we examine the models in the previous two sections as the intervals between bids become short.

In respect of each type of race (i.e. standard and asymmetrical) we consider a sequence of races defined as follows. In race 1 in the sequence, each player makes a bid each unit of time; we have already analysed this case. In race k in the sequence each player bids each kth of a unit of time. We preserve the alternating move structure throughout. Thus, as k becomes large, the process of action and reaction between rivals becomes more rapid. We are interested in what happens in the limit as k goes to infinity. This limiting case is of interest for several reasons. First, under suitable assumptions, the trigger zones collapse to form a curve, which can be characterised. Secondly, explicit examples can conveniently be solved in the limiting case; these may be illuminating. In particular, examples reveal clearly how different are standard and asymmetrical races. Thirdly, and rather speculatively, the limiting case can perhaps be regarded as the appropriate solution to the model in continuous time.

The present section contains an informal derivation of the limit of the equilibrium as k tends to infinity. A full statement of the technical conditions required to justify our analysis is given in Appendix B. One more substantive assumption should however be noted. We assume that $w_i(z)/z \to 0$ as $z \to \infty$. This means that it is impossible to move a strictly positive distance in zero time with a fixed budget.

Now let us consider race k in the sequence (the following applies equally to standard and asymmetrical races). A bid of an *amount* z implies expenditure at a rate kz, since the effort is applied for $1/k$ units of time. Expenditure at rate kz implies progress at rate $w_i(kz)$. Therefore, in race k, a bid of z moves player i a distance $w_i(kz)/k$ towards the finishing line.

Using this fact, we can define the $\{C_n^k\}$ sequence for race k in the natural way. Rather than state a formal definition, let us extend equation (1) to characterise the sequence $\{C_n^k\}$. If $C_{n+1}^k > C_n^k$ then

(2) $\quad C_n^k = C_{n-1}^k + w_A(k\Omega_A^k(C_{n-1}^k))/k,$

where $\Omega_A^k(x)$ is the value to A of a free run from x in race k.

Similarly, the $\{E_n^k\}$ sequence for race k is given by

(3) $\quad E_n^k = nw_B(kV_B)/k$

(cf. Definition 2 in section III).

Inspection of (2) and (3) reveals that our assumption that $w_i(z)/z \to 0$ as $z \to \infty$ implies that the trigger zones vanish, both in the standard and asymmetrical races. Consider first equation (2). The width of the nth trigger zone in race k is $C_n^k - C_{n-1}^k = w_A(k\Omega_A^k(C_{n-1}))/k$. Clearly $\Omega_A^k(\cdot) < V_A$, and therefore the RHS $\to 0$ as $k \to \infty$. The same is true for B's sequence $\{D_n^k\}$ in the kth standard race. Therefore the trigger zones vanish in the standard race as $k \to \infty$.

To show that the same is true for the asymmetrical race, consider equation (3). The height of the nth trigger zone in the kth asymmetrical race is $E_n^k - E_{n-1}^k = w_B(kV_B)/k$. Clearly the RHS $\to 0$ as $k \to \infty$, by our assumption. This completes the argument that the trigger zones vanish.

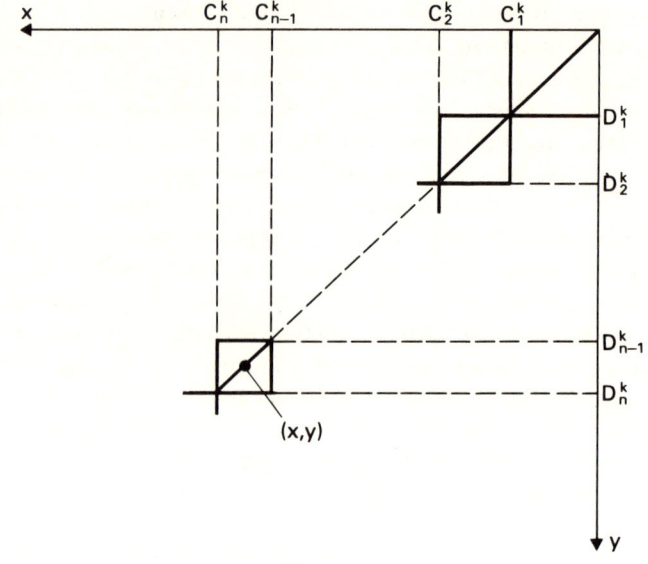

FIGURE 4
The Diagonals of Trigger Zones in Race k

Naturally the next step is to characterise the curve to which the trigger zones collapse. First we sketch how this is done for the standard race. Suppose that (x,y) lies on the diagonal of the nth trigger zone in race k: see Figure 4. Then the slope of the diagonal at (x,y) is given by

$$(4) \qquad \frac{dy}{dx} = \frac{D_n^k - D_{n-1}^k}{C_n^k - C_{n-1}^k} = \frac{w_B(k\Omega_B^k(D_{n-1}^k))}{w_A(k\Omega_A^k(C_{n-1}^k))}$$

from equation (2). If (x,y) lies on the limiting curve formed by the collapsed trigger zones, then the slope of this curve at (x,y) is given by

$$\frac{dy}{dx} = \lim_{k \to \infty} \left(\frac{w_B(k\Omega_B^k(D_{n-1}^k))}{w_A(k\Omega_A^k(C_{n-1}^k))} \right)$$

or

$$(5) \qquad \frac{dy}{dx} = \lim_{k \to \infty} \left(\frac{w_B(k\Omega_B(y))}{w_A(k\Omega_A(x))} \right)$$

where $\Omega_i(x)$ is the value to i of a free run from x in the limit as $k \to \infty$. That is, the slope of the limiting curve is the limit of the slopes of the diagonals that converge to it. The limiting curve is then characterised by equation (5).

It must be noted that informal arguments such as the present one can easily be mistaken: the slope of a limiting curve need not in general be the limit of the slopes of the curves that converge to it. However, we have derived an independent, rigorous, justification of that conclusion in the context of the

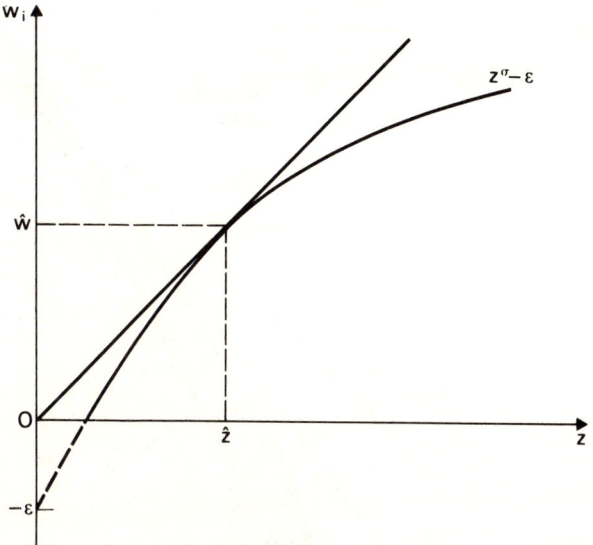

Figure 5
The Progress Function in the Example

present model. This rigorous argument is outlined in Appendix B.

The analysis for the asymmetrical race is much the same. The only difference is that V_B replaces $\Omega_B(y)$ in equation (5), due to the way that the $\{E_n^k\}$ sequence is defined.

The Example

Suppose that w_i has the form

(6) $\qquad w_i(z) = \max\{0, z^\sigma - \varepsilon\}$

for $i = A, B$, where $\varepsilon > 0$ and $0 < \sigma < 1$.

The most efficient rate of effort is $\hat{z} = (\varepsilon/(1-\sigma))^{1/\sigma}$. The value to A of a free run from x as $k \to \infty$ is therefore

(7) $\qquad \Omega_A(x) = V_A - \dfrac{x\hat{z}}{\hat{w}}$

$\qquad\qquad\quad = V_A - \gamma x$, say.

The Standard Race

Using (5), (6), and (7) we find that the equation of the limiting curve for the standard race is

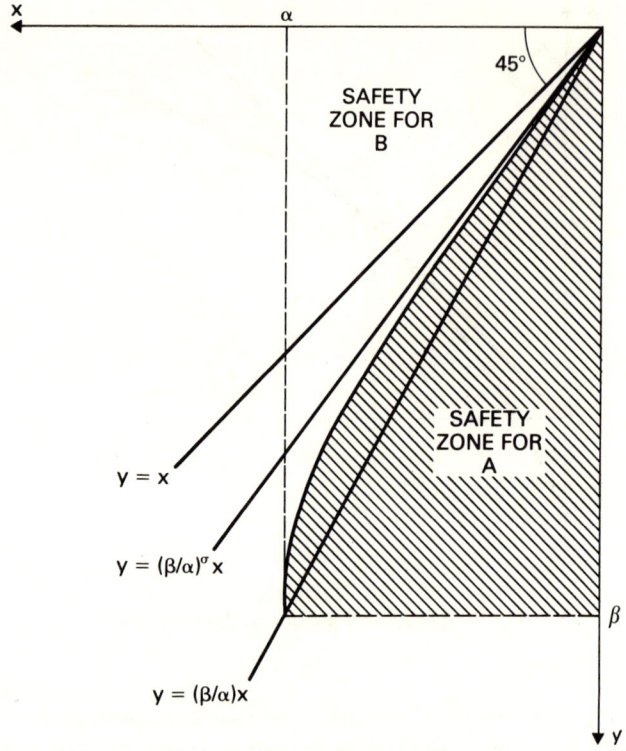

FIGURE 6
The Limiting Curve in the Standard Race

(8) $$\frac{dy}{dx} = \lim_{k \to \infty} \left(\frac{k^\sigma (V_B - \gamma y)^\sigma - \varepsilon}{k^\sigma (V_A - \gamma x)^\sigma - \varepsilon} \right) = \left(\frac{\beta - y}{\alpha - x} \right)^\sigma$$

where $\alpha = V_A/\gamma$ and $\beta = V_B/\gamma$. The solution to the differential equation (8) is

(9) $$y = \beta - ((\alpha - x)^{1-\sigma} - \alpha^{1-\sigma} + \beta^{1-\sigma})^{1/(1-\sigma)}$$

Assuming for instance that $\beta > \alpha$, the slope dy/dx increases with x and approaches infinity as $x \to \alpha$. At the origin the slope is $(\beta/\alpha)^\sigma$. The curve thus lies entirely to one side of the 45° line, reflecting the assumption that $\beta > \alpha$. Figure 6 sketches the curve.

The Asymmetrical Race

In this case the equation of the limiting curve is

$$\frac{dy}{dx} = \lim_{k \to \infty} \left(\frac{k^\sigma V_B^\sigma - \varepsilon}{k^\sigma (V_A - \gamma x)^\sigma - \varepsilon} \right)$$

(10) $$= \left(\frac{\beta}{\alpha - x} \right)^\sigma$$

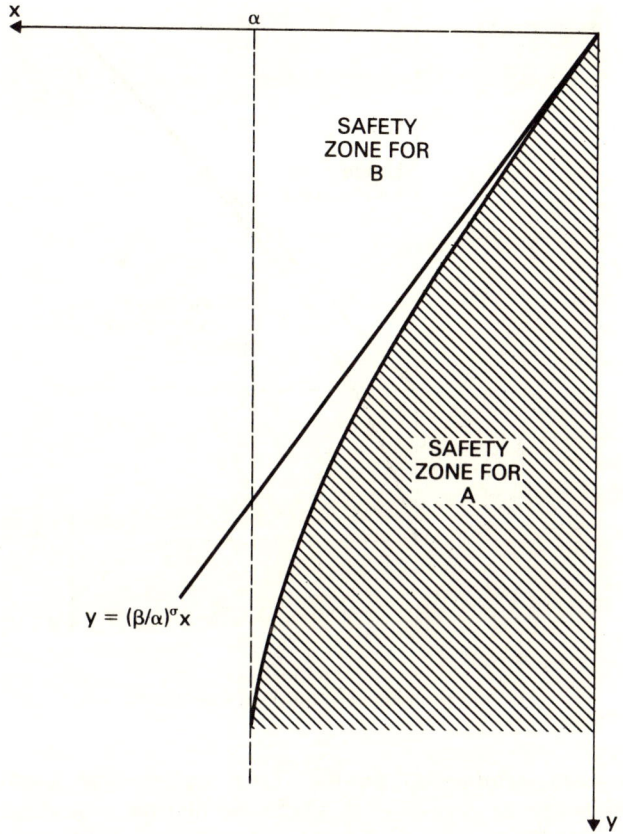

FIGURE 7
The Limiting Curve in the Asymmetrical Race

The solution to this differential equation is

(11) $$y = \frac{\beta^\sigma}{1-\sigma}(\alpha^{1-\sigma} - (\alpha-x)^{1-\sigma})$$

The slope of this curve is $(\beta/\alpha)^\sigma$ at the origin, is increasing in x, and goes to infinity as x goes to α. The curve is sketched in Figure 7.

The slope dy/dx for the asymmetrical race is everywhere steeper than it is for the standard race. The value of y at which $x = \alpha$ is therefore greater, and B's safety zone is larger. In Figure 8 we plot both curves for the case in which $V_A = V_B$ (that is $\alpha = \beta$).

VI. CONCLUSION

In a patent race between a firm already in a market and a firm attempting to enter it, there are several reasons why the incumbent and potential entrant

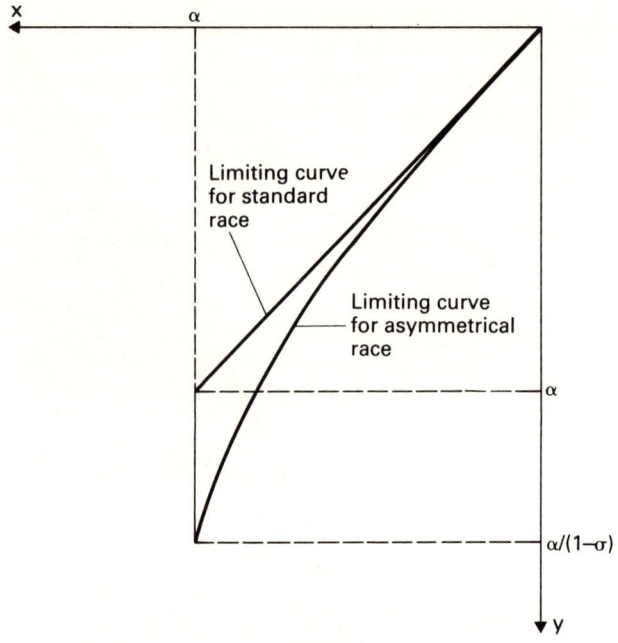

FIGURE 8
Comparison between the Two Limiting Curves

might be in an asymmetrical position. First, the two firms might value the patent differently. In particular, it is probable that the incumbent values the patent more highly than his rival, since monopoly persists if he wins the patent whereas there is competition if the rival is successful. Secondly, the firms might begin the race at different distances from the finishing line. For example, due to his past experience, the incumbent might have more knowledge than his rival at the outset of the race. Thirdly, the firms might differ in terms of R & D efficiency—that is, in terms of their ability to transform R & D effort into R & D output.

As well as these factors, there is another important asymmetry, which this paper has sought to explore. It is that the incumbent's aim is to *prevent* his rival from winning the patent, and not necessarily to win the patent himself. The rival, on the other hand, is out to *win* the patent. The analysis of our model reveals that this last asymmetry can be rather important. Indeed, it can happen that the rival is deterred from actively competing in the patent race even though he has the advantage over the incumbent in terms of all the three asymmetries described in the previous paragraph.

In this paper we have concentrated on the "pure" case, in which the incumbent's only concern is to prevent his rival from winning the patent. This is appropriate if, for example, the patent is for a technology no better than already possessed by the incumbent. If, however, the new technology is for a superior patent, then the incumbent has an incentive to win the patent in addition to his desire to stop the rival winning. The presence of this extra incentive in the "hybrid" case strengthens our conclusions regarding the pure case.

In summary, there are several sources of strategic advantage that an incumbent firm might enjoy in a patent race against a potential entrant into his market. An important one of these is that the incumbent is concerned to prevent the rival from winning, and not necessarily to obtain the patent for himself. This asymmetry appears to favour the incumbent considerably—especially if the players begin far from the finishing line. We suggest it as a possible ingredient for a theory of the persistence of monopoly.

CHRISTOPHER HARRIS AND JOHN VICKERS,
Nuffield College,
Oxford,
U.K.

APPENDIX A

In this appendix we prove that the sequences $\{C_n\}$ and $\{D_n\}$ exist. Since the analysis for $\{D_n\}$ is identical to that for $\{C_n\}$ we treat only $\{C_n\}$ explicitly. We also explore the properties of $\{C_n\}$ briefly. We drop the subscripts on w_A, V_A, and Ω_A since there is no risk of confusion.

Let us assume that w is increasing and continuous, that $w(0) = 0$, and that w exhibits increasing returns to scale for low effort levels, in the sense that there exists $\alpha > 0$ such that w is convex on the interval $[0, \alpha]$. Our first step is to show that $\Omega(x)$, the value of a free run from x, is well defined and continuous for all x.

Let $\omega_r(x)$ be the value of a run with r bids from x. A might choose to move to the finishing line with these r bids, or he might remain stationary. In particular, some of the bids may be zero. $\omega_r(x)$ is the solution to the problem

(A1) $\quad$ maximise $\displaystyle V - \sum_{i=1}^{r} a_i$
$\qquad a_1, a_2, \ldots, a_r$

$\qquad$ subject to $a_i \geq 0 \quad$ all i

$$V - \sum_{i=1}^{r} a_i \geq 0$$

$$\sum_{i=1}^{r} w(a_i) \geq x$$

when this problem is feasible, otherwise $\omega_r(x) = 0$. Standard arguments show that ω_r is well defined and continuous everywhere. Notice that $\omega_{r+1} \geq \omega_r$ for all r. Also, if there is a solution to the problem with $r+1$ bids in which one bid is zero then no loss of generality results from considering only the problem with r bids.

If either of the expressions $\Omega(x)$ and $\max\{\omega_r(x)\,|\,r\geqslant 1\}$ is well defined, then both expressions are well defined and each is equal to the other. Our strategy of proof is to show that there exists an $\mathcal{N}$ such that if $r > \mathcal{N}$ then there is a solution to the problem with r bids in which at least $r-\mathcal{N}$ of the bids are zero. It will follow that $\sup\{\omega_r\,|\,r\geqslant 1\} = \max\{\omega_r\,|\,1\leqslant r\leqslant\mathcal{N}\} = \omega_N$, and so that $\Omega = \omega_N$. In particular, Ω is well defined and continuous.

Let β be a value which yields a solution to the problem

(A2) $\qquad$ maximise $\dfrac{1}{a}w(a)$

$\qquad$ subject to $0 < a \leqslant V$

β is well defined because w is convex in a neighbourhood of the origin. β is one of the most efficient effort rates. We assume that $w(\beta) > 0$ in order to avoid trivialities. We also assume w.l.o.g. that $\beta > \alpha$, reducing α slightly if necessary. Further, let $\bar{x} = Vw(\beta)/\beta$. This is the distance that could be covered profitably if it were possible to proceed at the most efficient rate. If it is profitable to finish from x, then $\bar{x} \geqslant x$.

Fix r and consider the problem (A1). If it is infeasible then the number of non-zero bids that A will make in a run of length r from x is zero. We now show that if (A1) is feasible then there is an upper bound to the number of non-zero bids that A will make in such a run. The cases $w(\alpha) = 0$ and $w(\alpha) > 0$ must be considered separately.

Suppose that $w(\alpha) > 0$. Let the number of non-zero bids be m. Because w is convex in $[0, \alpha]$ we may assume w.l.o.g. that at most one of these bids is less than α. Moreover the total distance moved will be exactly x. Hence

$$x \geqslant (m-1)w(\alpha)$$

But (A1) is feasible, and so $x \leqslant \bar{x}$. We conclude that $m \leqslant (\bar{x}/w(\alpha)) + 1$.

Suppose instead that $w(\alpha) = 0$. Let K be the smallest integer such that $K\alpha \geqslant \beta$. Next, $w(a)/a$ is continuous for $a \in [\alpha, \beta]$, strictly positive for $a = \beta$, and zero for $a = \alpha$. Hence there exists γ, $\alpha < \gamma < \beta$, such that $w(\gamma) > 0$ and such that the efficiency $w(a)/a$ of any bid a in the range $\alpha \leqslant a \leqslant \gamma$ is at most $1/K$ of the efficiency of β. Now the number of non-zero bids not exceeding γ must be less than K. For suppose by way of example that to the contrary $\alpha \leqslant a_i \leqslant \gamma$ for $1 \leqslant i \leqslant K$. Then

$$\sum_{i=1}^{K} w(a_i) \leqslant Kw(\gamma) = K\gamma\frac{1}{\gamma}w(\gamma)$$

$$\leqslant K\gamma\frac{1}{K}\left(\frac{1}{\beta}w(\beta)\right)$$

$$< w(\beta)$$

$$\leqslant w(K\gamma)$$

A could therefore strictly increase his payoff by amalgamating the a_i, $1 \leqslant a_i \leqslant K$, into a single bid. This is a contradiction. Hence the number of non-zero bids not exceeding γ must indeed be less than K. Suppose that the number of non-zero bids is m. We have

$$x \geqslant (m-K)w(\gamma),$$

and, since $\bar{x} \geqslant x$, $m \leqslant K + \bar{x}/w(\gamma)$.

We have thus shown that, whether or not $w(\alpha) = 0$, there exists an upper bound $\mathcal{N}$ to the number of non-zero bids in a run of length r from x. In calculating $\Omega(x)$, then, we can restrict our attention to $\{\omega_r\,|\,1\leqslant r\leqslant\mathcal{N}\}$ w.l.o.g., and $\Omega = \omega_N$ is well defined and continuous.

It is now straightforward to show that $\{C_n\}$ is well defined. For suppose that C_{n-1}

is well defined. Then C_n is the solution to the problem

$$\text{maximise } c$$
$$\quad a,c$$
$$\text{subject to } a \geqslant 0$$
$$c - w(a) \leqslant C_{n-1}$$
$$a \leqslant \Omega(c - w(a)),$$

and consequently well defined.

We conclude this appendix with a few observations about $\{C_n\}$. Notice first that it is possible to finish profitably from x iff (A1) is feasible for $r = \mathcal{N}$. Hence there exists $C_\infty < \infty$ such that it is possible to finish profitably from x iff $x \leqslant C_\infty$. Since $\{C_n\}$ is increasing and $C_n \leqslant C_\infty$ for all n, $C_n - C_{n-1} \to 0$ as $n \to \infty$.

Next, the increments $C_n - C_{n-1}$ are decreasing in n, and strictly decreasing where they are strictly positive. In order to see this, suppose for a contradiction that $C_n - C_{n-1} > 0$ and that $C_{n+1} - C_n \geqslant C_n - C_{n-1}$. Any solution to the problem of finishing from C_{n+1} subject to moving to within C_n of the finishing line with the first bid is feasible in the analogous problem for C_n and C_{n-1}. However, in this latter problem it involves moving strictly beyond the finishing line, contradicting the construction of C_n, which is by definition the furthest distance from which it is profitable to finish subject to moving at least to within C_{n-1} of the finishing line with the first bid.

Thirdly, $C_n \to C_\infty$ as $n \to \infty$. The proof of this is almost identical to that of Property 3 in Harris and Vickers [1985] (set $\rho = 1$ in the proof in the Appendix of that paper).

Fourthly, $C_n \to C_\infty$ finitely as $n \to \infty$. For let $a_1, a_2, \ldots, a_r$ be a solution to the problem of finishing profitably from C_∞, and suppose w.l.o.g. that $a_i > 0$ for all i. There exists n_0 such that $C_\infty - C_n < w(a_1)$ for all $n \geqslant n_0$. Now, if $C_{n_0} = C_\infty$ there is nothing left to prove. Suppose therefore that $C_\infty - C_{n_0} > 0$. Then, since $a_1, a_2, \ldots, a_r$, which is the solution to the problem of finishing from C_∞ profitably, remains feasible when the additional constraint that $w(a_1) \geqslant C_\infty - C_{n_0}$ is introduced, we have that $C_{n_0+1} = C_\infty$. Hence $C_n \to C_\infty$ finitely as claimed.

Finally we prove the result, used in the text and in the following appendix, that if $C_{n+1} > C_n$ then $C_n = C_{n-1} + w(\Omega(C_{n-1}))$. For consider the problem of covering C_n subject to moving at least to within C_{n-1} of the finishing line with the first bid. If the constraint on the first bid binds then certainly $C_n = C_{n-1} + w(\Omega(C_{n-1}))$. If it does not, then, as in the previous paragraph, $C_{n+1} = C_n$. Thus the result claimed holds.

APPENDIX B

Let w_i^δ be player i's progress function when δ is the duration of a bid. In this appendix we show how a meaningful calibration for the w_i^δ can be derived from consideration of the continuous time case. We then examine the behaviour of the solution of the δth game as $\delta \to 0$.

If, in the continuous time case, player A's bid rate at time t is $a(t)$ then his total progress over the interval $[0, T]$ is

$$\int_0^T w_A(a(t))\, dt$$

and the cumulative cost to him over the same interval is

$$\int_0^T a(t)\, dt.$$

B's cumulative cost and progress are defined analogously in terms of his bid rate $b(t)$.

Naturally a player is awarded the prize only if he reaches the finishing line in finite time. With this understanding we define $\Omega_i(v)$ as the value to player i of a free run from v.

Consider the δth game. If we think of player i as choosing a bid rate z which, once chosen, must remain constant over an interval of length δ, then i's progress over that interval will be $\int_0^\delta w_i(z)\,dt$, or $\delta w_i(z)$. Thus we define

$$w_i^\delta(z) = \delta w_i(z)$$

The cost of this bid is $\int_0^\delta z\,dt$, or δz.

We impose the following conditions on w_A and w_B in addition to those already imposed in Appendix A.

(i) For each i, $\delta w_i(1/\delta) \to 0$ as $\delta \to 0$.
(ii) There exist $h:(0,\infty) \to (0,\infty)$ and functions $\bar{w}_A$ and $\bar{w}_B$ continuous on $(0,\infty)$ such that $\bar{w}_i(z) > 0$ for each i and all $z > 0$, and such that

$$h(\delta)\delta w_i\left(\frac{z}{\delta}\right) \to \bar{w}_i(z) \quad \text{as} \quad \delta \to 0$$

for each i and all $z \geqslant 0$.

The earlier assumptions guarantee the existence of Ω_i^δ and sequences $\{C_n^\delta\}$ and $\{D_n^\delta\}$ for the δth game. Condition (i) states that it is not possible to move a finite distance in zero time with a fixed budget. It guarantees that the trigger zones collapse. In conjunction with the earlier assumption that w_i is convex in a neighbourhood of the origin, condition (i) also guarantees the existence of Ω_i. Condition (ii) is purely technical, and is needed in order to give a rigorous derivation of the limiting "trigger line". h is independent of i, and in effect normalises $\delta w_i((1/\delta)z)$.

The Standard Race

Let $C_\infty^\delta = \max\{C_n^\delta \mid n \geqslant 0\}$ and let C_∞ be the maximum distance from which A can finish in the continuous time case. (In the notation of Appendix A, this distance is $\bar{x}$.) C_∞ is finite, $C_\infty^\delta \leqslant C_\infty$, and $C_\infty^\delta \to C_\infty$ as $\delta \to 0$. Then D_∞^δ and D_∞ can be defined analogously for B, and similar remarks apply. Also, $0 \leqslant \Omega_i^\delta \leqslant \Omega_i$ and $\Omega_i^\delta \to \Omega_i$ pointwise on $[0,\infty)$ for each i. In what follows we show how the limiting behaviour of the trigger zones can be characterised in the rectangle $[0,C_\infty) \times [0,D_\infty)$.

Observe first that the widths and heights of the trigger zones are dominated by

$$\delta w_A\left(\frac{1}{\delta}V_A\right) \quad \text{and} \quad \delta w_B\left(\frac{1}{\delta}V_B\right)$$

respectively, and so converge to zero uniformly with δ. It follows, first, that we can restrict our attention to the line traced out by the diagonals of the trigger zones, and secondly that we can ignore the possibility that

$$C_n^\delta - C_{n-1}^\delta \neq \delta w_A\left(\frac{1}{\delta}\Omega_A^\delta(C_{n-1}^\delta)\right)$$

for the last strictly positive increment $C_n^\delta - C_{n-1}^\delta$.

The line traced out by the diagonals of the trigger zones of the δth model, parameterised by s, can be described by the following pair of differential equations:

$$X_\delta'(s) = h(\delta)(C_n^\delta - C_{n-1}^\delta) \quad \text{if} \quad C_{n-1}^\delta \leqslant X_\delta(s) < C_n^\delta$$
$$Y_\delta'(s) = h(\delta)(D_n^\delta - D_{n-1}^\delta) \quad \text{if} \quad D_{n-1}^\delta \leqslant Y_\delta(s) < D_n^\delta$$

X_δ and Y_δ are strictly increasing as long as $X_\delta(s) < C_\infty^\delta$ and $Y_\delta(s) < D_\infty^\delta$. We can therefore invert them to obtain $Q_\delta: [0, C_\infty^\delta) \to [0, \infty)$ and $R_\delta: [0, D_\infty^\delta) \to [0, \infty)$ respectively. We analyse only Q_δ explicitly.

Let $\mathcal{N}(x, \delta)$ denote the maximum n such that $C_{n-1}^\delta \leq x < C_n^\delta$. Then Q_δ satisfies the differential equation

$$Q_\delta'(x) = \frac{1}{h(\delta)\,(C_{\mathcal{N}(x,\delta)}^\delta - C_{\mathcal{N}(x,\delta)-1}^\delta)} \qquad \text{for} \qquad 0 \leq x < C_\infty^\delta$$

Let

$$q(x, \delta) = h(\delta)\delta w_A\!\left(\frac{1}{\delta}\Omega_A(C_{\mathcal{N}(x,\delta)-1}^\delta)\right)$$

Then

$$Q_\delta(x) = \int_0^x \frac{1}{q(\xi, \delta)}\, d\xi$$

for $0 \leq x < C_\infty^\delta$. It can be shown that $q(\xi, \delta) \to \bar{w}_A(\Omega_A(\xi))$ uniformly in ξ over compact sub-intervals of $[0, C_\infty)$. Thus, if

$$Q(x) = \int_0^x \frac{1}{\bar{w}_A(\Omega_A(\xi))}\, d\xi,$$

we have that $Q_\delta \to Q$ pointwise on $[0, C_\infty)$.

Now Q_δ and Q are strictly increasing, Q is continuous, and $Q_\delta \to Q$ pointwise on $[0, C_\infty)$. It follows that $Q_\delta^{-1} \to Q^{-1}$ pointwise on $[0, \bar{s})$, where $\bar{s} = \sup\{Q(x) \,|\, x < C_\infty\}$. Let $X = Q^{-1}$. Then we have shown that $X_\delta \to X$ pointwise on $[0, \bar{s})$. In exactly the same way one can show that $R_\delta \to R$, where

$$R(y) = \int_0^y \frac{1}{\bar{w}_B(\Omega_B(\xi))}\, d\xi,$$

and that $Y_\delta \to Y$, where $Y = R^{-1}$ too is defined on $[0, \bar{s})$.

We have therefore shown that the line traced by the diagonals of the trigger zones of the δth model converges to the line $\{(X(s), Y(s)) \,|\, 0 \leq s < \bar{s}\}$. Then X and Y can be found directly from the differential equations

$$X'(s) = \bar{w}_A(\Omega_A(X(s)))$$
$$Y'(s) = \bar{w}_B(\Omega_B(Y(s)))$$

($s \in [0, \bar{s})$). This result underlies the discussion of section V.

The Asymmetric Race

In the asymmetric case the line traced by the diagonals of the trigger zones of the δth model converges to the line $\{(X(s), Y(s)) \,|\, 0 \leq s < \bar{s}\}$, where

$$X'(s) = \bar{w}_A(\Omega_A(X(s)))$$
$$Y'(s) = \bar{w}_B(V_B)$$

($s \in [0, \bar{s})$). Here X and $\bar{s}$ are exactly as before, and the argument which establishes the form of X is unchanged. The argument which establishes the form of Y is similar but rather simpler.

STRATEGIC INVESTMENT IN AN INDUSTRY WITH A COMPETITIVE PRODUCT MARKET*

Huw Dixon

I. INTRODUCTION

THIS PAPER explores the scope for, and effect of, strategic behaviour by firms in an industry where the product market is "competitive" in the usual sense that firms are effectively price-takers. Traditionally the literature on imperfect competition has concentrated on the product market, employing the notions of the Cournot equilibrium or monopolistic competition. The model presented shows that even if firms are unable to obtain any such market power in the product market, they can still influence the market outcome through investment behaviour which determines their actual cost structure. The ability of firms to thus influence the market outcome is directly related to their market share. This is a result which is not only of theoretical interest. It is sometimes argued that for some industries concentration does not lead to welfare loss because the market may be competitive even with only a few producers (see Fisher *et al.* [1983, pp. 24-25] for the U.S. computer industry and I.B.M.). The message of this paper is that even in such competitive industries concentration still matters since firms can still behave strategically with factors such as investment and R&D.

This paper considers a model of strategic investment in the context of a two stage dynamic equilibrium with two factors of production, capital and labour. In the first "strategic" stage, firms choose their capital stocks. In the second "market" stage the capital stocks are fixed, and a competitive equilibrium occurs. The two stages of the model can be seen as capturing the distinction between the long run and the short run. The equilibrium rests on the reasonable assumption that the capital decisions of firms are irreversible in the market stage. We are thus implicitly assuming that there is no rental market for capital. In the competitive market stage the price equates supply with demand. In essence, the choice of the capital stock in the strategic stage determines the supply function that the firm has in the market stage. Thus firms are able to influence the market equilibrium to their favour through their choice of capital stock. The resultant equilibrium can be interpreted as a Nash equilibrium in supply functions (see for example Grossman [1981], Dixon [1984a]).

In evaluating the welfare consequences of the model, it is necessary to realise that the cost structure of the firm is endogenous. The choice of capital

---

* This is part of my D.Phil thesis. I would especially like to thank my supervisor Jim Mirrlees for his guidance, and George Yarrow for useful comments and encouragement. Paul Geroski and an anonymous referee were also extremely helpful. The financial assistance of the ESRC is acknowledged.

determines the firms "short-run" cost function. If we were only to consider the *actual* cost structure of firms, then, since price equals marginal cost in the competitive market stage, the standard welfare analysis would tell us that there was no restriction of output, and no loss of consumer surplus. However, since investment alters the firm's actual cost structure, welfare considerations need to concentrate on possible rather than actual costs. In equilibrium we find that firms are able to restrict investment and output so that the price exceeds least cost, and there is a loss of consumer surplus relative to the socially optimal outcome. This is not the only source of welfare loss.

Because capital is used strategically in this model, there is an asymmetry between capital and labour. In equilibrium the strategic use of investment leads to a bias away from capital, so that there is undercapitalisation and an excessive labour-capital ratio. This results in inefficient production, in the sense that the actual costs of producing the firm's output are in excess of the minimum technically required.

The result of undercapitalisation provides an interesting contrast with existing models of the strategic use of investment. The model which most closely resembles ours is Brander and Spencer's model of R&D expenditure [1983]. The crucial difference between the models is the assumption made about the market stage: they assume that it is Cournot. Under this assumption, they show that there is the opposite factor bias, with overcapitalisation in equilibrium. Furthermore, whereas strategic behaviour improves social welfare in the Brander and Spencer [1983] model as compared with the non-strategic case, in the model presented it leads to a loss in social welfare. Overcapitalisation can also occur in Dixit's model of strategic entry deterrence [1980, pp. 103-4].

The assumption of a competitive market stage, coupled with constant returns to scale gives the model a particularly tractable and intuitive form. In section I of the paper the basic framework is presented. In section II we explore the general properties of the equilibrium. We show that the profit to sales ratio that is, the price-cost margin) is inversely related to the elasticities of demand and supply. In section III two specifications of the general model are presented. First we derive an explicit solution to the model in the case of identical firms with Cobb-Douglas technology and constant elasticity industry demand. This example enables us to relate the strategic investment model with the standard (one stage or non-strategic) Cournot equilibrium. Furthermore, depending on the technical parameter, the strategic investment equilibrium has Cournot and Bertrand outcomes as limiting cases. We also provide a linearised model in section III, which is particularly useful for explicitly analysing the welfare properties of the model. We are able to show, in this case at least, that the welfare loss due to strategic inefficiency may be large relative to the standard welfare "triangle".

The main body of this paper treats the number of firms as given: there is a given set of active incumbents. However, the impact of entry on the model is briefly discussed. Entry adds an additional welfare loss to the model, since sunk set-up costs will in general lead to more firms than are socially optimal in the industry.

I. A MODEL OF STRATEGIC INVESTMENT

We present the general model in this section, and will consider more specific cases in section III. All functions are assumed to be differentiable when required.

Firms have a standard two-input constant-returns production function:

A1: Each firm's production function $f_i : R_+^2 \to R_+$ is homogeneous to degree one and strictly concave in each input:

$$x_i = f_i(k_i, L_i) \qquad f_k, f_L > 0 > f_{LL}, f_{kk}$$

where k_i and L_i are capital and labour inputs of the ith firm.

This assumption is stronger than required, but it simplifies the analysis. We can then define the firm's cost function in the standard manner taking the factor prices w and r as parameters.

(a) *Long-Run Cost function*: $a \cdot x$

$$a(x) = \min_{L, k \in R_+} (w \cdot L + r \cdot k) \qquad \text{subject to} \qquad f(k, L) - x \geq 0$$

$$= a \cdot x$$

where a is (constant) least average cost.

(b) *Short-Run Cost Function*: $k \cdot c(x/k)$

$$C(K, x) = \min_{L \in R_+} (w \cdot L + r \cdot k) \qquad \text{subject to} \qquad f(k, L) - x \geq 0$$

Under constant-returns we can define $k \cdot c(x/k) = k \cdot C(1, x/k)$.

Concavity of f in L implies that c is convex in output-per-unit-capital x/k. Given the technology, we can then define the "short-run" supply function, again taking advantage of constant returns.

(c) *Supply Function*: $k \cdot s(p)$

$S(k, p)$ is the output which solves:

$$\max_{x, L \in R_+^2} [p \cdot x - w \cdot L - r \cdot k] \qquad \text{subject to} \qquad f(k, L) - x \geq 0$$

Under A1 this can be written as $k \cdot s(p)$.

Thus $s(p)$ is the profit-maximising output-per-unit-capital. Obviously, the strict convexity and differentiability of $c(x/k)$ imply that s is strictly increasing in p, and its second derivative s'' will be positive or negative depending on c'''. In effect, through its choice of k_i, the ith firm chooses the supply function it will have in the market-stage.

We consider a two stage model. In the first "strategic" stage, firms precommit their capital stock. In the second "market stage", firms' capital stocks are fixed, and a competitive equilibrium occurs. In order to define the competitive price we need to state our assumptions about the industry demand function.

A2: Industry demand $F: R_+ \to R_+$ is bounded, continuous, and strictly decreasing when positive.

The competitive price θ which occurs in the market stage is defined implicitly by the relation:

(1.1) $\qquad F(\theta) - \sum_{i=1}^{n} k_i \cdot s_i(\theta) = 0$

We can thus define the implicit function which gives the competitive price θ ruling in the market stage to the n-vectors of capital stocks $\underline{k}$ chosen in the strategic move, $\theta: R_+^n \to R_+$

(1.2) $\qquad \theta = \theta(\underline{k})$

Total differentiation of (1.1) yields:

(1.3) $\qquad \dfrac{\partial \theta}{\partial k_i} = \dfrac{s_i(\theta)}{F' - \sum_{j=1}^{n} k_j \cdot s'_j} < 0$

where primes denote derivatives with respect to price, which are evaluated at $\theta(\underline{k})$. The numerator s_i will vary between firms, whilst the denominator is common to all firms, and reflects the fact that as the price falls, firms' outputs will fall. If firms are identical then (1.1) and (1.3) simplify, since θ will depend only on the total capital stock Σk_j, as will $\partial \theta / \partial k_i$.

We are now in a position to define the firm's payoff function U_i, giving the profit earned as a function of the capital stocks chosen in the strategic move. First, however, we define the firm's profit-per-unit-capital conditional upon θ, $\pi: R_+ \to R$

(1.4) $\qquad \pi(\theta) = \theta \cdot s(\theta) - c(s(\theta))$

Thus π is the nett or supernormal rate of profit on capital, once the cost-per-unit-capital r has been covered (since r is included in $c(\cdot)$, from definition (b)). We now have the firm's profit-function $U_i: R_+^n \to R$.

(d) *Profit Function*: $U_i(\underline{k}) = k_i \cdot \pi(\theta(\underline{k}))$.

Having defined firms' payoffs in terms of their choices of k_i in the strategic move, we can define the equilibrium in the two stage model as a Nash equllibrium $\{\underline{k}^*, \theta^*\}$ in the game $[R_+, U_i : i = 1 \ldots n]$. The Nash equilibrium assumption seems perfectly natural here, since the capital decision is irreversible, so that firms are unable to react to each other. Whilst the model is formally defined as a Nash equilibrium in capital stocks, it is really a Nash equilibrium in supply functions. We will have more to say about this subsequently.

II. THE PROPERTIES OF THE EQUILIBRIUM

Supposing an equilibrium $\underline{k}^*$ to exist, what does it look like? We will restrict ourselves to those equilibria where all firms are producing, that is, $\underline{k}^* \gg 0$, and we shall denote the equilibrium market price $\theta^* = \theta(\underline{k}^*)$. Then $\underline{k}^*$ will be a Nash equilibrium if for all firms $i = 1 \ldots n$:

$$(2.1) \qquad U_{ki}|_{k^*} = \pi_i(\theta^*) + k_i^* \cdot \frac{d\pi}{d\theta} \cdot \frac{\partial \theta}{\partial k_i} = 0$$

where U_{ki} is the partial derivative of U_i with respect to k_i (since we shall never need cross-partials, this notation should be unambiguous). We can define the elasticity of θ with respect to k_i as:

$$(2.2) \qquad \varepsilon_i =_{\text{def}} -\frac{k_i}{\theta} \cdot \frac{\partial \theta}{\partial k_i}$$

substituting (2.2) into (2.1), and noting that by Hotelling's Lemma $d\pi/d\theta = s(\theta)$, at $\underline{k}^*$:

$$(2.3) \qquad \frac{\pi(\theta)}{\theta^* \cdot s_i(\theta^*)} = \varepsilon_i$$

Note that the LHS of (2.3) is the ith firm's profit to sales ratio. Hence in equilibrium, each firm's profit to sales ratio will be equal to the elasticity of the market price with respect to its own capital. Clearly, the profit to sales ratio must equal the price-average-cost-margin, and when we expand the LHS of (2.3) we obtain:

$$(2.4) \qquad \frac{\theta^* - \dfrac{c(s(\theta^*))}{s(\theta^*)}}{\theta^*} = \varepsilon_i$$

where $c(s(\theta))/s(\theta)$ is average cost. It should be noted that we have made no assumption of average-cost being equal to marginal cost to derive (2.4): the LHS is in principle a directly observable variable (if we leave aside problems of measuring profits, of course).

It is easily shown that the equilibrium price θ^* in the market stage will be greater than the long-run (least) average cost a_i for all firms that produce in equilibrium. If $\theta^* < a_i$, then the ith firm will make a loss if it produces anything at all, and if $\theta^* = a_i$ it will earn nothing. Since we restrict ourselves to $\underline{k}^* \gg 0$, the price must be greater than or equal to a_i. But if $\theta^* = a_i$, then the firm could reduce k_i slightly, thus increasing θ and hence earn positive profits.

In the case of identical firms (2.3) simplifies further. Since $\partial \theta / \partial k_i$ is then a function of total capital only, and so is identical across firms:

$$(2.5) \qquad \frac{\partial \theta}{\partial k_i} = \frac{s(\theta)}{F' - s' \cdot \Sigma k_j} \qquad j = 1 \ldots n$$

so that from (2.2) and (2.5) we have:

$$(2.6) \qquad \varepsilon_i = \frac{k_i}{\Sigma k} \cdot \frac{1}{\varepsilon_s - \varepsilon_d}$$

where ε_s and ε_d are the familiar price elasticities of supply and demand, $\varepsilon_s = (\theta/s) \cdot s'$, $\varepsilon_d = (\theta/F) \cdot F'$. Hence if all firms have an identical technology, then (2.3) becomes:

$$(2.7) \qquad \frac{\pi(\theta^*)}{\theta^* \cdot s(\theta^*)} = \frac{1}{n(\varepsilon_s - \varepsilon_d)}$$

Thus the profit to sales ratio equals the reciprocal of the sum of demand and supply elasticities (evaluated at θ^*), divided by the number of firms. In an industry with $\varepsilon_s = -\varepsilon_d = 1$, and fifteen firms, the profit to sales ratio would be $1/30^{\text{th}}$.

Equation (2.7) is clearly similar to the equilibrium condition in the Cournot–Nash model. As we argue in Dixon [1984a], perhaps the most natural and convincing interpretation of the standard Cournot model is that firms pre-commit both factors of production, so that in the strategic move firms choose a capacity, and in the market stage a competitive equilibrium (occurs that is, the price clears the market). Hence the symmetric Cournot equilibrium is given by:

$$(2.8) \qquad \frac{\theta^c - a}{\theta^c} = \frac{-1}{n \cdot \varepsilon_d}$$

Comparing (2.8) with the equilibrium condition for the strategic investment case, we can see that they differ in two important respects. First, on the LHS of (2.8) the price cost margin is given as a mark-up on a. Second, the RHS of (2.8) and (2.7) are directly comparable, and might lead us to expect that the profit to sales ratio in the strategic investment case will be less than in the Cournot case. However, even if this is so, we cannot infer that the equilibrium price will therefore be lower in the strategic investment case. For any given price θ, the Cournot profit to sales ratio is larger, since average costs are at their minimum. It is therefore quite possible that $\theta^* > \theta^c$ even though the inequality is reversed for the respective profit to sales ratios. No general comparison is presented in this paper.[1] However, in the linear model in section III, the Cournot price will always be the higher of the two. It can also be shown in the case of

[1] For a general treatment see Dixon [1984b, chapter 6, Theorem 6.1].

Cobb–Douglas firms and constant elasticity demand, that a sufficient condition for $\theta^c > \theta^*$ is inelastic demand ($\varepsilon_d > -1$). The presence of ε_s in (2.7) reflects the fact that in choosing its capital stock, the firm takes into account not only the downward slope of the demand curve, but also the reduction in (all) firms' outputs as θ falls. In the Cournot case, of course, these outputs are treated as constant.

An implication of the fact that $\theta^* > a_i$ is that firms will employ an inefficient technology, and incur costs in excess of a_i. The reason for this is that the firm is on its short-run cost curve in the market stage. Hence it will only employ least-cost technology if $\theta^* = a_i$. If $\theta^* > a_i$, then the firm will not be on its long-run cost-curve, and will in fact be *undercapitalised*: the firm's output capital ratio $s(\theta^*)$ is higher than the cost-minimising ratio $s(a)$, so that the firm employs an excessively labour intensive technology. Although the firm is maximising profits, the strategic structure of the model—and the resultant asymmetry between the firm's choice of capital and labour—implies that the firm does not employ the least-cost technology.

In order to bring out even more clearly the nature of the distortion, we can telescope the firm's decision into a simple optimisation programme:

$$(2.9) \quad \max_{k_i, L_i, x_i} \theta(k_i, k_{-i}) \cdot x_i - w \cdot L_i - r \cdot k_i \quad \text{subject to} \quad f(k_i, L_i) - x_i \geq 0$$

The firm chooses x_i and L_i freely as in the standard competitive case. The strategic nature of the firm's investment decision is captured by making θ a function of k_i (and k_{-i}). The first-order conditions yield

$$(2.10) \quad \frac{w}{r} = \frac{f_L}{f_k - \varepsilon_i \cdot s(\theta)} > \frac{f_L}{f_k}$$

From (2.9) and (2.10) we can see that the dependence of the competitive price in the firm's capital stock reduces the "marginal revenue product" from f_k to $f_k - \varepsilon_i \cdot s(\theta)$, and hence leads to a *lower* capital-labour ratio than required for least-cost production. When choosing k_i, the firm takes into account both its effect on the subgame price, and its effect on costs via the capital-labour ratio. At $\underline{k}^*$, if any firm were to increase its capital stock, the gains from a lower output-capital ratio in terms of reducing average costs would be outweighed by the resultant fall in θ. It should be clear from this simple treatment that the undercapitalisation result is general in this model, and does not depend at all on the assumption of constant returns in A1.

The symmetric industry equilibrium is depicted in Figure 1. The equilibrium price θ^* is determined by the intersection of the industry demand function and the supply function which results from the capital stocks chosen in the strategic stage. The U-shaped industry "short-run" average cost curve is marked AC. The strategic inefficiency due to under capitalisation is represented by the fact that average cost AC* is less than marginal cost in equilibrium. The industry profits $\Sigma k_i^* \cdot \pi(\theta^*)$ are given by the area A. The profit to sales ratio is given by

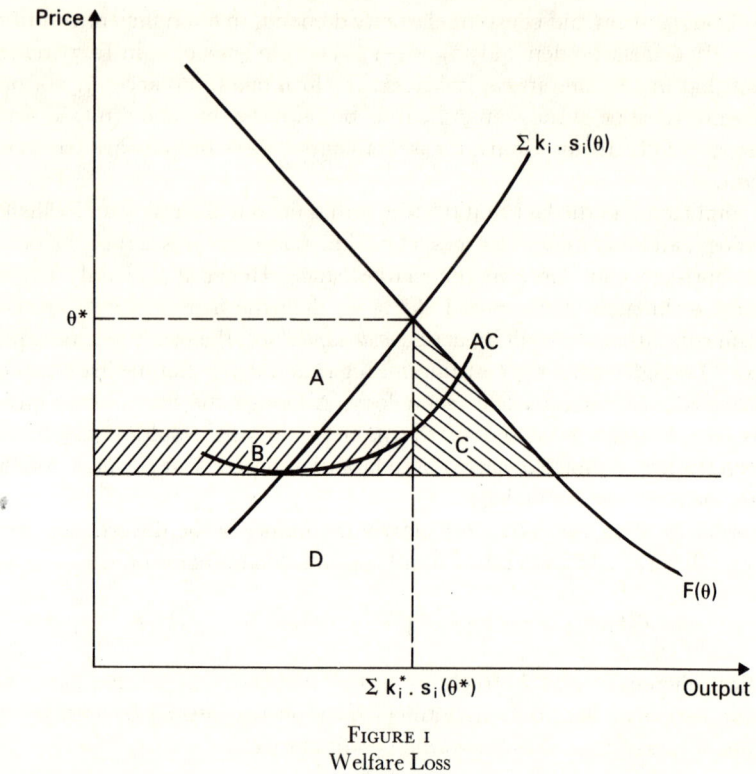

FIGURE 1
Welfare Loss

the ratio of area A to areas A, B, D. We shall now briefly consider the welfare losses in this framework employing the familiar consumer surplus approach, as in the "social costs of monopoly" literature (see Marshall [1920], Harberger [1954], Cowling and Mueller [1978] *inter alia*). Whilst this approach is open to serious criticism, it provides a useful first guide. In this model there will be two sources of lost consumers' surplus. Firstly we have the standard welfare loss given by the "triangle" under the demand curve, area C in the figure. Secondly we have the welfare loss due to strategic inefficiency, which is represented by area B in Figure 1, being the lost profits to shareholders $(AC^* - a) \cdot F(\theta^*)$. It should be noted that this strategic inefficiency is totally different in origin to the X-inefficiency as in Leibenstein [1966] and Comanor and Leibenstein [1969]. In the strategic investment model presented here the inefficiency is due to the dynamic structure of the model, not the fact that the best monopoly profit is a quiet life. In the market stage, the managers minimise costs: the inefficiency stems from the constraint the managers have imposed on themselves by their choice of capital in the strategic stage. In section III below, we show that in a linearised model (Case 2), the welfare loss due to strategic inefficiency may well be larger than the conventional triangle. This is not surprising, since the efficiency loss is $AC^* - a$ multiplied by the entire industry output.

We have now explored the properties of the strategic investment equilibrium. Even if the product market is perfectly competitive—or at least approximately so—the possibility of strategic commitment of capital would lead to prices above least-average cost.

The second important property of the model leads firms to choose undercapitalised technologies that are economically inefficient. It should be noted that this result only occurs because the firm is forced to separate its choice of capital and labour, and cannot choose them simultaneously. As we discuss in Dixon [1984a], were firms able to precommit both factors of production, and hence their capacity, then there would be no strategic factor bias, and the equilibrium of the two stage game would be Cournot. The strategic inefficiency is also related to the nature of the technology. Even in the case where firms precommit only capital, if the technology is Leontief or putty-clay, then in effect output and labour are thereby precommited, so that there will be a Cournot outcome with no strategic inefficiency. We should also note that the undercapitalisation result stems from the particular nature of the market subgame: had we assumed a Cournot equilibrium in the market stage, we would have obtained an overcapitalisation result, as in Brander and Spencer [1983].[2]

III. SOME EXPLICIT SOLUTIONS TO THE MODEL

In order to explore the mechanisms of the model more closely, it is useful to consider some specific functional forms. We will consider two cases. In case 1 we will explore the model in the case of identical firms with Cobb–Douglas technology, and constant elasticity demand. In case 2 we explore the model when firms may be different, but demand and supply functions are "linear". The second case is particularly simple for exploring the welfare loss due to strategic inefficiency. Consideration of these examples also gives us some ideas about existence in the model, since in both cases an equilibrium will exist under fairly weak conditions.

Case 1: Constant Elasticities: Cournot and Bertrand Outcomes as Limiting Cases of the Strategic Investment Model

In the case of identical firms, we recall the simple equilibrium condition (2.7):

$$\frac{\pi(\theta)}{\theta \cdot s(\theta)} = \frac{1}{n(\varepsilon_s - \varepsilon_d)}$$

Since the RHS of the equation is expressed in terms of ε_s and ε_d, we first consider the model when these are parameters. It will be recalled that ε_s is the elasticity of supply-per-unit capital $s(\theta)$ with respect to the market price.

[2] The market stage can be generalised to allow for a wider range of market outcomes. Yarrow [1985] has allowed for a conjectural variations model.

Cobb–Douglas technologies yield constant elasticity supply functions. Formally, if we specialise A5 to:

A1(a): $\quad x = L^\alpha \cdot k^{1-\alpha} : \varepsilon_s = \alpha/1-\alpha \qquad (0 < \alpha < 1)$

We also specialise A2 to constant elasticity of demand:

A2(a): $\quad F(p) = p^{-\beta} \qquad (\varepsilon_d = -\beta)$

Under A1(a) and A2(a), the profit to sales ratio will be uniquely determined by the three parameters of the model: n, α and β. Before proceeding to the explicit solution, however, it is necessary to consider whether or not an equilibrium exists: equation (2.8) merely tells us that the first order conditions are satisfied. Under A1–2 we know that there is a unique vector $\underline{k}^*$ which satisfies (2.8), in which all firms capital stocks are the same ($k_i^* = k^*$ for all i). Define ϕ where:

(3.1) $\quad \phi = (n-1) \cdot k^*/k_a$

and k_a is the competitive level of the capital stock ($a = \theta(k_a)$). Given that the other firms choose k^*, firm i will never want to choose its own capital stock so that the price is less than a, so we can restrict our attention to $k_i \leq (1-\phi) \cdot k_a$. Under what conditions will $\underline{k}^*$ so defined be an equilibrium? Proposition 1 gives a sufficient condition for the payoff function to be quasi-concave.

Proposition 1 (A1(a), A2(a)): *A unique symmetric equilibrium exists if*

$$\frac{1}{1-\phi} \geq \frac{1 - \varepsilon_d + 2 \cdot \varepsilon_s}{2 \cdot (\varepsilon_s - \varepsilon_d)}$$

The proof is given in the appendix. A sufficient condition for Proposition 1 to be satisfied is that demand is elastic. If there are more than a few firms, ϕ will be close to unity, so that we can be reasonably assured of existence.

Under A1(a) the profit to sales ratio is given by:

(3.2) $\quad \dfrac{\pi(\theta)}{\theta \cdot s(\theta)} = [1-\alpha] \left[1 - \left(\dfrac{a}{\theta}\right)^{1/1-\alpha} \right]$

We can now express (2.7) in terms of our parameters and solve for θ^*.

(3.3) $\quad \theta^* = a \cdot \left[1 - \dfrac{1}{n \cdot (\alpha + (1-\alpha) \cdot \beta)} \right]^{\alpha - 1}$

(3.3) is particularly useful if we wish to compare the strategic investment equilibrium with the Cournot equilibrium. Recall that in Dixon [1984a] we interpret the Cournot equilibrium as corresponding to the case where the firm precommits both factors of production, and hence chooses its capacity in the strategic move. In this case, firms will always choose a cost minimising capital labour ratio. Since there are constant returns to scale, the resultant Cournot equilibrium is:

$$(3.4) \quad \theta^c = a \cdot \left(1 - \frac{1}{n \cdot \beta}\right)^{-1}$$

Comparing (3.4) and (3.3) it can be seen that since $0 < \alpha < 1$, a sufficient condition for the Cournot price θ^c to exceed θ^* is that $\beta \leq 1$.

Having computed the equilibrium values $\{k^*, \theta^*\}$ under A1(a) and A2(b), we shall briefly consider how the equilibrium varies with the technological parameter α. When the firm chooses k_i in the strategic move, it chooses the supply function it will have in the market subgame. The parameter α determines the elasticity of the "short run" supply function $s(\theta)$: as $\alpha \to 1$, $\varepsilon_s \to +\infty$; as $\alpha \to 0$, $\varepsilon_s \to 0$. Thus α can be interpreted as representing the flexibility of production in the market stage. With Cobb–Douglas technology the limiting cases of $\alpha = 1$ or $\alpha = 0$ are not in themselves interesting, but they can act as a guide to the intuition for α close to 0 or 1. If $\alpha = 0$, then $x = k$ (for $L > 0$), so that output is totally determined by investment in the strategic move. We would thus expect a Cournot outcome, where the profit to sales ratio is $-1/\varepsilon_d$. If $\alpha = 1$, then $x = L$ ($k > 0$), so that precommitment does not affect the short run supply function, which would be perfectly elastic at $\theta = w$. In this case we would expect the Bertrand case of a zero profit to sales ratio.

The reasoning from these two cases is indeed correct, since from equations (3.3) and (3.4) it follows that:

$$\alpha \to 1 \quad \text{implies} \quad \frac{\theta^*}{a} \to \left[1 - \frac{1}{n}\right]^0 = 1 \quad (n \geq 2) \text{ "Bertrand"}$$

$$\alpha \to 0 \quad \text{implies} \quad \frac{\theta^*}{a} \to \left[1 - \frac{1}{n\beta}\right]^{-1} \quad (n \cdot \beta > 1) \text{ "Cournot"}$$

(Note that a itself varies with α.) Thus, depending on the elasticity of supply, the markup of price over least cost has the Cournot and the Bertrand values as limiting cases.

More can be said about the relationship with the Cournot case. If firms have constant returns Leontief technology, for example, then the output (or rather capacity) will be tied down in the strategic stage, and hence the Cournot equilibrium will occur. A further interesting property of the Leontief case is that there is no strategic inefficiency since, given its capacity, the firm will not employ labour over and above the minimum technically required, whatever the market price. Indeed, there will be no inefficiency for any technology for which the capacity is determined by the choice of capital stock. For example, if technology is putty-clay, then the capital labour ratio will be efficient, and the strategic investment equilibrium will be the Cournot equilibrium.

Case 2: The Welfare Loss in a Linear Model

In this section we show how the model works out in the linear case, where the supply and demand functions in the market subgame are linear. Linearity of the firm's supply-per-unit-capital function $s(p)$, can be seen as arising from a symmetric Cobb–Douglas technology (where the exponents on capital and labour are both 0.5). This is a special case of assumption A1(a), if we allow for non-identical firms:

A1(b): $\quad x_i = k_i^{0.5} \cdot L_i^{0.5}$

From this specification of the production function we can derive the functions $s(\theta)$, $\pi(\theta)$. These are best expressed using the parameter v, where v is defined as the least-cost or efficient output-capital ratio, so that $s(a) = v$.

$$(3.5) \qquad s(\theta) = \frac{v}{a} \cdot \theta$$

$$(3.6) \qquad \pi(\theta) = \frac{v}{2a}(\theta^2 - a^2)$$

On the demand side we give a special case of A2:

A2(b): $\quad F(p) = \max[0, \bar{p} - p]$

Thus we assume linearity and normalise so that $F' = -1$. Under these assumptions the market stage equilibrium condition implies the simple relation between capital stocks and price:

$$(3.7) \qquad \theta(\underline{k}) = \frac{\bar{p}}{1 + \Sigma k_i \cdot \omega_i} \qquad \text{where} \qquad \omega_i = v_i/a_i$$

Substitution of (3.7) into (3.6) yields the payoff function:

$$(3.8) \qquad U_i(\underline{k}) = \frac{\bar{p}^2}{2} \cdot \frac{\omega_i \cdot k_i}{1 + \Sigma \omega_j \cdot k_j} - r \cdot k_i$$

Thus U_i is strictly concave in k_i in this linear case. Hence an equilibrium exists. It can be shown that the equilibrium price is less than the Cournot price (Dixon [1984b, Theorems 5.1 and 6.1]).

One of the properties of the strategic investment equilibrium is that production is inefficient. The rest of this section of the paper is devoted to deriving explicit terms for this inefficiency in the linear case.

The excessive labour-capital ratio leads to average-costs in excess of minimum average costs a. Hence the strategic-inefficiency in production can be measured by:

$$(3.9) \qquad AC - a = \frac{(\theta - a)^2}{2\theta}$$

We are now in a position to derive an expression giving the total welfare loss in the strategic investment game as a function of θ^*. There are, we recall, two sources of "lost" consumer's surplus in the strategic investment model, as depicted in Figure 1. First, we have the standard welfare-loss given by the "triangle" under the demand curve, area A.

$$(3.10) \quad \Delta w_1 = \frac{(\theta - a)^2}{2}$$

Second, we have the additional efficiency loss given by area B. This reflects the consumer surplus lost to shareholders due to average costs exceeding their minimum. From (3.9) this area is given by:

$$(3.11) \quad \Delta w_2 = F(\theta) \cdot \left[\frac{c(s(\theta))}{s(\theta)} - a \right] = \frac{(\bar{p} - \theta) \cdot (\theta - a)^2}{2\theta}$$

Hence the total welfare-loss $\Delta w = \Delta w_1 + \Delta w_2$ is given by:

$$(3.12) \quad \Delta w = \frac{(\theta - a)^2}{\theta} \cdot \frac{\bar{p}}{2}$$

It is quite clear that the total welfare loss is strictly monotonic for $\theta \geqslant a$. However, whilst the standard welfare-loss triangle increases with θ, the strategic inefficiency Δw_2 is not monotonic. From (3.11) we can see that the strategic inefficiency is equal to zero both when output is zero ($\theta = \bar{p}$), and when AC $= a$ ($\theta = a$). We could reasonably expect that the welfare loss due to strategic inefficiency might be rather large relative to the standard welfare loss. If we compare (3.10-3), then:

$$\Delta w_2 = -[\Delta w_1/\varepsilon_d]$$

Thus the consumer surplus lost through strategic inefficiency equals the surplus lost via the triangle divided by the elasticity of demand. For $\varepsilon_d \geqslant -1$, the strategic inefficiency will represent the more important welfare loss. This is not so surprising, since the welfare loss due to strategic inefficiency is the excess cost multiplied by the entire industry output, so that even if the average cost is only slightly in excess of the minimum, it will be considerably magnified. The importance of strategic inefficiency in this model is not peculiar to this specification.

IV. STRATEGIC INVESTMENT AND ENTRY

The main body of this paper has assumed that there is a fixed set of active incumbents in the industry, with no entry or exit. This section provides a simple example of how entry might be modelled, and its welfare implications. It needs to be made quite clear from the outset that this section is more an outline than a detailed formal analysis. The special case considered provides an interesting illustration that is reasonably typical.

There are many ways of treating entry, depending on when entry is allowed.[3] We shall consider the simplest case: we add an extra entry move prior to the

---

[3] In effect, the treatment presented does not allow for entry after the investment decisions have been taken. This contrasts with models of entry deterrence where entry may occur after the incumbents have made their investment decision (e.g. Dixit [1980]).

strategic stage of the model. Firms incur sunk set-up costs $\mu > 0$. There is an infinite set of identical firms, which make their entry decision in some preordained order. Given the number of firms that decide to enter, a strategic investment equilibrium occurs. No entry occurs after the initial entry move. In evaluating the profits from entry, firms have perfect foresight.

With strictly positive set-up costs and constant returns to scale production, the model is of course the rather special case of natural monopoly (since the industry cost structure is super-additive (see Baumol et al. [1982]). Whilst this makes the analysis very simple, the qualitative results are generally valid.

Consider first the social optimum in this industry, which we shall take to be the Ramsey solution, which maximises the consumer surplus subject to the self-financing constraint. The Ramsey solution is the triplet $\{n_r, a_r, k_r\}$, the optimal number of firms, price, and capital stock respectively. Since the industry is a natural monopoly, the analysis is very simple, since we know that $n_r = 1$. Furthermore, it will be socially optimal to produce efficiently, with the output capital ratio v. Since demand is downward sloping, the Ramsey optimal price and capital stock are those which maximise output subject to the finance constraint:

(4.1) $\qquad$ max $\quad F(a_r)$

(4.2) $\qquad$ subject to $\quad k_r \cdot v \cdot (a_r - a) \geq \mu$

(4.3) $\qquad F(a_r) = k_r \cdot v$

How does the strategic investment equilibrium with entry compare with the Ramsey optimum? Let us denote this equilibrium by the triplet $\{n^*, K^*, \theta^*\}$, where K^* is the industry capital stock, and $\theta = \theta(K^*)$ (since firms are identical, the equilibrium is symmetric). These values are determined by the equilibrium condition (2.7) between the active incumbents, plus the entry condition. Both of these conditions can be summarised using the "outcome function" $\Omega(n)$, giving profits net of entry costs when there are n firms in the industry. For a broad class of standard models Ω is a uniquely defined, strictly decreasing function of n, and from (2.7) $\Omega \to 0$ as $n \to \infty$. The number of firms n^* is determined by $\Omega(n^*) \geq \mu \geq \Omega(n^*+1)$. This will in turn define the equilibrium capital stock in the industry.

Given this skeletal outline, we have enough information to compare the strategic investment equilibrium with the Ramsey optimum. There are four points of contrast which are of interest:

(i) *Excess Entry*: $n^* \geq n_r$. Unless entry costs are large, $n^* > n_r$.

To see why, note that if $\Omega(1) > \mu$, there will be more than one firm. Entry in excess of the social optimum will occur unless entry costs are large, where "large" means that $\mu > \Omega(2)$.

(ii) *Inefficiency in Production*: We know from the analysis in section II that the method of producing output will be inefficient, being under-capitalised. This is unchanged by entry, since $\theta^* > a$ for all finite n.

(iii) *Excessive Price*: $\theta^* > a_r$.

This must be so if the incumbents are to cover their entry costs μ. From (i), fixed costs in the industry $n^* \cdot \mu$ are at least as great as in the Ramsey case. But for $\theta > a$, production is inefficient by (ii). For any given price, therefore, industry profits are less than in the efficient Ramsey case (see (4.2)). Hence the equilibrium price θ^* must exceed the Ramsey price.

(iv) *Underinvestment*: $K^* < K_r$. There is less investment in the industry than in the Ramsey case.

This follows from (ii) and (iii). Since $\theta^* > a_r$, industry output is less than optimal. But $s(\theta^*) > v$ from (ii), so that $K^* < K_r$.

In the strategic investment model with entry, there are too many firms which underinvest and are inefficient. In essence there are too many firms producing too little output with too little capital. As should be quite clear from the analysis, the conclusions (i)–(iv) will apply beyond the case of fixed set-up costs plus constant returns technology. However, the case of natural monopoly is rather special.

What happens if firms have the more standard U-shaped long run average cost curves? These can be seen as arising from a diminishing returns to scale production function with strictly positive fixed or sunk costs. All comparisons

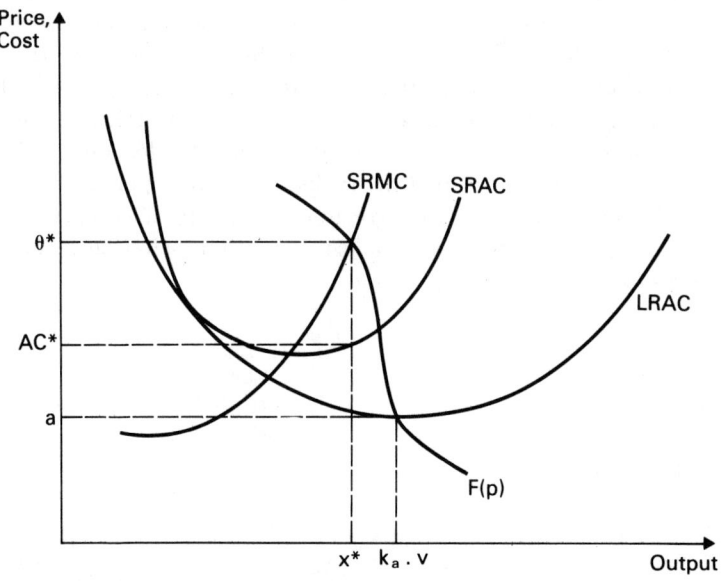

FIGURE 2
Chamberlinian Excess Capacity

(i)–(iii) will still be directly valid. The only important modification concerns comparison (iv). If we ignore the integer problem, in the Ramsey solution each firm will produce at the bottom of its "long run" average cost curve. This implies a certain capital stock for each firm, denoted k_a. However, in the strategic investment equilibrium the zero profit entry condition will mean that firms will produce at below the least cost capacity, as depicted in Figure 2, which depicts a symmetric equilibrium as in Figure 1, except that the LRAC is U-shaped. Thus we can extend (iv) to include the standard "Chamberlinian" undercapacity result. Not only are firms off their LRAC as in the constant returns case, but the output is below the minimum economic scale ($k^* < k_a$). With the introduction of a U-shaped cost function, we have a rather paradoxical result. Given the capital stocks chosen in equilibrium, there is overutilisation of capacity, an excessive output-capital ratio. This is due to strategic inefficiency. The entry condition, however, implies that the capital stock is too small, being less than the "capacity" level k_a.

V. CONCLUSION

There may still be a relationship between concentration and welfare loss even in an industry where conditions in the product market are competitive. Firms can employ such variables as investment to influence the market outcome, and their ability to do so is directly related to their "market share", interpreted as the firm's share in the industry capital stock. This leads to a price which is higher than the price that occurs when investment is not employed strategically, and there is a corresponding welfare loss due to the resultant restriction of output. The strategic use of investment in this way also gives rise to an additional inefficiency in production, since the technology will be too labour intensive. In the simple linear model presented in section III, the welfare loss due to this strategic inefficiency may be larger than the loss due to the price being too high. This suggests that the evaluation of monopoly power needs to go beyond a simple analysis of the conditions in the product market and the actual cost structure of firms, and to take into account such strategic behaviour and the distortions to which it gives rise.

HUW DIXON
Birkbeck College,
London University,
7–15 Gresse Street,
London W1P 1PA,
U.K.

APPENDIX

Proof of Proposition 1

We show that U_i is strictly quasi-concave in k_i. A necessary and sufficient condition for quasi-concavity is that *if* $U_{ki} = 0$ then the second partial U_{kki} is non-positive. Now,

$$U_{ki} = \pi(\theta) + k_i \cdot s(\theta) \cdot \frac{\partial \theta}{\partial k_i} = \pi(\theta) - \frac{1}{\varepsilon_s - \varepsilon_d} (\theta \cdot s(\theta) \cdot \sigma)$$

where

$$\sigma = \frac{K_i}{\Sigma k_j} \quad (j = 1 \ldots n),$$

σ being the ith firm's capital share. If $U_{ki} = 0$, then

$$\frac{\pi(\theta)}{\theta \cdot s(\theta)} = \frac{\sigma}{\varepsilon_s - \varepsilon_d}$$

If we evaluate U_{kki} when $U_{ki} = 0$ we find after some manipulation that:

$$\left. \frac{\partial U_i^2}{\partial k_i^2} \right|_{U_{ki}=0} = -\frac{1}{\varepsilon_s - \varepsilon_d} \cdot \frac{\pi(\theta)}{\Sigma k_j} \cdot \left[\varepsilon_s \cdot 2 \cdot \frac{(1-\sigma)}{\sigma} - \varepsilon_d \cdot \left(\frac{2-\sigma}{\sigma} \right) - 1 \right]$$

This will be non-positive if

$$\frac{1}{\sigma} \geq \frac{1 - \varepsilon_d + 2 \cdot \varepsilon_s}{2 \cdot (\varepsilon_s - \varepsilon_d)}$$

But $\sigma \leq 1 - \phi$ (for profits to be positive).

PRODUCT DIVERSITY AND MONOPOLISTIC COMPETITION UNDER UNCERTAINTY*

Norman J. Ireland

I. INTRODUCTION

Monopolistic competition with free entry is of course traditionally characterised by the individual firm producing at the tangency between average revenue and average cost curves. However if output has to be decided *ex ante* of the position of the average revenue curve being revealed, then this description is no longer adequate. In fact two additional factors need to be incorporated. The first is that the firm's attitude towards risk combined with stochastic variations of marginal revenue may imply an adjustment in optimal output. In particular, if the firm is risk averse then the possibility of an extra dollar marginal revenue will not counter-balance the (same probability) possibility of a dollar less marginal revenue. Thus desired output will be less. This result is well known in the theory of the firm, emanating from papers by Sandmo [1971] and Ishii [1977] amongst others.

If, as is likely, the uncertainty relates to demand conditions in the industry as a whole rather than being limited to demand for a particular firm's (differentiated) product, a second factor is also important. If firms are risk averse then the possibility of a positive profit of one dollar will not counter-balance the (same probability) possibility of a loss of one dollar. Thus at expected profit of zero, firms will leave the industry, decreasing the number of products available, and increasing the demand for those remaining. For the individual firm which remains in the industry while uncertainty is imposed on the industry's demand, two effects via demand are seen. One is the increase in demand for the firm's product due to decreased competition and the other is the lower evaluation of demand due to the risk aversion of the firm.

The effect of uncertainty on the output of the individual firm may be ambiguous in a totally general model as the two effects above influence desired output in different directions. Also the market equilibrium nature of the monopolistic competition model implies that if output is reduced in firms within the industry, this increases the incentive for new firms to enter the industry and may indeed mean that the number of firms increases rather than decreases with the onset of uncertainty. Thus both the level of output in an individual firm and the number of firms within the industry may respond with either sign to the introduction of uncertainty, although we can rule out the case where both

---

* The author is grateful to participants in the meeting of the Industrial Economics/Economic Theory Study Groups, Oxford 1984, and to the editors and referees of this Journal for a number of valuable comments.

increase. In this paper we wish to study and demonstrate these possibilities and investigate their welfare implications.

As we are considering the equilibrium of an industry composed of differentiated but similar products, we will take as our source of uncertainty the level of market demand. Thus next period's demand for all kinds of ice cream is dependent on random weather conditions; next period's demand for all makes of washing machine are dependent on unknown consumer preferences concerning washing machines and other commodities as well as on consumers' incomes. We will not be focussing primarily on uncertainty which arises over a specific firm's share in a given market demand—due for instance to incomplete consumer information, although the model can be interpreted in this way except in the analysis of welfare effects where a rather different approach would be needed.

In section II the model is outlined and basic assumptions are discussed. In section III an industry equilibrium is defined and studied for the "symmetric" case of identical firms. It is argued that, under very general assumptions, incorporating a Nash quantity-setting non-cooperative game augmented by conjectural variations embodied in agents' behaviour, an increase in uncertainty will result in a decrease in a measure of aggregate industry supply. In section IV we take a special case to investigate the composition of this decrease in terms of changes in number of firms (products) and output per firm (product). In section V, welfare aspects are considered and it is shown that, in a non-trivial set of circumstances, uncertainty will *increase* the expected net welfare created by the industry. Section VI summarises the conclusions.

II. THE MODEL

Providing that there are a sufficient number of candidate firms able to enter the industry at zero cost, we can define long run monopolistic competition equilibrium under uncertainty by requiring that the expected utility of a firm within the industry is the same as that obtained by a firm outside the industry, and that each firm conceives its output decisions as maximising its expected utility given its conjecture concerning the response (if any) of industry supply as a whole to such decisions. Each firm faces identical demand and cost conditions (i.e. firms are symmetric) and are affected by the same industry-wide uncertainty over demand. Thus we will define

(i) *Demand*. The price at which a typical (j^{th}) firm can sell its product is p_j given by

(1) $\qquad p_j = \alpha f(x, z) \qquad f_x \leqslant 0; f_z < 0$

where α is of the form

(2) $\qquad \alpha = \mu + \sigma r$

In (2), r is a random variable with mean zero and variance one. Thus the parameters μ and σ^2 are the mean and variance of α. The function $f(x, z)$ is differentiable with negative partial derivative with respect to a measure of industry supply, z, and non-positive partial derivative with respect to the firm's own output, x. Note that to the extent that firms supply differentiated products, z is not merely the sum of individual firms' outputs. For instance, a one per cent increase in the number of producing firms combined with a one per cent fall in output per firm may well increase z, even though total quantity supplied by the industry is unchanged, due to the greater variety of choice available.

Thus if there are n producing firms

(3) $\quad z = g(x, n) \quad g_x > 0; g_n > 0$

(ii) *Cost*. We will define

(4) $\quad c_j = c(x) \quad c_x > 0; c(0) > 0$

as the cost incurred by the typical (j^{th}) firm. We will assume that (4) is sufficiently convex (or not concave) that second-order conditions hold where necessary. Also we will assume that there are no interproduct economies of scale (economies of scope, see Waterson [1983]). Thus each firm will produce at most one product.

(iii) *Entry and Exit*. There are an arbitrarily high number of potential firms. The decision to exit or enter the industry is taken on the basis of the expected utility from participation. If the initial Nash equilibrium of production plans of firms currently in the industry yields a level of expected utility per firm not equal to the level that can be obtained from non-participation, then entry or exit takes place and a new Nash equilibrium of the revised group of participating firms is reached. This process is repeated until the expected utility of participating firms is the same as that of non-participating firms. We will take the latter level as zero without loss of generality. Only when equilibrium is reached does output take place, and only after output has been produced is the actual demand regime (value of α) revealed.

(iv) *Conjectural Variations*. The nature of the Nash equilibrium of participating firms is that each firm maximises its expected utility given other firms' behaviour but assuming a specific response of the rest of the industry to changes in its output. This conjectured response is to the effect that if the firm increases (decreases) its output by one per cent, it believes that total industry supply as measured by the index z increases (decreases) by η per cent, where η is common for all firms and is a constant conjectural elasticity defined by[1]

(5) $\quad \eta = \dfrac{dz}{dx}\dfrac{x}{z}$

Of course, the industry's actual response may be very different to that conjectured. In this sense, conjectural variations are not "rational" (see Perry [1982]) unless $\eta = 0$. In this case of competitive pricing (Spence [1976]) or

---

[1] A similar treatment of a constant elasticity η is used in Ireland [1983a]. Koenker and Perry [1981] use a rather different formulation of conjectural variation.

large group of firms (Dixit and Stiglitz [1977]), the rest of the industry is perceived by a firm to "make room" for increases in its output, so that z is unaffected. More generally we will consider that $0 \leq \eta \leq \bar{\eta}$, indicating a range of possible conjectural elasticities representing the degree of apparent collusion in the industry (Cubbin [1983]). The value of η which would imply that the industry's behaviour mimicked joint profit maximisation of participating firms would depend on the nature of z, that is the form of (3). Also the value of η may combine conjectures over entry and exit with those over other firms' output responses. In the absence of such conjectures over entry and exit, a pure Nash equilibrium would involve a value for η of $1/n$.

III. THE INDUSTRY EQUILIBRIUM UNDER UNCERTAINTY

Given the assumptions stated in the last section, we require for an industry long-run equilibrium that:

(6) $\quad E\{V(\pi)\} = 0$

and

(7) $\quad E\{V_\pi(\pi) \cdot \pi_x^*\} = 0$

where $V(\cdot)$ is the (typical) firm's utility function which is increasing in profit, π, and also strictly concave to represent the firm's decision-maker's risk aversion. Equation (6) is thus a generalisation of the zero profit condition for free entry and exit. Equation (7) is the marginal utility from the conjectured marginal profit (distinguished as π_x^*) from producing (and selling) an additional unit, and incorporates the conjectural elasticity η. Thus

(8) $\quad \pi = \alpha f(x, z) x - c(x)$

and

(9) $\quad \pi_x^* = \alpha f(x, z) \{1 - \varepsilon - \eta \theta\} - c_x(x)$

where $\quad \varepsilon = -f_x x/f > 0$
$\quad \theta = -f_z z/f > 0$

and η is defined by (5).

If x were fixed then (6) would imply that z is lower under uncertainty than under certainty, since in the former case $E(\pi) > 0$ due to the concavity of $V(\cdot)$, and $\sigma > 0$. Similarly if z were fixed then (7) would imply that output per firm is less under uncertainty as the single competitive firm analysis of Sandmo [1971] would be applicable. Furthermore any increase in uncertainty $(d\sigma > 0)$ would imply less z (if x was fixed) and less x (if z was fixed); the latter result provided that the coefficient of absolute risk aversion is non-increasing in income (a commonly accepted proposition) is due to Ishii [1977]. As our model is based on the notion that neither x nor z can be taken as fixed, a comparative analysis of their simultaneous responses to increased uncertainty requires (6) and (7) to be considered simultaneously determining x and z, while (3) then yields the number of active firms n. Obviously the equilibrium (x, z, n) will depend on the amount of uncertainty, specifically on the parameter σ. To facilitate analysis, we write (6) and (7) in the implicit form:

(6') $\quad \phi(x, z; \sigma) = 0$

(7') $\quad \psi(x, z; \sigma) = 0$

Total differentiation of the implicit functions (6') and (7') yield

(10) $\quad \begin{pmatrix} \phi_z & \phi_x \\ \psi_z & \psi_x \end{pmatrix} \begin{pmatrix} dz/d\sigma \\ dx/d\sigma \end{pmatrix} = \begin{pmatrix} -\phi_\sigma \\ -\psi_\sigma \end{pmatrix}$

We will argue that the following sign pattern holds:

(10') $\quad \begin{pmatrix} - & + \\ - & - \end{pmatrix} \begin{pmatrix} dz/d\sigma \\ dx/d\sigma \end{pmatrix} = \begin{pmatrix} + \\ + \end{pmatrix}$

where the $+$ sign for ϕ_x is replaced by a zero value if $\eta = 0$, as then ϕ_x is simply ψ and thus zero. The value of ϕ_z and ψ_z reflect the fact that both expected utility and the expected utility from the marginal unit produced is less if industry supply is greater as price becomes depressed. In fact $\psi_z < 0$ represents an assumption as it is conceivable that the marginal revenue curve could shift up while the average revenue shifted down. In this case it may be that $\psi_z \geqslant 0$, but we will discount this possibility, although in fact our analysis could be extended, via a dynamic stability of equilibrium argument, to incorporate it. We also have $\psi_x < 0$ as a second-order condition if $\eta > 0$ does not affect the sign. On the right hand side, $\phi_\sigma < 0$ because of the concavity of $V(\cdot)$ and $\psi_\sigma < 0$, assuming non-increasing absolute risk aversion, following the argument of Ishii [1977]. Note that the sign pattern is consistent with the cases discussed above where one of x and z is fixed.

By Cramer's rule we have immediately that

$$dz/d\sigma < 0$$

and

$$dx/d\sigma \text{ is ambiguous.}$$

Thus we can state

Proposition 1. A mean-preserving increase in risk (variance of α) will reduce the equilibrium level of an index of industry supply, providing the coefficient of absolute risk aversion of the firm is non-increasing in profit.

Proposition 1 is a result for the industry in Nash equilibrium which is analogous to the Sandmo/Ishii results for the single competitive firm. We will see in the next section that the apparent ambiguity in response of the typical firm's output is confirmed and that both output per firm and number of firms can change in either direction. Proposition 1, however, assures us that at least one of these will decrease with uncertainty.

Before proceeding to a more specific analysis, it should be pointed out that comparative statics of (6) and (7) with respect to μ would yield a negative right-hand-side vector. Then $dz/d\mu > 0$ while $dx/d\mu$ is ambiguous, (although the sign of $dx/d\mu$ is not necessarily opposite to the sign of $dx/d\sigma$). However this yields the result that an upward shift in demand increases the supply of industry services but the source of this increase—whether from increased output per firm or an increase in the number of firms or both—is not determined.

IV. A SPECIFIC CASE

In the introduction, we conjectured that uncertainty might increase output per firm (by reducing the number of firms) or increase the number of firms (by reducing output per firm). In the last section, a fairly general analysis allowed us to conclude that an index of industry supply would always fall in response to increased uncertainty, but the possibility that both output per firm and number of firms do not decrease simultaneously remains. In this section we will show within a simple and tractable example that the following three possibilities can exist for feasible ranges of parameters:

(i) uncertainty leads to fewer firms and lower output per firm in long-run monopolistic competition equilibrium,
(ii) uncertainty leads to less firms and more output per firm in long-run monopolistic competition equilibrium,
(iii) uncertainty leads to more firms and less output per firm in long-run monopolistic competition equilibrium.

Although our example will be far from general, it will suffice to show that these three cases can all easily exist and that (ii) and (iii) are not mere curiosities. A particular reason for demonstrating this is the possibility that uncertainty may change the constituents of industry services so that although these decrease, reducing net welfare, the mix of constituents may improve in terms of efficiency to such an extent that net welfare is increased overall. We will return to this topic in the next section where we will also consider some more general issues in welfare and regulation.

As well as taking a particular welfare function to generate a specific demand system, our analysis will also be simplified by only investigating the effect of the onset of small uncertainty from an initial certainty equilibrium. Thus we compare (6') and (7') at $\sigma = 0$ and $\sigma = d\sigma > 0$. When $\sigma = 0$, (6') and (7') are solved by x and z which equate π and π_x^* ((8) and (9)) to zero and are independent of firms' utility functions. On the other hand, a slight complication occurs because both (6') and (7') have zero derivatives with respect to σ at $\sigma = 0$. The reason for this is that moving from $\sigma = \sigma_1 > 0$ has the same effect as moving from $\sigma = 0$ to $\sigma = -\sigma_1$ if the distribution of r is symmetric and as $\sigma_1 \to 0$ any significance of asymmetry disappears. Thus the functions (6') and (7') are flat with respect to σ at $\sigma = 0$. In order to avoid this problem but retain tractability we will expand (6′) and (7′) in second-order Taylor's expansions around $\sigma = 0$, evaluate expectations, and then use an exogenous shift in σ^2 from zero in order to assess the implications of uncertainty for the industry equilibrium. A similar expansion is involved in Ireland [1980] and developed in Aaftink, Ireland and Sertel [1982], and although results are only valid for the effect of the first "small" amount of uncertainty, they are indicative of likely behaviour and can also show where non-ambiguous results are not possible. Our current problem has the additional complication that it is not only the behaviour of individual agents which is affected by the imposition of uncertainty, but also the number of agents.

Second-order expansions of (6) and (7) yield, after taking expectations,

(6″) $\quad EV(\pi) \simeq [V(\pi)] + \dfrac{1}{2}\left[V_{\pi\pi}(\pi)\left(\dfrac{\partial \pi}{\partial \alpha}\right)^2\right]\sigma^2$

(7″) $\quad E\{V_\pi(\pi)\pi_x^*\} \simeq [V_\pi(\pi)\pi_x^*] + \left[V_{\pi\pi}(\pi)\dfrac{\partial \pi_x^*}{\partial \alpha}\dfrac{\partial \pi}{\partial \alpha}\right]\sigma^2$

where all terms in square brackets are evaluated at $\sigma = 0$ and at the certainty equilibrium values of x and z. Setting (6″) and (7″) to zero and taking comparative statics at $\sigma^2 = 0$ brings us back to a system such as (10), that is,

(11) $\quad \begin{pmatrix} [V_\pi(\pi)\pi_z] & [V_\pi(\pi)\pi_x] \\ \left[V_\pi(\pi)\dfrac{\partial \pi_x^*}{\partial z}\right] & \left[V_\pi(\pi)\dfrac{\partial \pi_x^*}{\partial x}\right] \end{pmatrix}\begin{pmatrix} dz \\ dx \end{pmatrix} = \begin{pmatrix} \dfrac{1}{2}\left[\dfrac{\partial \pi}{\partial \alpha}\right] \\ \left[\dfrac{\partial \pi_x^*}{\partial \alpha}\right] \end{pmatrix}\left[-V_{\pi\pi}(\pi)\dfrac{\partial \pi}{\partial \alpha}\right]d\sigma^2$

Dividing through (11) by $V_\pi(\pi)$ and defining the coefficient of absolute risk aversion as $A = -V_{\pi\pi}(\pi)/V_\pi(\pi)$ yields, again using [ ] to denote evaluation at $\alpha = \mu$ and the certainty equilibrium,

(12) $\quad \begin{pmatrix} [\pi_z] & [\pi_x] \\ \left[\dfrac{\partial \pi_x^*}{\partial z}\right] & \left[\dfrac{\partial \pi_x^*}{\partial x}\right] \end{pmatrix}\begin{pmatrix} \dfrac{dz}{d\sigma^2} \\ \dfrac{dx}{d\sigma^2} \end{pmatrix} = \begin{pmatrix} \dfrac{1}{2}\left[\dfrac{\partial \pi}{\partial \alpha}\right] \\ \left[\dfrac{\partial \pi_x^*}{\partial \alpha}\right] \end{pmatrix}\left[A\dfrac{\partial \pi}{\partial \alpha}\right]$

The specific demand system we will use is derived from the gross welfare function

(13) $\quad W = \alpha(z - \tfrac{1}{2}z^2)$

and the industry services index

(14) $\quad z = \sum_{i=1}^{n} x_i^\beta$

Equations (13) and (14) imply a constant elasticity of substitution between products of $1/(1-\beta)$. Then, ignoring income effects, marginal welfare of good

j is the price that consumers are willing to pay for good j, that is

(15) $\qquad p_j = \alpha(1-z)\beta x_j^{\beta-1} \qquad j = 1, 2, \ldots, n$

We will assume that cost functions for all firms are identical, and for the typical (j^{th}) firm is equal to $cx_j^{\beta} + C$. The restriction that the exponent on x_j in costs is the same as that on x_j in (14) is purely to allow algebraic solutions; note however that it encompasses (i) the case of homogeneous products ($\beta = 1$) and constant marginal cost, and (ii) the case of heterogeneous products ($\beta < 1$) and diminishing marginal cost. As all x_j will be the same in equilibrium by symmetry, the j subscript may be dropped, giving profit for the typical firm as:

(8') $\qquad \pi = x^{\beta}\{\alpha(1-z)\beta - c\} - C$

The certainty equilibrium is defined by (8') and (9') set equal to zero, where

(9') $\qquad \pi_x^* = \beta x^{\beta-1}\{\alpha(1-z)\beta - c\} - x^{\beta}\alpha\beta\eta z/x$
$\qquad\quad = \beta x^{\beta-1}\{\alpha\beta(1-z) - \alpha\eta z - c\}$

and $\sigma^2 = 0$ implies $\alpha = \mu$. Note that $\eta > 0$ (that is, non-competitive pricing) is required for second-order conditions. The certainty equilibrium is the solution to (8') and (9') and is

(16) $\qquad z = (\mu\beta - c)/(\mu(\beta+\eta))$

(17) $\qquad x^{\beta} = C(\beta+\eta)/(\eta(\mu\beta - c))$

We use (8') and (9') in (12) and obtain, using (16) and (17), and simplifying:

(12') $\qquad \begin{pmatrix} -\mu & \eta\dfrac{(\mu\beta-c)/x}{\beta+\eta} \\ -\mu(\beta+\eta) & 0 \end{pmatrix} \begin{pmatrix} \dfrac{dz}{d\sigma^2} \\ \dfrac{dx}{d\sigma^2} \end{pmatrix} = \begin{pmatrix} \dfrac{1}{2}\dfrac{\mu\eta+c}{\mu(\beta+\eta)} \\ \dfrac{c}{\mu} \end{pmatrix} [A\partial\pi/\partial\alpha]$

where $[A\partial\pi/\partial\alpha] > 0$. Using Cramer's rule we have

(18) $\qquad \dfrac{dz}{d\sigma^2} = -[A\partial\pi/\partial\alpha]c/\{\mu^2(\beta+\eta)\}$

(19) $\qquad \dfrac{1}{x}\dfrac{dx}{d\sigma^2} = [A\partial\pi/\partial\alpha]\dfrac{\frac{1}{2}(\mu\eta-c)}{\mu\eta(\mu\beta-c)}$

From (14) and the fact that symmetry implies $x_i = x$ for all i:

$$\frac{d\log n}{d\sigma^2} = \frac{d\log z}{d\sigma^2} - \beta\frac{d\log x}{d\sigma^2}$$

Hence we obtain from (18) and (19) by using (16)

(20) $\qquad \dfrac{d\log n}{d\sigma^2} = [A\partial\pi/\partial\alpha]\dfrac{\{-c\eta - \beta(\mu\eta-c)/2\}}{\eta\mu(\mu\beta-c)}$

Thus we have

Proposition 2. The imposition of uncertainty can give rise to any one of the following three responses of long-run equilibrium:

(i) the number of firms and output per firm will both fall;
(ii) the number of firms will fall but output per firm will rise;
(iii) the output per firm will fall but the number of firms will rise.

We have proved Proposition 2 by using a specific example and small uncertainty. For this example, (19) and (20) hold so that

$$\frac{dx}{d\sigma^2} \gtreqless 0 \quad \text{as} \quad \eta \gtreqless \frac{c}{\mu}$$

$$\frac{dn}{d\sigma^2} \gtreqless 0 \quad \text{as} \quad \eta \lesseqgtr \frac{c}{\mu}\frac{\beta\mu}{2c+\beta\mu} = lc/\mu$$

so that case (i) above holds if $lc/\mu < \eta < c/\mu$, case (ii) holds if $\eta \geq c/\mu$ and case (iii) holds if $\eta < lc/\mu$.

The fact that the same example can contain all three cases for feasible parameter values demonstrates that no case can be dismissed as obscure or pathological.[2]

V. WELFARE ASPECTS

Under certainty, a rough and ready measure of welfare in a partial equilibrium model would be the sum of consumers' and producers' surpluses. Under uncertainty, however, it would be necessary to deduct that part of producers' surplus or profit which compensates producers for running risks to which they are averse. This is a "deadweight" loss of uncertainty, and if all profits in long run equilibrium are required to be used for such compensation then expected net welfare (ENW) may be described as

(21) $\quad \text{ENW} = E\{W - p\sum x\}$

On the other hand the proportion of profits necessary to compensate producers may be quite small. Two scenarios may illustrate this. First consider that firms' decisions are taken by managers as agents for society. Managers decide what goods to produce (that is, entry and exit) and how much to produce. They are rewarded on the basis of profits—either by a performance-linked income schedule or by reputation which affects their future income streams—but this reward itself is an insignificant part of a firms' profits and losses. The latter is (virtually) fully distributed to consumers who also receive income from other industries, have fully-diversified asset portfolios, and who are

---

[2] Of course not every welfare-based demand system generates all three possibilities. For instance, among a fairly small set of tractable alternatives, the constant elasticities model (see for instance Koenker and Perry [1981]), where $W = \alpha z^\theta$ and z is of the form (14), does *not* permit case (ii) although it does permit cases (i) and (iii).

essentially risk-neutral as a result. A second possibility is that firms are controlled by a small subset of stock holders (a single stock holder for example) who have a small proportion of the total stock but whose holding is a large part of their personal portfolio of assets, and thus they require a positive expected profit as compensation for risk-bearing.[3]

The limit of either case is such that virtually all profit is distributed to risk neutral consumers; firm controllers have the same long run expected utility, and so expected net welfare is

$$(22) \quad \text{ENW} = E\{W - p\sum x + n\pi\}$$
$$= E\{W - nc(x)\}$$

and consumers consider the profit-generating aspects of their (personal) expenditure as insignificant, so that they choose consumption levels to maximise consumers' surplus $W - p\sum x$, given α.

The correct model certainly lies between (21) and (22), but we will confine our attention here to these two polar cases in order to analyse the welfare effects of introducing uncertainty into a monopolistic competition equilibrium.

It will be anticipated that if all profits are "deadweight" loss, and ENW is (21), then, for a very large class of models, uncertainty reduces ENW. In particular if $z = \sum_j x_j^\beta$ then $p_j = W_z \beta x_j^{\beta-1}$, all j, and ENW $= W - W_z z\beta$. Then as W is concave in z, $d\text{ENW}/dz > 0$, so that $d\text{ENW}/d\sigma^2 < 0$ as z declines with the imposition of uncertainty. If, however, there is little deadweight loss from uncertainty it is *a priori* not inconceivable that the changes in the number of firms and output per firm resulting from the imposition of uncertainty may well give rise to increased ENW as defined by (22). In the example of the last section, expected net welfare would then be:

$$(22') \quad \text{ENW} = \mu(z - \tfrac{1}{2}z^2) - cz - nC$$

as $c(x) = cx^\beta + C$. The optimum $n^0 = 1$ and $z^0 = 1 - c/\mu$ is found from maximising (22') with respect to n and x given the constraint $n \geq 1$. Industry services, supplied in a monopolistic competition long run equilibrium under certainty, given by (16), is less than z^0 as $\beta \leq 1$ and $\eta > 0$, and we might assume this undersupply of industry services to hold more generally. The imposition of general demand uncertainty would decrease the industry supply of services and thus tend to reduce welfare by moving to a socially worse position. However this is not the complete story as we have also seen that the number of firms/output per firm mix is likely to be radically changed by uncertainty. We may consider a situation where economies of scale exist and products are fairly homogeneous. Would it then be possible that uncertainty would drive out sufficient firms that those remaining could expand their

---

[3] The connection between firm behaviour and the asset portfolio of controlling shareholders in relation to mergers is considered in a number of papers including Bradburd [1980] and Ireland [1983b]. (Note however that an additional restriction of an upper bound on s is required for the proof of Proposition 1 of the latter to be correct.)

outputs to take advantage of economies of scale and thereby increase expected welfare because of increased efficiency?

We will attack this question in two ways. First we will investigate a general model but with homogeneous goods. We will show that ENW will increase with uncertainty if and only if output per firm increases with uncertainty. This we will state as Proposition 3. We will then argue that this case can occur by referring to our example of section II. Then we will see how, within this example, the result can be extended to differentiated products provided the conjectural variation elasticity increases in compensation.

If the industry's products are homogeneous, we have $\beta = 1$ and can write

$$z = xn$$

and expected net welfare can be written as

(23) $\quad$ ENW $= \mu G(z) - nc(x) \qquad G_z > 0; G_{zz} < 0$

Now we have

(24) $\quad \dfrac{d\text{ENW}}{d\sigma^2} = \dfrac{\partial \text{ENW}}{\partial x}\dfrac{dx}{d\sigma^2} + \dfrac{\partial \text{ENW}}{\partial n}\dfrac{dn}{d\sigma^2}$

and

(25) $\quad \dfrac{\partial \text{ENW}}{\partial x} = \mu G_z n - nc_x(x)$

(26) $\quad \dfrac{\partial \text{ENW}}{\partial n} = \mu G_z x - c(x)$

Now $\mu G_z \equiv p_j$, the price for the homogeneous products, as μG_z is the utility of the marginal unit of the commodity. In zero-profit equilibrium under certainty (26) is thus zero. Also as $\eta > 0$, the (conjectural) profit-maximising output per firm is given by $\mu G_z - c_x(x) + \mu G_{zz} \eta z/x = 0$. Thus as $G_{zz} < 0$, (25) is positive. We then have from (24):

Proposition 3. In long run equilibrium, if products are homogeneous then expected net welfare defined by (22) is decreased by the addition of small uncertainty if output per firm decreases as a result of the uncertainty, and is increased if output per firm is increased.

Note that as products are homogeneous, a Chamberlinian equilibrium under certainty will be characterised by too small an output level compared with the social optimum due to a too-small firm output level. Increasing output per firm improves efficiency (increased economies of scale) and there is no loss of variety from the smaller number of firms as products are homogeneous.

With differentiated products, $\partial \text{ENW}/\partial n \neq 0$ and the result of uncertainty on ENW is a trade-off between the effects of less total supply and less variety on the one hand and increased efficiency from increasing returns to scale on the other. To see this, we can find $d\text{ENW}/d\sigma^2$ for our example. It will be simplest to consider (22') as a function of z and n. Thus

$$(25) \qquad \frac{d\text{ENW}}{d\sigma^2} = (\mu(1-z)-c)\frac{dz}{d\sigma^2} - Cn\frac{d\log n}{d\sigma^2}$$

Some tedious substitution from (16), (17), (18) and (20) yields

$$\frac{d\text{ENW}}{d\sigma^2} = \frac{[A\partial\pi/\partial\alpha]}{\mu^2(\beta+\eta)^2}\{\eta\mu(-c(1-\beta)+\beta(\mu\beta-c)/2)$$
$$-c(c(1-\beta)+\beta(\mu\beta-c)/2)\}$$

Thus

$$\frac{d\text{ENW}}{d\sigma^2} \gtrless 0 \qquad \text{as} \qquad \eta \gtrless s\frac{c}{\mu}$$

where

$$s = \frac{c(1-\beta)+\beta(\mu\beta-c)/2}{-c(1-\beta)+\beta(\mu\beta-c)/2}$$

provided that $-c(1-\beta)+\beta(\mu\beta-c)/2 > 0$, that is $\dfrac{c}{\mu} < \dfrac{\beta^2}{2-\beta}$

and $\dfrac{d\text{ENW}}{d\sigma^2} < 0$ otherwise.

Obviously if $\beta = 1$ (homogeneous products) then $s = 1$ and $d\text{ENW}/d\sigma^2$ has the sign $dx/d\sigma^2$ (see Proposition 2) thus confirming: Proposition 3. If $\beta < 1$ (differentiated products), then our example also has reducing marginal costs (as β is also the exponent in the cost function). Although η is required to be bigger then $s(c/\mu)$ where $s > 1$ for $\beta < 1$, and thus the parameter range allowing $d\text{ENW}/d\sigma^2$ to be positive is smaller with differentiated products, it is still easy to find combinations of parameter values which do allow this result. For instance $c/\mu = \frac{1}{2}$, $\beta = 0.9$ yields $s = 1.769$ and $\eta > 0.885$ implies $d\text{ENW}/d\sigma^2 > 0$; $c/\mu = 0.2$, $\beta = 0.9$ yields $s = 1.136$ and $\eta > 0.227$ implies $d\text{ENW}/d\sigma^2 > 0$.

Thus there are non-trivial cases when the removal of uncertainty by insuring the price function so that $\alpha \equiv \mu$ is not in the social interest, and these cases prevail where the conjectural variation is large so that the industry is behaving in a fairly "collusive" way even if overt collusion is not taking place. A final point relates to the case of zero marginal cost, that is $c = 0$. The welfare maximum is then $z^0 = 1$ (the bliss point) and $n = 1$. The industry equilibrium given by (16) and (17) still exists as $\eta > 0$ but we then see that $d\text{ENW}/d\sigma^2 > 0$ as $sc/\mu = 0$, and thus $\eta > sc/\mu$, all $\eta > 0$. In this case the level of industry services is the same after the imposition of uncertainty ($dz/d\sigma^2 = 0$ from (18)) and so the only result is a shift in the mix of services so that more benefit is obtained from economies of scale.

VI. CONCLUSION

We have argued that to consider that demand uncertainty leads to lower output per firm or that it leads to fewer participating firms is too simplistic. If simultaneous adjustment to uncertainty is allowed then all we can be confident of is that at least one of these responses will occur. Indeed the same simple example showed the possibility that either output per firm or number of firms could respond positively to the onset of (small) uncertainty.

The possibility of a fall in the provision of industry services being accompanied by a large change in the number of firms to output per firm mix led to the possibility that uncertainty might in fact increase net welfare by virtue of a more efficient mix provided there was little "deadweight" loss from uncertainty. This possibility would be indicated in our example by (i) a high value of β and thus a high value of the elasticity of substitution among products, (ii) low marginal cost compared to fixed cost, (iii) high demand and (iv) high conjectural elasticity. The last two suggest an industry equilibrium with a large number of firms as the high conjectural elasticity will imply fairly low outputs of participating firms. High substitutability plus high fixed cost mean that welfare is improved by moving to a few firms/high output per firm mix, and thus the introduction of uncertainty may achieve a better expected net welfare outcome.

This study is partial equilibrium in character. It does not consider economic problems outside the industry in question and is limited in application. However the need to allow for demand uncertainty in models of monopolistic competition which treat more complex problems such as that of intra-industry trade (see Krugman [1980]) is considerable; it is hoped to extend the analysis of this paper in those directions.

NORMAN J. IRELAND,
Department of Economics,
University of Warwick,
Coventry CV4 7AL,
U.K.

WELFARE LOSSES IN OLIGOPOLY AND MONOPOLISTIC COMPETITION

G. K. YARROW

I. INTRODUCTION

ESTIMATES OF the magnitudes of monopoly welfare losses (MWL) appearing in the economics literature have tended to differ quite widely. At one end of the spectrum we find figures of the order of 0.1 % of GNP quoted by Harberger [1954] in his pioneering study, while at the other extreme Cowling and Mueller [1978] have derived estimates of around 10 % of gross corporate product from some of their measures. Two of the major sources of such differences lie in the treatment of (a) the general equilibrium aspects of deviations between prices and marginal costs, and (b) the impact of market power on the cost levels of firms; but, unfortunately, the tendency of writers to adopt rather different analytical frameworks often makes it difficult to accurately assign the variations in the estimates to specific factors.

In the present paper the issue of monopoly welfare loss is considered in the context of a differentiated goods model based upon work on monopolistic competition by Spence [1976] and by Dixit and Stiglitz [1977]. Within a set of common assumptions about demand, the effects of varying cost conditions and differing equilibria on the level of MWL are examined. On this basis, four major factors connected with suboptimal resource allocation can be identified: (a) supernormal profits, (b) product differentiation, (c) suboptimal scale, and (d) factor bias. The first of these needs little explanation: its association with welfare loss has been well explored in structure-conduct-performance theory and is used extensively in applied anti-trust economics. Attention will therefore be focused upon the remaining three, all of which can produce MWL in zero-profit equilibria.

The paper is organised as follows. Section II sets out and discusses the differentiated goods framework which will be used throughout the rest of the analysis. It is also shown how a simple transformation of variables reduces the model to the homogeneous goods case and thereby makes immediately available a number of familiar results from the structure-conduct-performance literature. In Section III the focus is on welfare analysis of monopolistic competition. The results here are essentially restatements of earlier work, although the transformation of variables helps to clarify their foundations. Section IV extends the analysis to incorporate additional decision variables such as advertising, research and development, etc., while section V considers the case where market conditions will not sustain a large number of firms in equilibrium and suboptimal scale effects become important. Factor bias is analysed in section VI and it is shown that its direction and magnitude are strongly affected by the "degree of competitiveness" between firms in their price-output decisions. Finally, section VII outlines a case where firms behave in a joint-profit maximising manner with respect to output choice but competitively with respect to product selection, and a lower bound for the resulting MWL is derived.

The technical analysis throughout the paper is informal: the aim is to pinpoint the central issues by covering a number of areas, rather than by looking in detail at the full implications of any individual piece of analysis.

II. THE COMMON FRAMEWORK

Consumers' preferences are assumed to be represented by a utility function:

$$(1) \quad U(x, \underline{q}) = x + h\left(\sum_k q_k^\alpha; \alpha\right),$$

where x is the quantity of some numeraire commodity, q_i is the output of variety i of a differentiated product, $0 < \alpha < 1$, $h'(.) > 0$ and $h''(.) < 0$. The inverse demand function of product variety i is therefore given by

$$(2) \quad p_i = \partial U/\partial q_i = \alpha h'(.) q_i^{\alpha - 1}$$

From the outset it is worth noting certain restrictive features of this specification: (a) income effects in the demands for differentiated goods are zero; (b) demand for every commodity is strictly positive at any finite price vector; (c) the demand functions are symmetric and, *ceteris paribus*, a change in the output of any variety will have the same proportionate effect on the demand for each of the other varieties (that is, there are no "near neighbour" effects).

These limitations are not considered vital for the issues to be tackled below and the demand model has the merit of allowing a straightforward parameterisation of the degree of product differentiation. To see this, consider the elasticities of the price of variety i with respect to other outputs and own output:

$$(3) \quad -(q_j/p_i)(\partial p_i/\partial q_j) = -\alpha(h'' q_j^\alpha/h') = \alpha e(.) s_j,$$

and

$$(4) \quad -(q_i/p_i)(\partial p_i/\partial q_i) = 1 - \alpha + \alpha e(.) s_i,$$

where $e(.)$ is the absolute value of the elasticity of $h'(.)$ and $s_i = q_i^\alpha / \Sigma q_k^\alpha$ is a type of market share measure. Thus, α is an obvious measure of the degree of substitutability in demand or product differentiation between the varieties, with *smaller* values of α implying *greater* differentiation and $\alpha = 1$ corresponding to the homogeneous goods case (where the own- and cross-price elasticities are equal).

Following Spence [1980], given the above assumptions, significant simplifications of analysis can be obtained via the substitutions

(5) $\quad z_i = q_i^\alpha$, and $z = \sum_k z_k$

Referring back to the utility function, it is immediately apparent that, from the consumers' viewpoint, these transformed output variables of the firms are perfect substitutes for one another. Henceforth, z_i will be labelled the *utility-output* of firm i, to distinguish it from the physical output level q_i.

If each variety of the differentiated commodity is produced by one, single-product firm, the revenue of the latter is

(6) $\quad p_i q_i = \alpha h'(.) q_i^\alpha = \alpha h'(.) z_i = \hat{p}(z) z_i$

where $\hat{p}(z) = \alpha h'(.)$ will be referred to as the *pseudo inverse demand curve* for the product. Thus, in utility-output space, the firm can be viewed as producing a commodity which is a perfect substitute for the outputs of other firms in the market—the unit "price" for the commodity $\hat{p}$ being a function only of the total output on offer, z. This allows the effects of product differentiation to be incorporated exclusively on the cost sides of the models and thereby makes instantly available a number of insights derived from the familiar homogeneous good analyses.

Turning, then, to cost conditions, it will be assumed initially that the total costs of firm i are given by

(7) $\quad C_i = f + c q_i = f + c z_i^\phi, \quad \phi = 1/\alpha > 1$

That is, the cost per physical unit of output is a declining function of output, but the average cost curve for utility-output is U-shaped. The unit cost of utility-output is minimised where

(8) $\quad z_i = z(m) = \{[f/c]/[\phi - 1]\}^{1/\phi}$

Adapting traditional terminology, $z(m)$ will be called the minimum efficient scale (m.e.s.) of the firm; the scale of operations here being measured in terms of the variable z_i. The physical output level corresponding to $z(m)$ is

(9) $\quad q(m) = [f/c]/[\phi - 1]$

Note that, as in standard analysis, the minimum efficient scale is an increasing function of the ratio of fixed to (physical) unit variable costs of production. The novel feature of the model is the dependence of m.e.s. on product differentiation. As ϕ increases from 1 (differentiation is increased), $z(m)$ falls, although the two variables will be positively related for sufficiently high levels of product differentiation. On the other hand, from (9), m.e.s. measured in physical output units is always a decreasing function of differentiation.

To summarise then, working in utility-output space we find that the differentiated products model with scale economies in production is equivalent to a homogeneous good model with cost conditions characterised by U-shaped average cost curves.

III. WELFARE LOSS AND MONOPOLISTIC COMPETITION

With free entry the market for the differentiated good will tend to be characterised by a large number of firms/varieties whenever the minimum efficient scale is very small in relation to the size of the market. To be more precise, define the market size $z(s)$ as the quantity of utility-output demanded when price is equal to minimised average cost:

(10) $\quad z(s) = \hat{p}^{-1}(f/z(m) + cz(m)^{\phi-1})$

Then the regions of parameter space producing monopolistically competitive equilibria are defined by the condition that

(11) $\quad z(m) \ll z(s)$,

where $z(m)$ is given by equation (8).

Necessary conditions for the monopolistic competition zero-profit equilibria are that, for each firm in the market, marginal revenue be equal to marginal cost and price be equal to average cost. For Nash quantity setting equilibria these become

(12) $\quad \hat{p}\{1 - s_i e(z)\} = c\phi z_i^{\phi-1}$

and

(13) $\quad \hat{p} z_i = f + c z_i^{\phi}$

where $e(z)$, as defined earlier, is the inverse elasticity of $\hat{p}(.)$ ($= -[z/\hat{p}][d\hat{p}/dz]$). But, with a large number of firms in the market, the term $s_i e(z)$ can be neglected. Hence, in utility-output space, (12) and (13) reduce to the conditions: price = marginal cost = average cost. This, of course, is just the familiar long run equilibrium position of the competitive firm.

Working with the transformed output variables makes it clear, therefore, that, from the social welfare perspective, each firm will operate at the optimum scale (cf. Dixit and Stiglitz [1977]), producing utility-output at the minimum unit cost. In the space of physical output, however, the diagrammatic representation would show the equilibrium of the firm occurring at the customary Chamberlinian tangency point, where the downward sloping demand curve for the firm's product touches the negatively sloped average cost curve. The usual excess capacity argument is now revealed to be misleading because of its neglect of consumers' preferences for variety. When these tastes are properly incorporated into the analysis the output level of each firm in the market is socially optimal.

If output per firm is socially optimal it might be tempting to conclude that the monopolistic competition equilibrium is a first-best optimum, but this would be incorrect. The market supply curve of utility-output will be horizontal at a price equal to minimised unit costs (OG) and the equilibrium market output (z^*) will be given by the point at which this line crosses the pseudo

WELFARE LOSSES IN OLIGOPOLY AND MONOPOLISTIC COMPETITION

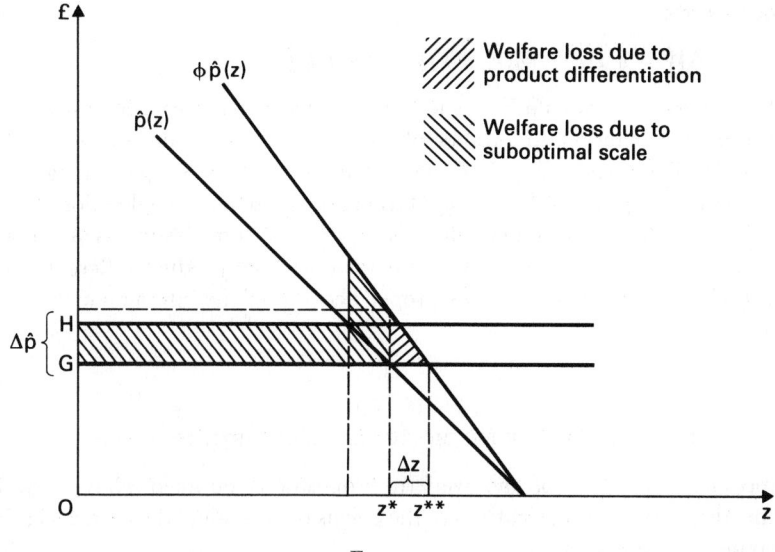

FIGURE 1

demand curve (see Figure 1). Next consider the marginal utility of transformed output. From (1) and (6):

(14) $\qquad \partial U/\partial z = h'(.) = \phi \hat{p}$

The marginal utility curve therefore lies above the pseudo demand curve and the first-best level of market output is given by z^{**} in Figure 1—where marginal utility is equal to marginal cost. Thus, although each firm produces at the socially optimal output level, the monopolistic competition equilibrium implies too few firms in the market. That is, the market is offering insufficient product variety to consumers (see Dixit and Stiglitz [1977]).

The source of the market failure in this case is the assumed absence of price discrimination. If firms could charge a constant price per unit of utility-output to consumers, the marginal utility and demand curves in utility output space would coincide and the resulting equilibrium would be a first-best optimum. But constancy of $\hat{p}$ across customers implies a non-linear pricing scheme for units of physical output.

Welfare loss arising from the lack of price discrimination can be estimated by the area of the shaded triangle shown in Figure 1. When product differentiation is low it is given approximately by

(15) $\qquad \Delta W = \Delta \hat{p} \Delta z/2 = [\phi - 1]\hat{p}\Delta z/2 = [\phi - 1]^2 R/[2e]$

where R is the industry's total revenue. This measure can be re-expressed in terms of the firm ($\eta(F)$) and market ($\eta(I)$) demand elasticities for output measured in physical units (given from (4) by setting s_i equal to zero and unity respectively):

(16) $\Delta W = \eta(I)R/\{2[\eta(F)-1][\eta(F)-\eta(I)]\}$

As an illustrative calculation, when $e = 1$ and $\phi = 1.1$ (corresponding to firm and market demand elasticities for physical output of 11 and 1 respectively), the welfare loss is about 0.5% of total revenue, which is the sort of magnitude that would be produced by the Harberger approach. Application of the Cowling and Mueller formula, which is based upon firm elasticities of demand only, would give misleading results in this case (low product differentiation, high $\eta(F)$) because it fails to take proper account of the interactions between firms.

IV. EXTENSIONS OF THE MONOPOLISTIC COMPETITION MODEL

Immediate extensions of the welfare propositions outlined above can be obtained for certain specifications of the effects of additional decision variables. Suppose, for example, that

(17) $U = x + h\left(\sum_k g(v_k)^\alpha q_k^\alpha\right), \quad g'(.) > 0,$

where v_i is an output-augmenting variable such as quality of the product, number of brands offered by the firm, number of advertising messages, product improving research and development inputs, etc. Letting $z_i = g(v_i)^\alpha q_i^\alpha$ it can quickly be shown that the revenue of firm i can again be written as $R_i = p(z)z_i$. Now suppose that costs are

(18) $C_i = f + rv_i + cq_i = f + rv_i + cz_i^\phi/g(v_i)$

Since the variable v_i does not affect revenue the model can be solved sequentially, first finding the level of v_i which minimises the costs of producing a given utility output and then treating profit as a function of utility output only. From (18) the cost minimising condition for choice of v_i is

(19) $r - cz_i^\phi g'(v_i)/g(v_i)^2 = 0$

Substituting for v_i from (19) into (18) gives total costs as a function of utility-output only and the analysis can then proceed as before. Thus, if market conditions are such as to sustain a large number of firms, the resulting levels of the product augmenting variable will constitute a constrained social optimum.

The most important implication arising from the addition of output-augmenting variables to the model is the effect on the minimum efficient scale of operations. Equation (18) shows that increases in v_i will, for any output level, increase fixed costs $(f + rv_i)$ and reduce variable costs $(cz_i^\phi/g(v_i))$, thereby tending to increase m.e.s. For example, let

(20) $C_i = f + rv_i + cv_i^{-\mu}z_i^\phi$

Then, solving (19) for v_i,

(21) $v_i = [\mu c/r]^{1/[1+\mu]} z_i^{\phi/[\mu+1]}$,

and hence,

(22) $C_i = f + k z_i^{\phi/[\mu+1]}$

Unit costs of utility-output will therefore decline with scale (that is, there is no minimum efficient scale) if

(23) $\mu > \phi - 1$

In other words, if products are not highly differentiated, relatively small opportunities for augmentation will yield natural monopoly conditions. In less extreme circumstances, the existence of opportunities for quality improvement, advertising, research and development, etc., will render small numbers of equilibria somewhat more likely. Fewness will, of course, imply deviations from constrained social optima (see section V).

V. FREE ENTRY EQUILIBRIA WITH SMALLER NUMBERS

When minimum efficient scale is a non-trivial fraction of market size the resulting equilibria will tend to exhibit individual market shares which are not negligibly small. In utility-output space the firm's marginal revenue will differ significantly from average revenue, and the latter curve will slope downwards. Ignoring problems connected with the restriction of the number of firms in the market (n) to an integer value, the equilibrium of the firm in utility-output space will be as shown in Figure 2. We now have a true excess capacity result:

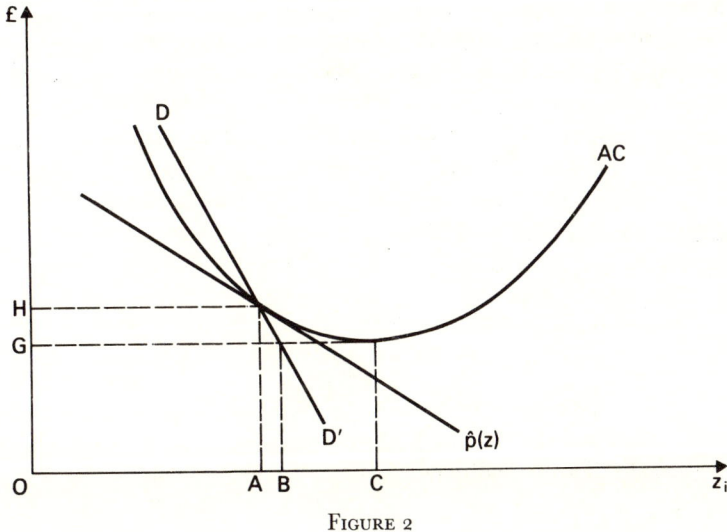

FIGURE 2

the unit cost of producing utility-output (which already incorporates the necessary allowance for consumer preferences for variety) is not minimised. Firms each produce too low an output and the magnitude of the resulting unit cost increase is represented by the distance GH. Translating into the market equilibrium diagram (Figure 1), we find a monopoly welfare loss *relative to the constrained optimum* and due to *suboptimal scale* given by the shaded region indicated.

In Figure 2 the line DD' shows the constant share of the market pseudo-demand curve for the firm. In a symmetric equilibrium it follows that total utility-output should be increased by a fraction AB/OA to take it to its constrained optimum level, while each firm's output would have to increase by a fraction AC/OA ($>AB/OA$) to minimise the costs of producing that output level. Hence, the number of firms/varieties would need to fall by a fraction BC/OA. In other words the equilibrium in this case features too many varieties of the product when judged from a second-best welfare benchmark: there is too much product differentiation. Indeed, if $BC/OA > (z^{**}-z^*)/z^*$ (see Figure 1) the number of products on offer would exceed that appropriate for a first-best result.

A second reason for suboptimal scale is the possibility that the equilibrium may be less "competitive" than that of the Cournot–Nash case. Thus, consider a conjectural variations approach where each firm expects a unit increase in its utility-output will lead to an increase in utility-output of ψ by each of its rivals. When $\psi = 0$ this reduces to the Nash quantity setting equilibrium, but there are reasons for believing that the latter will not always offer an appropriate way to proceed. Suppose, for example, that decisions are sequential: in some first period firms decide whether or not to enter the market at a (sunk) cost of f, and that subsequently those firms which have entered play a price-output game in which their (physical) unit costs of production are equal to c. In practice, price-output games will usually extend over durations of time in which there will be opportunities for several moves, and they can often be approximated by a sequence of repeated one-shot games. Now Nash equilibria of repeated games with limited information can closely resemble collusive solutions of one-period games (Kreps and Wilson [1982]). Hence, we might think of the value of ψ in the simpler, static conjectural variations analysis as being a crude parameterisation of the outcome of extended competition.

Adopting the conjectural approach, (12) and (13) become

(24) $\quad p\{1-e\psi-e[1-\psi]/n\} = c\phi z_i^{\phi-1}$

and

(25) $\quad pz_i = f + cz_i^\phi$

Dividing (24) by (25) we find that

(26) $\quad z_i = \{[f/c][1-\lambda]/[\phi+\lambda-1]\}^{1/\phi}$

where $\lambda = e\psi + e[1-\psi]/n$. The proportionate increase in the unit costs of utility output over the minimum level is therefore

$$[\phi-1]^{1-1/\phi}/\{[\phi+\lambda-1]^{1-1/\phi}[1-\lambda]^{1/\phi}\}-1$$

The number of firms (n) is, of course, endogenous and depends upon the values of the various parameters. Suppose that the latter are such as to imply $\lambda = 0.2$, and that $\phi = 1.1$ (the focus is again upon relatively low levels of product differentiation). Then the proportionate increase in unit costs is 10.8%. Ignoring the integer problem, it follows that monopoly welfare loss as a fraction of revenue exceeds 9.2%, which is considerably in excess of the levels calculated in the previous section.

As ψ increases, so that the second period equilibrium becomes "less competitive", n will increase: the prospect of greater returns in the price-output game will attract more firms into the market. Entry will continue until supernormal profit is bid away and we are left with the traditional cartel result: even though profits are zero there will be welfare loss arising from an excessive number of firms and suboptimal scale—the greater expenditures on entry costs implying greater than minimum unit costs (cf. Posner [1975]). Generally, both the welfare loss and excessive product variety will increase as the second-period equilibrium becomes more collusive.

VI. FACTOR BIAS

In the two-stage interpretation of the preceding models the entry cost f was assumed to have no effect on the second-stage marginal costs of the firms. More generally the first-period decisions may well involve expenditures which *do* influence subsequent marginal costs. Thus, if the outlays rv_i in the analysis of section IV are incurred at stage 1 and are not recoverable, the values chosen will affect the parameters of the later competitive game. In considering their initial decisions, therefore, firms will take account of these strategic effects and, in general, we will find that profit maximisation no longer implies cost minimisation (in the sense of selecting the least cost method of producing any given level of utility-output).

The tendency for firms not to employ cost-minimising input combinations in conditions of strategic interdependence leads to a third source of monopoly welfare loss, which will be referred to as factor bias. It should, however, be noted that factor bias will not occur in the extreme case of *pure* monopoly where there are no strategic incentives to vary the input vectors from their cost-minimising values. Oligopoly welfare loss might therefore be a better term for this type of inefficiency.

In order to simplify the analysis it will henceforth be assumed that $r = 1$ and that the pseudo inverse demand curve is iso-elastic:

(27) $\quad \alpha h'(.) = \beta[.]^{-e}$

The profit function of firm i thus becomes

(28) $\quad \Pi_i = \beta[\,.\,]^{-e} z_i - f - v_i - c z_i^\phi / g(v_i)$

Now the first-stage decisions are heavily conditioned by expectations concerning the nature of the later competition. Suppose, as before, the second-stage outcome is parameterised by (constant) conjectural coefficients ψ_{ij}, where ψ_{ij} is the conjectured rate of change of firm j's utility-output with respect to firm i's output. In other words, the first-order condition for profit maximisation by firm i at stage 2 is

(29) $\quad \beta[\,.\,]^{-e} - e\beta z_i[\,.\,]^{-e-1}\left[1 + \sum_{j \neq i} \psi_{ij}\right] - \phi c z_i^{\phi-1}/g(v_i) = 0$

Consider next the first-order conditions for profit maximisation with respect to v_i (the stage 1 decision). Differentiating (28) with respect to v_i, and remembering that v_i is a parameter of the second stage game and that variations in its level will affect outputs according to the equations in (29),

(30) $\quad \{\beta[\,.\,]^{-e} - e\beta z_i[\,.\,]^{-e-1} - \phi c z_i^{\phi-1}/g(v_i)\}\, dz_i/dv_i$

$\qquad - \beta e z_i[\,.\,]^{-e-1} \sum_{j \neq i} dz_j/dv_i - 1 + [c z_i^\phi/g(v_i)^2]g'(v_i) = 0$

Substituting from (29) this reduces to

(31) $\quad e\beta z_i[\,.\,]^{-e-1}\left\{\sum_{j \neq i} \psi_{ij} dz_i/dv_i - \sum_{j \neq i} dz_j/dv_i\right\} - 1 + [c z_i^\phi/g(v_i)^2]g'(v_i) = 0$

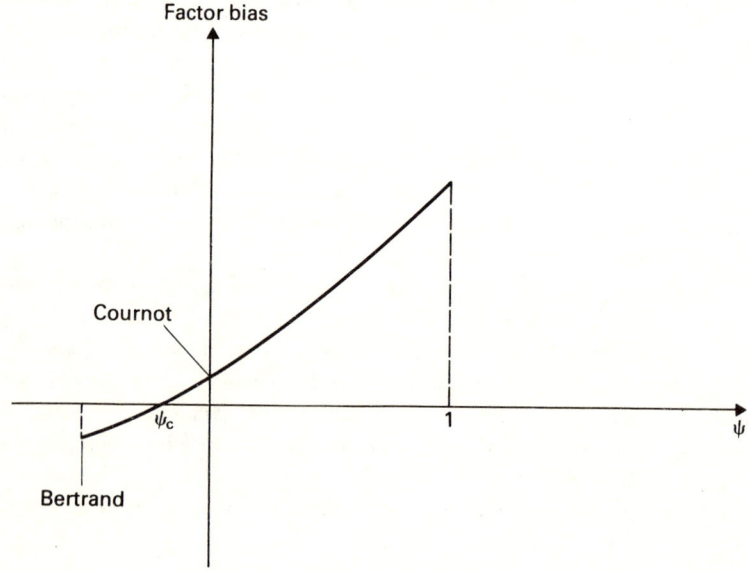

FIGURE 3

If the first term in (31) is zero we have the familiar cost-minimisation condition for the determination of v_i. In general, however, the first term will not be zero: it represents the strategic payoffs from changes in the first-period, non-recoverable expenditure. In the Cournot–Nash case the conjectural coefficients are all zero and the first term will typically (but not invariably) be negative. That is, an increase in v_i will reduce firm i's second-period marginal costs, inducing an accommodating reduction in rivals' outputs at stage 2. Expressed in terms of reaction functions, an increase in v_i will shift firm i's second-period reaction function outwards and, provided that the aggregate, second-period reaction function of rivals is negatively sloped, the equilibrium output of competitors will fall.

The effect of an additional negative term in equation (31) is equivalent in its impact to either a lower first-period marginal cost for the first-period variable or, alternatively, to a higher marginal payoff for that variable. Under normal assumptions it can therefore be expected that the outcome will tend to be a higher, optimal first-period expenditure than would be implied by the cost minimisation condition.

Differentiating the first-order conditions in (29) totally with respect to z_i and using (30),

$$(32) \quad [dz_i/dv_i] \Big/ \left[\sum_{j \neq i} dz_j/dv_i \right] = 1 \Big/ \left[\sum_{j \neq i} dz_j/dz_i \right]$$

Hence, when $\psi_{ij} = dz_j/dz_i$, we find that the first expression in (31) is zero. But $\psi_{ij} = dz_j/dz_i$ are the conditions for first-order consistent conjectural equilibrium (CCE) (see Bresnahan [1981]). Thus, if the second-period equilibrium is expected to be of the first-order CCE type, there will be no factor bias.

In the symmetric case, where $\psi_{ij} = \psi$ for all i and j, the magnitude of factor bias, measured by the difference between the optimal v/z ratio and its cost minimising value, can be expressed as a function of ψ. Figure 3 illustrates a typical case. Factor bias is zero at the CCE value of ψ, say ψ_c, which is intermediate between the Bertrand and Cournot values of the conjectural coefficient. As ψ increases (decreases) from ψ_c, the factor bias increases (decreases). Intuitively, the strategic value of higher initial expenditures becomes greater as the second-period equilibrium becomes less competitive: the extra output achieved by virtue of the associated reductions in rivals' output having a higher payoff when the second-period equilibrium is more collusive because of the greater gap between price and marginal cost. At very competitive second-period equilibria (such as Bertrand), factor bias is negative: firms choose lower v/z ratios than are implied by cost minimisation because, although each expects to lose volume relative to its competitors as a result of its own decision, the increase in price cost margins from the lower aggregate output more than compensates.

We are now in a position to examine, informally, the effects of factor bias on welfare. Take first the case when $\psi > \psi_c$. Here there are two counterbalancing

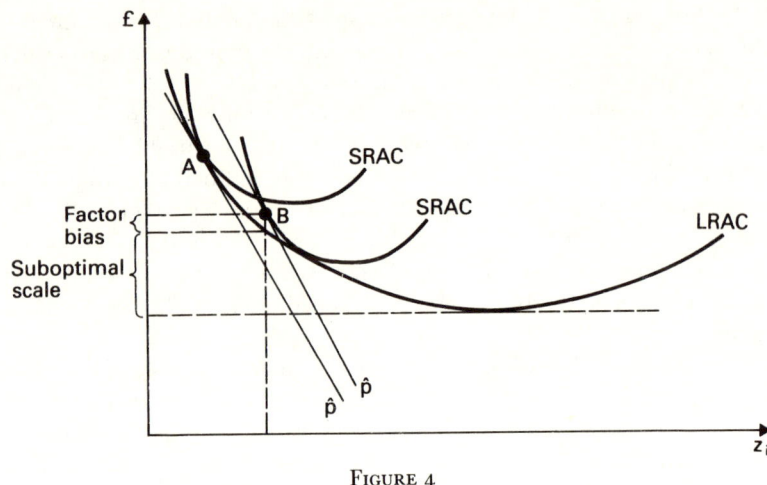

FIGURE 4

effects. Clearly the upward shift in the firms' cost curves resulting from excessive first-period expenditures will imply monopoly welfare losses. But these same increases in expenditures tend to reduce second-period marginal costs and thus imply increased equilibrium output levels for each firm which can offset some of the effects of suboptimal scale. Figure 4 shows a free entry, zero-profit equilibrium at A for the case where v_i and z_i are chosen simultaneously, the short run average cost curve showing the relationship between unit costs and utility-output when v_i is fixed at its long run equilibrium value. Now higher first-period expenditures in the sequential case will be associated with an equilibrium position such as B. Long run unit costs of producing the given output level are not minimised at this point and there are fewer, but larger, firms in the market as compared with A. In both cases, of course, economic profits are zero.

The diagram also shows a breakdown of the difference between market price and the lowest attainable unit cost into an effect due to suboptimal scale (which is lower than in the equivalent, one-stage model) and an effect due to factor bias. In the case illustrated the final outcome exhibits a lower market price (implying higher social welfare) than the equivalent non-sequential model. Although firms are no longer cost minimisers, the ability to sink costs in the first stage has here contributed to a better welfare outcome. The precise welfare results will vary from case to case however, and no claim for generality is being made on behalf of the one illustrated.

When $\psi < \psi_c$ the effect of sequential decisions on monopoly welfare loss is less ambiguous. The ability to sink first-period expenditures will tend to reduce the output level of each firm in equilibrium (increasing the number of firms in the market and raising MWL from the suboptimal scale effect) *and* raise the cost of producing that output level because of factor bias.

VII. FACTOR BIAS: A LIMITING CASE

It has been argued that factor bias tends to be greater the more collusive is the expected solution to the second-stage game and this section will sketch out a solution in a limiting case where firms act as joint maximisers with respect to their price/output decisions. It is assumed that each firm can choose to produce as many products as it likes and that product selection decisions are taken in the first period. Product selection decisions are, however, taken non-cooperatively and it is assumed that the outcome is a Nash equilibrium. The aim will be to place a lower bound on the level of monopoly welfare loss arising from excessive costs in this (admittedly extreme) case.

The costs of firm i are assumed to be given by

$$(33) \quad C_i = f + bm_i^\gamma + cm_i q_i = f + bm_i^\gamma + cm_i^{1-\phi} z_i^\phi,$$

where m_i is the number of products offered by firm i. The expression bm_i^γ represents the costs of bringing product varieties on to the market and will be referred to as the product development cost. The term $cm_i q_i$ represents production costs ($m_i q_i$ being the total output of the firm). Note that, to maintain the analytical convenience of symmetry, it is being assumed that firms produce the same number of units of each of their products.

Fixing z_i, the first-order condition for cost minimisation is

$$(34) \quad \gamma b m_i^{\gamma-1} - c[\phi - 1] m_i^{-\phi} z_i^\phi = 0$$

Hence, the conventional long run cost function can be written as

$$(35) \quad C_i = f + k z_i^{\phi \gamma / [\phi + \gamma - 1]},$$

where k is a constant depending upon the cost parameters. The unit cost curve of utility output will therefore have a minimum point when $\phi \gamma > \phi + \gamma - 1$. The corresponding, cost-minimising ratio of product development to production costs is, from (34),

$$(36) \quad \bar{\theta} = [bm_i^\gamma]/[cm_i^{1-\phi} z_i^\phi] = [\phi - 1]/\gamma$$

In period 2 the output levels of the firms are chosen to maximise joint profits. Hence,

$$(37) \quad \beta[1-e]z^{-e} = \phi c m_i^{1-\phi} z_i^{\phi - 1}$$

and

$$(38) \quad m_i/m_j = z_i/z_j$$

That is, market shares of the firms (in units of transformed output) are proportional to the number of products that each chooses to offer. Thus, in choosing the number of varieties in period 1 against an assumption of given numbers of rivals' products, a firm is directly selecting its market share, although it will recognise that an increase in, say m_i, will also increase the total output of commodities on the market and thereby depress market price. Solving equations (37) and (38) for the firms' outputs:

(39) $\quad z_i = \{\beta[1-e]/[\phi c]\}^{1/[\phi+e-1]} m_i M^{-e/[\phi+e-1]}$

where $M = \Sigma_k m_k$ is the total number of varieties on the market.

In period 1 firm i chooses the profit-maximising value of m_i. The first-order conditions for Nash equilibrium are

(40) $\quad \{\beta z^{-e} - c\phi m_i^{1-\phi} z_i^{\phi-1}\} dz_i/dm_i - e\beta z_i z^{-e-1} dz/dm_i$
$$- \gamma b m_i^{\gamma-1} + c[\phi-1] m_i^{-\phi} z_i^{\phi} = 0$$

As before, it is the first two terms which produce the deviation from the cost-minimising input combination. From (37), followed by differentiation of (39), they can be written as

(41) $\quad e\beta z^{-e}\{dz_i/dm_i - [dz/dm_i]/n\} = e\beta z^{-e} \rho M^{-e/[\phi+e-1]}\{1-1/n\}$
$$= e\beta z^{-e}[z_i/m_i]\{1-1/n\}$$
$$= e\phi c\{1-1/n\} m_i^{-\phi} z_i^{\phi}/[1-e],$$

where $\rho = \{\beta[1-e]/\phi c\}^{1/[\phi+e-1]}$. Substituting back into the condition for the optimal number of products, (40), and rearranging we find that

(42) $\quad \theta = [bm_i^{\gamma}]/[cm_i^{1-\phi} z_i^{\phi}] = \{\phi - 1 + e\phi[1-1/n]/[1-e]\}/\gamma$

Comparing with the cost minimisation condition (36), the ratio of product development costs to production costs has been increased by the third term on the right hand side of (42). For example, if $\phi = 1.1$, $e = 0.5$, $\gamma = 1$, and $n = 5$, the ratio rises from 0.1 to 0.98. That is, cost minimisation implies that product development costs at a given output level are a tenth of production costs, but the strategic advantages of product proliferation in the sequential model indicate that development costs will rise to about the same magnitude as production costs.

It is now straightforward to calculate the proportionate increase in variable costs (that is, total costs less f) at any output level and thereby obtain a lower bound for the ratio of welfare loss to revenue. Let $\bar{m}$ be the cost minimising number of products offered by a firm for a given level of output z. The ratio of variable costs is

(43) $\quad [bm^{\gamma} + cm^{1-\phi} z^{\phi}]/[b\bar{m}^{\gamma} + c\bar{m}^{1-\phi} z^{\phi}] = [m/\bar{m}]^{1-\phi}[1+\theta]/[1+\bar{\theta}]$
$$= [\theta/\bar{\theta}]^{[1-\phi]/[\phi+\gamma-1]}[1+\theta]/[1+\bar{\theta}]$$

from the definitions of θ and $\bar{\theta}$ (see (36)). Thus, for the parameter values specified in the preceding paragraph the proportionate deviation of unit variable costs from their minimum level for the given output is 46.3%. In the absence of market failures elsewhere this number places a lower bound on the magnitude of welfare loss in this particular case.

VIII. CONCLUSIONS

The most important implication of the above analysis is that the magnitude of monopoly welfare loss can be substantial in zero-profit equilibria. In this sense some support is provided for the view that resource misallocations resulting from monopoly power are a significant policy problem, despite the sorts of numbers generated by the Harberger approach.

Large levels of MWL appear to be most likely where market conditions are such that costs are inflated, either via suboptimal scale or non-cost-minimising input choices, as a result of competition for monopoly positions. Thus, relatively "collusive" solutions to price-output subgames produce more intense competition in earlier stages of the game (entry, choice of non-price variables, etc.) leading to a transformation of monopoly rents into costs. Market conditions would be most likely to produce such "substitution of competition" results where the effective number of repetitions of the price-output subgame is large (price and output changes can be made quickly with little cost) while the number of repetitions of earlier subgames is small (for example, sunk costs are more significant). Case by case analysis of individual markets would therefore be in order to establish the precise characteristics of competition in each.

G. K. YARROW,
Hertford College,
Oxford,
U.K.

THE SUPPLY OF QUALITY ON A MARKET FOR "EXPERIENCE GOODS"

THOMAS VON UNGERN-STERNBERG
CARL CHRISTIAN VON WEIZSÄCKER

I. INTRODUCTION

THIS PAPER is concerned with the analysis of markets for experience goods, that is, markets where consumers are imperfectly informed about the quality of the products they buy. Renewed interest in models of this kind was sparked off by Akerlof's seminal article "The Market for Lemons" in 1970.[1] He showed that in certain kinds of markets quality uncertainty on the part of consumers could lead to market failure in the form of an insufficient supply of high quality products, or even market breakdown (no trade takes place at all). The market Akerlof focused on to illustrate his point is the market for second hand cars. This is no accidental choice. The second hand car market is characterized by the fact that most suppliers appear on the market only once. This means that they do not have the possibility to build up reputations or goodwill with the consumers. This restriction is of some importance. The two factors leading to market failure in the presence of imperfectly informed consumers are (1) moral hazard and (2) adverse selection.[2] Moral hazard arises from the fact that if the producers' sales volume is totally independent of the quality of the products they sell, they will maximize profits by supplying only cheap low cost products. Adverse selection arises from the fact that suppliers of the cheapest low quality products will drive from the market any producer who for whatever reason wishes to supply higher quality products. The crucial assumptions giving rise to both of these sources of market failure are: (a) high quality products are more expensive to produce than low quality products, and (b) the sales volume of each supplier is independent of the quality he supplies. (As consumers cannot observe quality, the producer's choice of quality cannot have any influence on his sales volume.)

In most real world situations suppliers stay on the market for considerably longer than one "period". They then have the possibility to build up reputations or goodwill with the consumers. This is due to the following mechanism. While the consumers cannot directly observe a product's quality at the time of purchase, they may try to draw inferences about this quality from the past experience they (or others) have had with this supplier's products. The inferences will be of the kind: "If a producer has supplied good quality in the past,

---

[1] Akerlof [1970]. The term "experience good" for products whose qualities cannot be observed prior to purchase was created by Nelson, cf., Nelson [1970] and [1974].
[2] Akerlof [1970] focuses mainly on the adverse selection part of the issue. Arrow [1963] concentrates mainly on moral hazard aspects.

he will supply good quality in the future."[3] Under certain circumstances the supplier has an incentive not to disappoint these expectations. The expectations then establish a link between the quality a producer supplied (in the past) and his sales volume (in the present and future). The greater the quality a producer supplies at a given price, the greater the sales volume he can achieve. This reduces the scope for market failure due to moral hazard and/or adverse selection.

Under what circumstances will suppliers have an incentive not to cheat their customers by supplying low quality products? To answer this question one has to study the following trade-off: By cheating his customers and supplying low quality today, the producer can increase his current profits. Via the goodwill mechanism he would also decrease his future profits.[4] In a steady state equilibrium this means: The only way to induce a supplier not to make profits now by cheating the consumers by selling them low quality products is for him to make positive profits in each of the future periods. Future profits (in the sense of variable revenue minus variable costs) are compatible with a situation of free market entry only if the sunk costs of market entry are sufficiently high. Markets with quality uncertainty in which high quality products are supplied must thus in steady state equilibrium be characterized by the following properties. In each of the periods (1) variable revenue must be greater than variable costs, and (2) the *sunk* set-up costs of market entry must be sufficiently high.[5]

The interactions described in the last paragraph are analysed in some detail in Klein and Leffler [1981] and von Ungern-Sternberg and von Weizsäcker [1981]. The essential difference between these two models is as follows: Klein and Leffler assume that their firms act as quantity setters, that is, each firm acts as a price taker and chooses its output level till price equals marginal cost. Ungern-Sternberg and Weizsäcker assume instead that the firm is a quantity taker, that is, total demand and the number of suppliers on the market determine how much each of them can sell at the exogenously given price. Both of the above cited works have one weakness in common. They both study how high the market price has to be for a given quality level to be supplied, or, to put it slightly differently, what quality is forthcoming, when a given price is being charged. Statements about quality supplies are made *for an exogenously given price level*, and statements about the price level are made *for an exogenously given quality level*. This structure of the models means that they are unable to answer one of the questions one is most interested in, namely: *Will the market undersupply or oversupply quality?* To answer questions of this kind *one needs a model in which both the price charged by each producer and the quality he supplies are endogenously*

---

[3] cf., von Weizsäcker [1980a] and [1980b]. Because of the ubiquity of this kind of expectations formation he refers to it as the "extrapolation principle".
[4] This point is stressed in Farrel [1980], von Weizsäcker [1980a] and [1980b], Klein and Leffler [1981], von Ungern-Sternberg and von Weizsäcker [1981], Shapiro [1983], von Ungern-Sternberg [1984a].
[5] cf., Klein and Leffler [1981] and von Ungern-Sternberg and von Weizsäcker [1981].

determined. The aim of this paper is to fill just this gap. We construct a model with consumer quality uncertainty in which each producer endogenously determines both the price he charges and the quality he supplies. The model is similar to the one developed by Spence [1975] to study the quality choice of a firm in an environment with no uncertainty. As a result of this similarity it is very easy to pinpoint those quality distortions, which are due to imperfect information and the goodwill mechanism, and clearly separate them from those which would occur even in the absence of imperfect information on the part of consumers.

Our main conclusion is that the consumers' inability to observe quality directly does not, in the presence of goodwill, lead to the market undersupplying quality. On the contrary: the quality supplied is closer to what is socially optimal than would be the case in an environment of perfect information. The interactions leading to this result can be briefly summarized as follows. Spence [1975] shows that with fully informed consumers the quality supplied by a monopolist (or any other producer facing a downward-sloping demand curve) is determined by the consumers' valuation of quality of the last unit they buy, that is, the consumers' *marginal valuation of quality*. What is relevant from a social point of view, however, is not this marginal valuation but the additional utility the consumers derive from the extra quality on every one of the units they buy, that is, the consumers' *average valuation of quality*. Thus, if the marginal valuation of quality is lower than the average valuation, quality is undersupplied and in the opposite case it is oversupplied. Only if marginal and average valuation coincide is the "monopolist's" quality choice socially correct.[6]

How will quality uncertainty and the goodwill mechanism affect these results? The producer's choice of quality (and price) now affects two variables: First, *how much* each of his customers will buy from him, and second, *how many* customers he will actually have. The goodwill mechanism determines the number of consumers buying from a given producer. We thus have to ask ourselves: What are the factors determining whether a consumer recommends a given supplier to the other consumers? Surely it is not price alone. A low price producer selling terrible quality will hardly be recommended. Neither is it quality alone. A high quality supplier charging exorbitant prices is just as unlikely to be recommended. *The most reasonable approximation seems to us to say that consumers recommend those products to each other, which they believe to be yielding them the highest surplus*. This assumption leads directly to our results. The effect quality has on total consumer surplus is measured by the average valuation of quality. If a producer were interested only in the number of consumers buying from him his quality choice would therefore be guided only by the consumers' average valuation of quality. If the producer were interested only in the sales volume to each one of his customers, his quality choice would be guided only

---

[6] cf., Spence [1975, pp. 418–422]. Spence works with the consumers' inverse demand functions, rather than the direct demand functions, which are more convenient for our purposes. These are, however, mere notational differences.

by the consumers' marginal valuation of quality. As the producer is interested in both the total number of customers and the sales volume to each one of them, his quality choice will be guided by some kind of "weighted mean" of the consumers' marginal and average valuation of quality. If the marginal valuation of quality is lower than the average valuation, the quality supplied in a situation of imperfect information will still be lower than the social optimum. It will, however, be somewhat higher than would be the case in a situation of perfect information. A similar argument holds for the case where there would be an oversupply of quality in the presence of perfectly informed consumers. The quality supplied in the presence of imperfect consumer information will still be higher than is socially optimal but somewhat closer to the social optimal.

All of this does not, of course, imply that less information improves the working of the market as a whole. The goodwill mechanism implies that the equilibrium price charged by each producer will be higher, the less informed are the consumers.[7] The basic lesson to learn from this model is thus as follows: In models without a goodwill mechanism, imperfect quality information causes market failure due to an undersupply of high quality products. In markets where the goodwill mechanism does work, imperfect information will still cause market failure. Market failure does not, however, take the form of excessively low quality, but rather of prices above marginal costs. This conclusion might seem somewhat curious at first sight, but it fits everyday observations quite well. Clothing, sport goods, cars, restaurant meals, etc., are all to a certain extent "experience goods". We doubt, however, that cars (for example) would be of higher quality if customers could perfectly observe their various characteristics prior to purchase. It seems much more plausible that increased information would lead to more intensive competition and this would cause the price level to fall.

In the next section of this paper we derive the interactions just described in a formal model. Section III contains some concluding remarks.

II. THE MODEL

We consider a model of a market for an experience good which can be produced in different qualities q.

The assumptions concerning the supply side are:

(i) There are N suppliers i, $i = 1 \ldots N$ of this good. Each of them produces according to a per period total cost function $TC_i(x_i, q_i)$ where x_i is the quantity he sells, and q_i the quality he supplies. The producers do *not* (necessarily) all have the same cost functions. All the cost functions do however have the

---

[7] cf., the works cited in footnote 4.

property that:

(1) $\quad \dfrac{\partial TC_i}{\partial x_i} = c_i(q_i) \quad$ with $c'_i > 0$ and $c''_i > 0 \quad \forall i$

that is, all the per period production functions exhibit constant returns to scale and increasing costs of quality.

(ii) The producers' decision variables are the price they charge and the quality they supply in all the periods they stay on the market. These two determine their (expected) sales volume. The producers act as Nash competitors in their choice of price and quality.

(iii) The discount rate used by all the producers is r. To simplify that notation we introduce

$$R_T = \sum_{t=1}^{T} (1+r)^{-t}$$

The assumptions concerning the demand side are:

(iv) In every period there are Q *identical* new consumers entering in the market. The consumers entering in the market in period t will be called the consumers of generation t. Each generation of consumers stays on the market for $(T+1)$ periods.

(v) Each consumer's demand for the good is decreasing in price and increasing in quality. Demand for a product of quality q sold at a price p is denoted by

(2) $\quad x = D(p, q)$

The associated surplus is denoted by

(3) $\quad S = S(p, q) = \displaystyle\int_p^\infty D(v, q)\, dv$

We introduce the common notation

$$\dfrac{\partial x}{\partial p} = D_1, \quad \dfrac{\partial x}{\partial q} = D_2, \quad \dfrac{\partial S}{\partial p} = S_1 \quad \text{and} \quad \dfrac{\partial S}{\partial q} = S_2$$

Note for later use that

$$\dfrac{\partial x}{\partial q} \bigg/ \dfrac{\partial x}{\partial p} = \dfrac{D_1}{D_2}$$

gives us the consumer's *marginal valuation of quality*, that is, the amount he is willing to pay for an increase in the quality of *the last* unit he buys. Similarly

$$\dfrac{\partial S}{\partial q} \bigg/ \dfrac{\partial S}{\partial p} = \dfrac{\partial S}{\partial q} \bigg/ D(p, q) = \dfrac{S_2}{S_1}$$

gives us the consumer's *average valuation of quality*, that is, the amount he would be willing to pay for an increase in the quality of *all* the units he buys.

The goodwill mechanism in this model works as follows:

(vi) In the first period each consumer randomly[8] visits one producer and samples *one unit of his good*. At the end of the first period each consumer meets a number of other consumers of his generation, and they exchange information about the price and the quality of the products they have sampled. As a result of this exchange of information each consumer then chooses one producer from whom he will buy in the remaining T periods he stays on the market. Each consumer will obviously choose that producer whom he believes to be supplying the "best" product, that is, *the producer whom he believes to be selling the product yielding the greatest surplus*. We assume that the information consumers exchange contains a certain amount of noise, so that *the number of customers who end up buying from any given supplier i is a continuous increasing function of the surplus his product yields*.[9]

Denote by f_i the fraction of a generation who will end up buying from supplier i. Introducing the notation $S_i = S(p_i, q_i)$ we have

(4) $\quad f_i = f(S_i, S_1, \ldots, S_{i-1}, S_{i+1}, \ldots, S_N)$

with $\partial f/\partial S_i = f_1 > 0$ and $\partial f/\partial S_j < 0$, $i \neq j$. For consistency we must, of course, have $\sum_{i=1}^{N} f_i = 1$.

(vii) Once the consumers have been allocated to the various suppliers according to the mechanism described above, each of them buys from his supplier according to his demand function $x_i = D(p_i, q_i)$.

Equilibrium

We shall not prove the existence of a unique equilibrium in the model described above, but content ourselves with the analysis of the properties it must exhibit: The sales volume of producer i to any given generation of consumers is

(5) $\quad V = Q\left[\dfrac{1}{N} + Tf(S_i, .)x_i\right]$

The present value of profits he earns on any given generation of consumers is

(6) $\quad \Pi_i = [p_i - c_i(q_i)]Q\left[\dfrac{1}{N} + R_T f(S_i, .)x_i\right]$

---

[8] Given the information the consumers have, it is rational for them to choose the producer from which they buy this first unit at random. While they may know that the stores charging a higher price sell better quality (on average), this tells them nothing about which producer offers the best price–quality combination.

[9] The structure of the model is similar to many of the "brand choice" models in the management science literature cited. In that literature the transition matrices among different brands are often exogenously specified. We assume that there exists an objective measure of quality, and that the probability of purchase is an increasing function of quality and a decreasing function of price.

Given the Nash assumption, profit maximization implies[10] choosing p_i and q_i such that

$$\frac{\partial \Pi_i}{\partial p_i} = 0 \rightarrow$$

(7) $\quad R_T[f_1 S_1 x_i + f(S_i,.)D_1] = -\dfrac{[1/N + R_T f(S_i,.)x_i]}{[p_i - c_i(q_i)]}$

$$\frac{\partial \Pi_i}{\partial q_i} = 0 \rightarrow$$

(8) $\quad R_T[f_1 S_2 x_i + f(S_i,.)D_2] = \dfrac{\partial c_i/\partial q_i [1/N + R_T f(S_i,.)x_i]}{[p_i - c_i(q_i)]}$

Taking the quotient of (7) and (8), we obtain

(9) $\quad \dfrac{\partial c_i}{\partial q_i} = \dfrac{x_i f_1 S_2 + f(S_i,.)D_2}{x_i f_1 S_1 + f(S_i,.)D_1}$

Define $x_i f_1 = a$ and $f(S_i,.) = b$. Equation (9) can then be rewritten

(10) $\quad \dfrac{\partial c_i}{\partial q_i} = \dfrac{a S_2 + b D_2}{a S_1 + b D_1} = A$

where both a and b are strictly positive numbers.

It is shown in the Appendix that

(11) $\quad$ if $\dfrac{S_2}{S_1} < \dfrac{D_2}{D_1}$, then $\dfrac{S_2}{S_1} < A < \dfrac{D_2}{D_1}$

and

(12) $\quad$ if $\dfrac{S_2}{S_1} > \dfrac{D_2}{D_1}$, then $\dfrac{S_2}{S_1} > A > \dfrac{D_2}{D_1}$

Equation (9) is the main result of this paper. Let us turn to its interpretation: Recall from the definitions following equation (3) that S_2/S_1 gives the consumers' *average valuation of quality*, that is, it is the *social incentive to produce quality*. A social planner facing the total cost function $TC_i(x_i, q_i)$, will choose his quality level such that

(13) $\quad \dfrac{\partial c_i}{\partial q_i} = \dfrac{S_2}{S_1}$

---

[10] When formulating the problem in this way we are assuming that the producer's profit maximization problem does have an *interior* solution. In particular it must be the case that the new consumers coming on the market each period will not buy from a producer if the price he charges is exorbitantly high. What we are assuming essentially is that it does not pay the producer to charge a very high price and supply the lowest possible quality compatible with the production technology he has chosen. Denote by p^{max}, the maximum price at which consumers are willing to buy the product and by $c_i(\beta_1)$ the marginal cost of producing the lowest possible quality. We are assuming then that the per period profits obtained by selling quality β_1 at a price p^{max} yields lower per period profits than the interior solution we are discussing.

The socially optimal quality choice, that is, the quality choice satisfying equation (13) will be denoted q_i^s. Similarly D_2/D_1 gives the consumers' *marginal valuation of quality*, that is, it is the private incentive to produce quality in a situation of complete information. A monopolist would then choose his quality level such that

$$(14) \qquad \frac{\partial c_i}{\partial q_i} = \frac{D_2}{D_1}$$

The monopolist's quality choice, that is, the quality choice satisfying equation (14) will be denoted q_i^m. Spence [1975] has shown that whenever $D_2/D_1 < S_2/S_1$, the monopolist has an insufficient incentive to produce quality. The quality forthcoming will be too low, that is, $q_i^m < q_i^s$. When $D_2/D_1 > S_2/S_1$, the monopolist has too great an incentive to produce quality. The quality forthcoming will be too high, that is, $q_i^m > q_i^s$.

Equations (9) and (10) and their interpretations (11) and (12) give a supplier's incentive to produce quality in a situation of *imperfect* information. Denote the producer's optimal quality choice by q_i^*. Equation (11) tells us that if in a situation of perfect information there is a private incentive to produce excessively high quality, this incentive will persist in a situation of incomplete information. The incentive will, however, be somewhat lower, that is, $q_i^m < q_i^* < q_i^s$. Similarly equation (12) tells us that if in a situation of perfect information there is an insufficient private incentive to produce quality, again this tendency will persist in a situation of imperfect information. The incentive to produce quality will, however, be somewhat higher, that is, $q_i^s < q_i^* < q_i^m$.

The main conclusion we derive from the above analysis is as follows: *With a functioning goodwill mechanism one cannot say that imperfect consumer information will lead to the market undersupplying quality.* While the market will not, of course, always choose the socially optimal quality level, this fact cannot be ascribed to the information problem *per se*. The same kind of problems arise even in situations of perfect information. The result that imperfect information leads to quality levels closer to the social optimum can be explained as follows: In a situation of imperfect information a producer's choice of quality level affects two variables: First, the surplus he yields to the consumers and thus, via the goodwill mechanism, his total number of customers. And, second, his sales volume to each customer. A social planner is interested only in the first of these effects; a monopolist selling to customers with perfect information only in the second. A supplier selling on a market with imperfect information has to take both factors into account. It is thus hardly surprising that his quality choice will lie somewhere in between the social optimum and the monopolist's.

Further Interpretations

Apart from this main result, the above model has some further interesting properties that one would expect to find in any model of a market for an experience good. Substituting the producer's optimal quality choice q_i^* into (7) we obtain:

$$(15) \quad [p_i - c_i(q_i^*)] = -\frac{[1/\mathcal{N} + R_T f(S_i,.)x_i]}{R_T[f_1 S_1 x_i \eta f(S_i,.) D_1]}$$

Equation (15) has the following properties:

(i) $[p_i - c_i(q_i^*)] > 0$. As in all models of the goodwill mechanism with quantity taking suppliers, high quality products will be forthcoming only if price is greater than marginal cost, that is, if the producers make positive per period profits. This result together with the preceding analysis shows that imperfect information on the part of consumers does indeed lead to market failure. In the presence of the goodwill mechanism, the market failure does not, however, take the form of low quality, but of excessively high prices (that is, prices above marginal costs).

$$(ii) \quad \frac{\partial [p_i - c_i(q_i^*)]}{\partial R_T} < 0$$

The lower R_T, that is the higher the interest rate, the higher will be the price cost margin charged by each producer. Again this is an intuitively plausible result. The greater the interest rate, the greater is the incentive to "cheat" the new customers entering each period by charging a high price, even if this does imply a loss of sales volume in future "repeat purchases".

$$(iii) \quad \frac{\partial [p_i - c_i(q_i^*)]}{\partial f_1} < 0$$

The greater f_1, that is the stronger the sales volume reacts to a given increase in the surplus to the consumers, the lower will be the equilibrium price cost margin. In the special case, where $D_2/D_1 = S_2/S_1$, the social incentive to provide quality coincides with the private incentive. We will then of course have $q_i^S = q_i^* = q_i^m$. In such a situation an increase in f_1 will leave the choice of quality unchanged, and lead to a simple reduction in price.[11]

III. CONCLUSION

The analysis can, of course, be extended in several directions. However, it should be clear from the formulation of the problem adopted here that the producer's quality choice depends critically on the exact specification of the repeat purchase function. The specification we have adopted, while certainly somewhat *ad hoc*, is the most plausible first approximation we could think of. However, if price were given a preponderant weight in the goodwill function, this would bias the results in the direction of excessively low quality. The opposite would occur if quality were the main determinant of the total number

---

[11] Analogous results are derived in a somewhat different framework and discussed in much greater detail in von Ungern-Sternberg and von Weizsäcker [1981] and von Ungern-Sternberg [1984a, chapters 4–6].

of customers. The fact that the price level can usually be exactly observed, but quality only with some noise, does not seem to bias the results against the provision of quality. That, at least, is the result explicitly derived in von Ungern-Sternberg [1984b] in an admittedly somewhat more restrictive framework.

The essential message of our current knowledge of the goodwill mechanism is certainly that the market does have powerful self-correcting mechanisms for "lemons"-type problems which are due to adverse selection and moral hazard. It is imperative that we understand the working of these mechanisms. Such an understanding is a necessary prerequisite for formulating a government's role in helping the consumers with their search for information. As the calls for government intervention to regulate markets are, at least in Germany, getting continuously stronger, the workings of the perhaps too invisible hand of the goodwill mechanisms should be made somewhat more visible by the profession.

THOMAS VON UNGERN-STERNBERG ACCEPTED NOVEMBER 1984
AND CARL CHRISTIAN VON WEIZSÄCKER,
Department of Economics,
Universität Bern,
Gesellschaftsstr. 27,
Bern 3012,
Switzerland.

APPENDIX

We shall restrict ourselves to proving only one of the four inequalities in (11) and (12). The other three can be proven in the same way:

Theorem: If

(A1) $\quad \dfrac{S_2}{S_1} < \dfrac{D_2}{D_1}$

and $a > 0$ and $b > 0$, then

(A2) $\quad \dfrac{S_2}{S_1} < \dfrac{aS_2 + bD_2}{aS_1 + bD_1}$

Proof: There exists a positive constant α, such that we can write

(A3) $\quad D_2 = \alpha S_2$

As $S_2/S_1 < D_2/D_1$, then there must also exist some positive constant k such that we can write

(A4) $\quad D_1 = \alpha(S_1 - k)$

Substituting (A3) and (A4) into (A2) and simplifying, we obtain:

(A5) $\quad \dfrac{S_2}{S_1} < \dfrac{S_2(a + \alpha b)}{S_1(a + \alpha b) - \alpha k}$

As both α and k are greater than zero, A5 is obviously correct. QED

BIBLIOGRAPHY

AAFTINK, J., IRELAND, N. J. and SERTEL, M. R., 1982, 'On Cournot–Nash Equilibria with Exogenous Uncertainty', Warwick Economic Research Paper No. 210 (July), forthcoming *Journal of Optimisation Theory and Applications*.

AKERLOF, G. A., 1970, 'The Market for Lemons: Qualitative Uncertainty and the Market Mechanism', *The Quarterly Journal of Economics*, 84, 3 (August), pp. 488–500.

ANDERSON, J., 1984, 'Identification of Interactive Behaviour in Air Service Markets: 1973–76', *Journal of Industrial Economics*, 23, 4 (June), pp. 489–508.

APPELBAUM, E., 1979, 'Testing Price Taking Behaviour', *Journal of Econometrics*, 9, pp. 283–294.

APPELBAUM, E., 1982, 'The Estimation of the Degree of Oligopoly Power', *Journal of Econometrics*, 19, pp. 287–299.

AREEDA, P. and TURNER, D. F., 1975, 'Predatory Pricing and Related Practices Under Section 2 of the Sherman Act', *Harvard Law Review*, 88, 4 (February), pp. 697–733.

AREEDA, P. and TURNER, D. F., 1976, 'Scherer on Predatory Pricing: A Reply', *Harvard Law Review*, 89, 5 (March), pp. 891–900.

ARROW, K. J., 1963, 'Uncertainty and the Welfare Economics of Medical Care', *The American Economic Review*, 53, 5 (December), pp. 465–491.

D'ASPREMONT, C. and GERARD-VARET, L., 1979, 'Incentives and Incomplete Information', *Journal of Public Economics*, 11, pp. 25–34.

AUMANN, R. J., 1960, 'Acceptable Points in Games of Perfect Information', *Pacific Journal of Mathematics*, 10, pp. 381–417.

BAKER, J. and BRESNAHAN, T., 1984, 'Estimating the Demand Curve Facing a Single Firm: Estimates for Three Brewing Firms', Research Paper 54, Stanford Workshop on the Economics of Factor Markets.

BAKER, J. and BRESNAHAN, T., 1985, 'The Gains from Merger or Collusion in Product-Differentiated Industries', *Journal of Industrial Economics*, this issue.

BASAR, T. and HO, Y. C., 1974, 'Information Properties of the Nash Solutions of Two Nonzero-sum Games, *Journal of Economic Theory*, 7, 4 (April), pp. 370–387.

BAUMOL, WM. J., 1979, 'Quasi-Permanence of Price Reductions: A Policy for Prevention of Predatory Pricing', *Yale Law Journal*, 89, 1 (November), pp. 1–26.

BAUMOL, WM. J., PANZAR, J. C. and WILLIG, R. D., 1982, *Contestable Markets and the Theory of Industry Structure* (Harcourt, Brace, Jovanovitch, San Diego).

BEATH, J. and ULPH, D., 1984, 'The Welfare Economics of Vertical Products Differentiation', mimeo, University of Bristol.

Beer Marketer's Insights, annual.

BERNHEIM, B. D., 1984, 'Rationalisable Strategic Behaviour', *Econometrica*, 52, 4 (July), pp. 1007–1028.

BIGGADIKE, E. R., 1976, *Corporate Diversification Entry, Strategy and Performance* (Harvard University Press, Cambridge).

BRADBURD, R. M., 1980, 'Conglomerate Power without Market Power: the Effect of Conglomeration on a Risk Averse Quantity Adjusting Firm', *American Economic Review*, 70, 3 (June), pp. 483–488.

BRANDER, J. and SPENCER, B., 1983, 'Strategic Commitment with R & D: the Symmetric Case', *Bell Journal of Economics*, 14, 1 (Spring), pp. 225–235.

BRESNAHAN, T. F., 1980, 'Competition and Collusion in the American Automobile Industry: The 1955 Price War', mimeo, Stanford University.

BRESNAHAN, T. F., 1981, 'Departures from Marginal-Cost Pricing in the American Automobile Industry: Estimates for 1977–1978', *Journal of Econometrics*, 11, pp. 201–227.
BRESNAHAN, T. F., 1981, 'Duopoly Models with Consistent Conjectures', *American Economic Review*, 71, 5 (December), pp. 934–945.
BRESNAHAN, T. F., 1981, 'Competition and Collusion in the American Automobile Industry: The 1955 Price War', mimeo, Stanford University.
BRESNAHAN, T. F., 1982, 'The Oligopoly Solution Concept is Identified', *Economics Letters*, 10, 1, pp. 87–92.
BRODLEY, J. F. and HAY, G. A., 1981, 'Predatory Pricing: Competing Economic Theories and the Evolution of Legal Standards', *Cornell Law Review*, 23, 4 (April), pp. 738–803.
BROWN, D. and HEAL, G., 1979, 'Equity, Efficiency and Increasing Returns', *Review of Economic Studies*, 46, 4 (October), pp. 571–586.
BULOW, J. and PFEIDERER, P., 1983, 'A Note on the Effect of Cost Changes on Prices', *Journal of Political Economy*, 91, 1 (February), pp. 182–185.
CAVES, R. and PUGEL, T., 1980, 'Intraindustry Differences in Conduct and Performance: Viable Strategies in U.S. Manufacturing Industries', Monograph Series in Finance and Economics, N.T.U. Graduate School of Business Administration.
CHAMBERLIN, E. H., 1929, 'Duopoly: Value when Sellers are Few', *Quarterly Journal of Economics*, 43, pp. 63–100.
CHAMBERLIN, E. H., 1933, *The Theory of Monopolistic Competition* (Harvard University Press, Cambridge, Mass.).
CLARKE, R. N., 1983, 'Duopolists Don't Wish to Share Information', *Economics Letters*, 11, pp. 33–36.
CLARKE, R. N., 1983, 'Collusion and the Incentives for Information Sharing', *Bell Journal of Economics*, 14, pp. 383–394.
CLARKE, R., DAVIES, S. and WATERSON, M., 1984, 'The Profitability-Concentration Relation: Market Power or Efficiency?', *Journal of Industrial Economics*, 32, 4 (June), pp. 435–450.
COMANOR, W. and LEIBENSTEIN, H., 1969, 'Allocative Efficiency, X-inefficiency, and the Measurement of Welfare Losses', *Economica*, N.S. 36, 143 (August), pp. 304–309.
COWLING, K. and CUBBIN, J., 1972, 'Hedonic Price Indexes for Cars in the U.K.', *Economic Journal*, 82, 327 (September), pp. 963–978.
COWLING, K. and WATERSON, M., 1976, 'Price Cost Margins and Market Structure', *Economica*, 43, 171, pp. 267–274.
COWLING, K. and MUELLER, D., 1978, 'The Social Costs of Monopoly Power', *Economic Journal*, 88, 352 (December), pp. 727–748.
CRAWFORD, V. and SOBEL, J., 1982, 'Strategic Information Transmission', *Econometrica*, 50, pp. 1431–1451.
CUBBIN, J., 1975, 'Quality Change and Pricing Behaviour in the U.K. Car Industry, 1956–1968', *Economica*, 42, 165 (February), pp. 43–58.
CUBBIN, J., 1983, 'Apparent Collusion and Conjectural Variations in Differentiated Oligopoly', *International Journal of Industrial Organisation*, 1, pp. 155–163.
CYERT, D. and DEGROOT, M., 1973, 'An Analysis of Cooperation and Learning in a Duopoly Context', *American Economic Review*, 63, 1, pp. 24–37.
DANSBY, R. and WILLIG, R., 1979, 'Industry Performance Gradient Indices', *American Economic Review*, 69, 3, pp. 249–260.
DASGUPTA, P. and STIGLITZ, J., 1980, 'Industrial Structure and the Nature of Innovative Activity', *Economic Journal*, 90 (June), pp. 266–293.
DASGUPTA, P., 1982, 'The Theory of Technological Competition', ICERD Discussion Paper No. 82/46 (May), London School of Economics, International Centre for Economics and Related Disciplines.

DASGUPTA, P., 1984, 'The Theory of Technological Competition', in F. Matthewson and J. Stiglitz (eds.), *New Developments in the Analysis of Market Structure* (M.I.T. Press, Boston, Mass.).
DEMSETZ, H., 1974, 'Two Systems of Belief about Monopoly', in Goldschmid *et al.* (eds.), *Industrial Concentration: The New Learning* (Little and Brown, Boston).
DE PALMA, A., GINSBURGH, V., PAPAGEROGIOU, Y. and THISSE, J.-F., 1983, 'The Principle of Minimum Differentiation Holds under Sufficient Heterogeneity', CORE, Discussion Paper, No. 8339, Louvain-la-Neuve.
DICKSON, V., 1983, 'Collusion and Price-Cost Margins', *Economica*, 49, 193 (February), pp. 39–42.
DIXIT, A., 1980, 'The Role of Investment in Entry Deterrence', *Economic Journal*, 90, 357 (March), pp. 95–106.
DIXIT, A., 1982, 'Recent Developments in Oligopoly Theory', *American Economic Review*, 72, 2 (May), papers and proceedings, pp. 12–17.
DIXIT, A. K. and STIGLITZ, J. E., 1977, 'Monopolistic Competition and Optimum Product Diversity', *American Economic Review*, 67, 3 (June), pp. 297–308.
DIXON, H. D., 1984a, 'Cournot and Bertrand Outcomes as Equilibria in a Strategic Metagame with Precommitment', Birkbeck Discussion Paper, No. 166.
DIXON, H. D., 1984b, *Approximate Bertrand Equilibria and Strategic Precommitment*, D. Phil. Thesis, Oxford.
DIXON, H. D., 1985, 'Strategic Investment in an Industry with a Competitive Product Market', *Journal of Industrial Economics*, this issue.
DOLBEAR, F., LAVE, L. and BOWMAN, G., 1968, 'Collusion in Oligopoly: An Experiment on the Effect of Numbers and Information', *Quarterly Journal of Economics*, 82 (May), pp. 240–259.
EASLEY, D., MASON, R. T. and REYNOLDS, R. J., 1981, 'A Dynamic Analysis of Predatory Pricing with Rational Expectations', Working Paper 250, Cornell University.
EASLEY, D., MASON, R. T. and REYNOLDS, R. J., 1984, 'Preying for Time: Additional Analysis', mimeo, Cornell University.
EASLEY, D., MASON, R. T. and REYNOLDS, R. J., 1985, 'Preying for Time', *Journal of Industrial Economics*, this issue.
EATON, B. C. and LIPSEY, R. G., 1975, 'The Principle of Minimum Differentiation Reconsidered: Some New Developments in the Theory of Spatial Competition', *Review of Economic Studies*, 42, 1 (January), pp. 27–49.
EATON, B. C. and LIPSEY, R. G., 1976, 'The Non-Uniqueness of Equilibrium in the Löschian Location Model', *American Economic Review*, 66, 1 (March), pp. 77–93.
EATON, B. C. and LIPSEY, R., 1978, 'Freedom of Entry and the Existence of Price Profit', *Economic Journal*, 80 (September), pp. 455–469.
EATON, B. C. and LIPSEY, R., 1980, 'Exit Barriers and Entry Barriers: The Durability of Capital as a Barrier to Entry', *Bell Journal of Economics*, 11, 2 (Autumn), pp. 721–729.
EATON, B. C. and LIPSEY, R., 1981, 'Capital, Commitment and Entry Equilibrium', *Bell Journal of Economics*, 12, 2 (Autumn), pp. 593–604.
EISENBERG, B. S., 1980, 'Information Exchange Among Competitors: the Issue of Relative Value Scales for Physicians' Services', *Journal of Law and Economics*, 23, 2 (October), pp. 441–460.
EISENSTAT, P., MASON, R. T. and RODDY, D., 'An Economic Analysis of the Associated Milk Producers, Inc. Monopoly', filed with the court in *U.S. v. Associated Milk Producers, Inc.*, 394 F. Supp. 29 (W.D. Mo. 1975) aff'd 534 F.2d 113 (8th Cir., 1976), 628 pp.
ELLISON, R. I. and UHL, K. P., 1964, 'Influence of Beer Brand Identification on Taste Perception', *Journal of Marketing Research* (August), pp. 321–332.
ELZINGA, K. G., 1982, 'The Beer Industry', in Walter Adams (ed.), *The Structure of American Industry* (6th edition, Macmillan, New York).

ENCAOUA, D., GEROSKI, P. and JACQUEMIN, A., 1984, 'Strategic Competition and the Persistence of Dominant Firms: A Survey', in F. Matthewson and J. Stiglitz (eds.), *New Developments and the Analysis of Market Structure* (M.I.T. Press, Boston, Mass.).
FARREL, J., 1980, 'Prices as Signals of Quality', unpublished Ph.D. dissertation.
FISHER, F. M., MCGOWAN, J. J. and GREENWOOD, J. E., 1983, *Folded, Spindled and Mutilated: Economic Analysis and U.S. v. IBM* (M.I.T. Press, Cambridge and London).
FOURAKER, L. and SIEGEL, S., 1963, *Bargaining behavior* (McGraw-Hill, New York).
FRIEDMAN, J. W., 1963, 'Individual Behavior in Oligopolistic Markets: An Experimental Study', *Yale Economic Essays*, 3, pp. 359–417.
FRIEDMAN, J. W., 1969, 'On Experimental Research in Oligopoly', *Review of Economic Studies*, 36, pp. 399–415.
FRIEDMAN, J. W., 1970, 'Equal Profit as a Fair Division', in H. Sauermann (ed.), *Beiträge zur Experimentellen Wirtschaftsforschung*, II (J. C. B. Mohr (Paul Siebeck), Tübingen), pp. 19–32.
FRIEDMAN, J. W., 1971, 'A Non-Cooperative Equilibrium for Supergames', *Review of Economic Studies*, 38, pp. 1–12.
FRIEDMAN, J. W., 1972, 'On the Structure of Oligopoly Models with Differentiated Products', in H. Sauermann (ed.), *Beiträge zur Experimentellen Wirtschaftsforschung*, III (J. C. B. Mohr (Paul Siebeck), Tübingen), pp. 28–63.
FRIEDMAN, J. W., 1977, *Oligopoly and the Theory of Games* (North-Holland Publishing Co., Amsterdam).
FRIEDMAN, J. W., 1983, *Oligopoly Theory* (Cambridge University Press, Cambridge).
FRIEDMAN, J. W. and HOGGART, A. C., 1980, *An Experiment in Non-Cooperative Oligopoly* (JAI Press, Greenwich, Connecticut).
FUDENBERG, D., GILBERT, R. J., STIGLITZ, J. E. and TIROLE, J., 1983, 'Preemption, Leapfrogging and Competition in Patent Races', *European Economic Review*, 22, pp. 3–31, Special Issue on Market Competition, Conflict and Collusion.
FUDENBERG, D. and TIROLE, J., 1984, 'Dynamic Models of Oligopoly', mimeo, Stanford University.
GAL-OR, E., 1982, 'Information Sharing in Oligopoly', University of Pittsburgh, Working Paper.
GEROSKI, P., 1982, 'Interpreting a Correlation Between Profits and Concentration', *Journal of Industrial Economics*, 30, 3 (March), pp. 305–318.
GEROSKI, P., 1982b, 'The Empirical Analysis of Conjectural Variations in Oligopoly', mimeo, Université Catholique de Louvain.
GEROSKI, P., 1983, 'Some Reflections on the Theory and Application of Concentration Indices', *International Journal of Industrial Organization*, 1, pp. 79–94.
GEROSKI, P. and ULPH, A., 1984, 'A Model of the Crude Oil Market in Which Conduct Varies Over Time', mimeo, University of Southampton.
GEROSKI, P. and JACQUEMIN, A., 1984, 'Dominant Firms and Their Alleged Decline', *International Journal of Industrial Organisation*, 2, pp. 1–27.
GEROSKI, P., INGHAM, A. and ULPH, A., 1984, 'Asymmetric Information and Entry: The Case of Learning by Observing', mimeo, University of Southampton.
GILBERT, R. J., 1981, 'Patents, Sleeping Patents and Entry Deterrence', in S. C. Salop (ed.), *Strategy, Predation and Antitrust Analysis*, Federal Trade Commission, pp. 205–269.
GILBERT, R. J. and NEWBERY, D., 1982, 'Pre-emptive Patenting and the Persistence of Monopoly, *American Economic Review*, 72, 3 (June), pp. 514–526.
GILBERT, R. J. and NEWBERY, D., 1984a, 'Uncertain Innovation and the Persistence of Monopoly: Comment', *American Economic Review*, 74, 1 (March), pp. 238–242.
GILBERT, R. J. and NEWBERY, D., 1984b, 'Pre-emptive Patenting and the Persistence of Monopoly: Reply', *American Economic Review*, 74, 1 (March), pp. 251–253.

GOLLOP, F. and ROBERTS, M., 1979, 'Firm Interdependence in Oligopolistic Markets', *Journal of Econometrics*, 10, pp. 313–331.
GREEN, E. J., 1980, 'Non-Cooperative Price Taking in Large Dynamic Markets', *Journal of Economic Theory*, 22, 2 (April), pp. 155–182. Reprinted in A. Mas-Collell (ed.), *Non-Cooperative Approaches to the Theory of Perfect Competition* (Academic Press, 1982), pp. 37–64.
GREEN, E. J. and PORTER, R. H., 1984, 'Noncooperative Collusion under Imperfect Price Information', *Econometrica*, 52, 1 (January), pp. 87–100.
GREER, D. F., 1971, 'Product Differentiation and Concentration in the Brewing Industry', *Journal of Industrial Economics*, 19, 3 (July), pp. 201–219.
GREER, D. F., 1979, 'A Critique of Areeda and Turner's Standards for Predatory Practices', *The Antitrust Bulletin*, XXIV, 2 (Summer), pp. 233–261.
GREER, D. F., 1981, 'The Causes of Concentration in the Brewing Industry', *Quarterly Review of Economics and Business*, 21, 4 (Winter), pp. 87–106.
GROSSMAN, S., 1981, 'Nash Equilibrium and the Industrial Organisation of Market with Large Fixed Costs', *Econometrica*, 49, 5 (September), pp. 1149–1172.
GROSSMAN, G. and SHAPIRO, C., 1984, 'Information Advertising with Differentiated Products', *Review of Economic Studies*, 51, 1 (January), pp. 63–81.
HARBERGER, A., 1954, 'Monopoly and Resource Allocation', *American Economic Review*, Papers and proceedings, 44 (May), pp. 77–87.
HARRIS, C. J. and VICKERS, J. S., 1985, 'Perfect Equilibrium in a Model of a Race', *Review of Economic Studies*, 52, pp. 193–209.
HARRIS, C. J. and VICKERS, J. S., 1985, 'Patent Races and the Persistence of Monopoly', *Journal of Industrial Economics*, this issue.
HARSANYI, J. C., 1967–68, 'Games with Incomplete Information Played by Bayesian Players', *Management Science*, 14, 11 (July), Parts I, II, III, pp. 159–182, 320–334, 486–502.
HART, O. D., 1983, 'Monopolistic Competition in the Spirit of Chamberlin: A General Model', *I.C.E.R.D. Discussion Paper, 83/82*, LSE.
HATTEN, K. J. and SCHENDAL, D. E., 1977, 'Heterogeneity Within an Industry: Firm Conduct in the U.S. Brewing Industry 1952–71', *Journal of Industrial Economics*, 26, 2 (December), pp. 99–114.
HAY, D., 1976, 'Sequential Entry and Entry Deterring Strategies in Spatial Competition', *Oxford Economic Papers*, 28, 2 (July), pp. 240–257.
HAZILLA, M. and KOPP, R. J., 1983, 'Substitution between Energy and Other Factors of Production', *Resources of the Future*.
HOGARTY, T. F. and ELZINGA, K. G., 1972, 'The Demand for Beer', *Review of Economics and Statistics*, 54, 2 (May), pp. 195–198.
HOGGATT, A. C., 1959, 'An Experimental Business Game', *Behavioural Science*, 4, pp. 192–203.
HOGGATT, A. C., 1967, 'Measuring the Cooperativeness of Behaviour in Quantity Variation Duopoly Games', *Behavioural Science*, 12, pp. 109–121.
HOLAHAN, W. L., 1978, 'Cartel Problems: Comment', *American Economic Review*, 68, 5 (December), pp. 942–946.
HOTELLING, H., 1929, 'Stability in Competition', *Economic Journal*, 39 (March), pp. 41–57.
IRELAND, N. J., 1980, 'The Analogy between Parameter Uncertainty and Parameter Changes', *Economics Letters*, 6, pp. 301–308.
IRELAND, N. J., 1983a, 'Monopolistic Competition and a Firm's Product Range', *International Journal of Industrial Organization*, 1, pp. 239–252.
IRELAND, N. J., 1983b, 'A Note on Conglomerate Merger and Behavioural Response to Risk', *Journal of Industrial Economics*, 31, 3 (March), pp. 283–290.

IRELAND, N., 1985, 'Product Diversity and Monopolistic Competition under Uncertainty', *Journal of Industrial Economics*, this issue.
ISHII, Y., 1977, 'On the Theory of the Competitive Firm under Price Uncertainty: A Note', *American Economic Review*, 67, 4 (September), pp. 768–769.
IWATA, G., 1974, 'Measurement of Conjectural Variations in Oligopoly', *Econometrica*, 42, 5 (September), pp. 947–966.
JOSCOW, A., 1983, 'A Welfare Analysis of Industry Product Variety', mimeo, Yale University.
JOSKOW, P. L. and KLEVORICK, A. K., 1979, 'A Framework for Analyzing Predatory Pricing Policy', *Yale Law Journal*, 89, 2 (December), pp. 213–270.
JUST, R. and CHERN, W., 1980, 'Tomatoes, Technology and Oligopoly', *Bell Journal of Economics*, 11, 2 (Autumn), pp. 584–602.
KAMIEN, M. I. and SCHWARTZ, N. L., 1982, *Market Structure and Innovation* (Cambridge University Press, New York and Sydney).
KEITHAHN, C., 1978, 'Staff Report of the Federal Trade Commission', *The Brewing Industry*, December.
KELTON, C. M. L. and KELTON, W. D., 1982, 'Advertising and Intra-industry Brand Shift in the U.S. Brewing Industry', *Journal of Industrial Economics*, 30, 2 (March), pp. 293–303.
KIRMAN, WM. and MASSON, R. T., 1984, 'Capacity Signalling to Deter Entry', unpublished paper, Cornell University.
KLEIN, B. and LEFFLER, K., 1981, 'Non Governmental Enforcement of Contracts: The Role of Marketforces in Assuring Quality', *The Journal of Political Economy*, 88, 4 (August), pp. 615–641.
KOENKER, R. W. and PERRY, M. K., 1981, 'Product Differentiation, Monopolistic Competition and Public Policy', *Bell Journal*, 12, 1 (Spring), pp. 217–231.
KOLLER, R. H., III, 1971, 'The Myth of Predatory Pricing: An Empirical Study', *Antitrust Law and Economics Review*, 4, 4 (Summer), pp. 105–123.
KREPS, D. M., MILGROM, P. and WILSON, R., 1982, 'Rational Cooperation in the Finitely Repeated Prisoners' Dilemma', *Journal of Economic Theory*, 27, pp. 245–252.
KREPS, D. M. and WILSON, R., 1982a, 'Sequential Equilibria', *Econometrica*, 50, pp. 863–894.
KREPS, D. M. and WILSON, R., 1982b, 'Reputation and Imperfect Information', *Journal of Economic Theory*, 27, 2 (August), pp. 253–279.
KREPS, D. M. and SCHEINKMAN, J. A., 1983, 'Quantity Precommitment and Bertrand Competition Yield Cournot Outcomes', *Bell Journal of Economics*, 14, 2 (Autumn), pp. 326–337.
KRUGMAN, P., 1980, 'Scale Economies, Product Differentiation and the Pattern of Trade', *American Economic Review*, 70, 5 (December), pp. 950–959.
LAITNER, J., 1980, 'Rational Duopoly Equilibria', *Quarterly Journal of Economics*, 95, 4 (December), pp. 641–662.
LAMBIN, J., NAERT, P. A. and BULTEY, A., 1975, 'Optimal Marketing Behaviour in Oligopoly', *European Economic Review*, 6, pp. 105–128.
LANCASTER, K., 1975, 'Socially Optimal Product Differentiation', *American Economic Review*, 65, 4 (September), pp. 567–585.
LANCASTER, K., 1979, *Variety, Equity and Efficiency* (Columbia University Press, New York).
LANE, W., 1980, 'Product Differentiation in a Model with Endogenous Sequential Entry', *Bell Journal of Economics*, 11, 1 (Spring), pp. 237–260.
LEE, L.-F. and PORTER, R. H., 1984, 'Switching Regression Models with Imperfect Sample Separation Information—With an Application on Cartel Stability', *Econometrica*, 52, 3 (March), pp. 391–418.

LEE, T. and WILDE, L., 1980, 'Market Structure and Innovation: A Reformulation', *Quarterly Journal of Economics*, 94, 2 (March), pp. 429–436.

LEIBENSTEIN, H., 1966, 'Allocative Efficiency versus X-efficiency', *American Economic Review*, 56 (June), pp. 392–415.

LERNER, A., 1934, 'The Concept of Monopoly and the Measurement of Monopoly Power', *Review of Economic Studies*, 11 (June), pp. 157–175.

LOURY, G., 1979, 'Market Structure and Innovation', *Quarterly Journal of Economics*, 93, 3 (August), pp. 395–410.

LUCE, R. D. and RAIFFA, H., 1966, *Games and Decisions* (Wiley).

MACLEOD, W. B., 1984, 'The Core and Oligopoly Theory', CORE, Louvain-la-Neuve, mimeo (revised version of CORE Discussion Paper No. 8331).

MACLEOD, W. B., NORMAN, G. and THISSE, J.-F., 1984, 'Competition, Collusion and Free Entry in Spatial or Differentiated Product Markets', CORE Discussion Paper No. 8436, Louvain-la-Neuve.

MCCONNELL, J. D., 1968, 'An Experimental Examination of the Price-Quality Relationship', *Journal of Business*, 41 (October), pp. 439–449.

MCGEE, J. S., 1980, 'Predatory Pricing Revisited', *Journal of Law and Economics*, XXIII, 2 (October), pp. 289–330.

MCKINNON, R. I., 1966, 'Stigler's Theory of Oligopoly: A Comment', *Journal of Political Economy*, 74, pp. 281–285.

MADDALA, G. S., 1983, *Limited-Dependent and Qualitative Variables in Econometrics* (Cambridge University Press, Cambridge).

MARRIS, R. AND MUELLER, D. C., 1980, 'The Corporation, Competition and the Invisible Hand', *Journal of Economic Literature*, 18, 1 (March), pp. 32–63.

MARSHALL, A., 1920, *Principles of Economics* (Macmillan (8th Ed.), London).

MEADE, J., 1974, 'The Optimal Balance between Economies of Scale and Variety of Products: An Illustrative Model', *Economica*, 41, 164 (November), pp. 359–367.

MILGROM, P. and ROBERTS, J., 1982a, 'Predation, Reputation, and Entry Deterrence', *Journal of Economic Theory*, 27, 2 (August), pp. 280–312.

MILGROM, P. and ROBERTS, J., 1982b, 'Limit Pricing and Entry under Incomplete Information: An Equilibrium Analysis', *Econometrica*, 50, 2 (March), pp. 443–459.

MUELLER, D., 1981, 'Economies of Scale, Concentration and Collusion', mimeo, F.T.C.

MYERSON, R., 1984, 'Two-Person Bargaining Problems with Incomplete Information', *Econometrica*, 52, pp. 461–487.

NELSON, P., 1970, 'Information and Consumer Behaviour', *The Journal of Political Economy*, 78, 2 (March/April), pp. 311–329.

NELSON, P., 1974, 'Advertising as Information', *The Journal of Political Economy*, 82, 4 (July/August), pp. 729–754.

NERMUTH, M., 1979, *Information Structures in Economics*, Studies in the Theory of Markets with Imperfect Information, Lecture Notes in Economics and Mathematical Systems No. 196 (Springer-Verlag, Berlin).

NOVSHEK, W. and SONNENSCHEIN, H., 1980, 'Small Efficient Scale as a Foundation for Walrasian Equilibrium', *Journal of Economic Theory*, 22, pp. 243–255.

NOVSHEK, W. and SONNENSCHEIN, H., 1982, 'Fulfilled Expectations Cournot Duopoly with Information Acquisition and Release', *Bell Journal of Economics*, 13, pp. 214–218.

OKADA, A., 1980, 'Information Exchange Between Oligopolists', Department of Systems Science, Tokyo Institute of Technology, Research Report B-83, June, 1980.

ORDOVER, J. and WILLIG, R., 1981, 'An Economic Definition of Predation: Pricing and Product Innovation', *Yale Law Review*, 91, 1 (November), pp. 8–53.

ORNSTEIN, S., 1981, 'Antitrust Policy and Market Forces as Determinants of Industry Structure: Case Histories in Beer and Distilled Spirits', *The Antitrust Bulletin*, 26 (Summer), pp. 281–313.

ORR, R. and MACAVOY, P., 1965, 'Price Strategies to Promote Cartel Stability', *Economica*, 44, pp. 186–197.
OSBORNE, D. K., 1976, 'Cartel Problems', *American Economic Review*, 66, 5 (December), pp. 835–844.
PALFREY, T. R., 1982, 'Risk Advantages and Information Acquisition, *Bell Journal of Economics*, 13, pp. 219–224.
PATINKIN, D., 1947, 'Multi-Plant Firms, Cartels, and Imperfect Competition', *Quarterly Journal of Economics*, 61 (February), pp. 173–205.
PEARCE, D. G., 1984, 'Rationalisable Strategic Behaviour and the Problem of Perfection', *Econometrica*, 52, 4 (July), pp. 1029–1050.
PERLOFF, J. and SALOP, S., 1983, 'Equilibrium with Product Differentiation', mimeo.
PERRY, M. K., 1982, 'Oligopoly and Consistent Conjectural Variations', *Bell Journal of Economics*, 13, pp. 197–205.
PHLIPS, L., 1983, *The Economics of Price Discrimination* (Cambridge University Press, Cambridge).
PHLIPS, L. and THISSE, J. F., 1982, *Symposium on Spatial Competition and the Theory of Differentiated Markets*, *Journal of Industrial Economics*, 31, 1/2 (September, December).
PHLIPS, L. and RICHARD, J.-F., 1984, 'A Dynamic Oligopoly Model with Demand Inertia and Inventories', CORE Discussion Paper No. 84, Université Catholique de Louvain, Louvain-la-Neuve.
PLOTT, C. R., 1982, 'Industrial Organization Theory and Experimental Economics', *Journal of Economic Literature*, 20, pp. 1485–1527.
PORTER, R. H., 1983a, 'Optimal Cartel Trigger Price Strategies', *Journal of Economic Theory*, 29, 2 (April), pp. 313–338.
PORTER, R. H., 1983b, 'A Study of Cartel Stability: The Joint Executive Committee, 1880–1886', *The Bell Journal of Economics*, 14, 2 (Autumn), pp. 301–314.
PORTER, R. H., 1985, 'On the Incidence and Duration of Price Wars', *Journal of Industrial Economics*, this issue.
POSNER, R. A., 1975, 'The Social Costs of Monopoly and Regulation', *Journal of Political Economy*, 83, 4 (August), pp. 807–828.
POSNER, R. A., 1976, *Antitrust Law: An Economic Perspective* (University of Chicago Press, Chicago).
PRESCOTT, E. and VISSCHER, M., 1977, 'Sequential Location among Firms with Foresight', *Bell Journal of Economics*, 8, 2 (Autumn), pp. 378–393.
REES, R., 1984, 'The Theory of Principal and Agent', forthcoming *Bulletin of Economic Research*.
REES, R., 1985, 'Cheating in a Duopoly Supergame', *Journal of Industrial Economics*, this issue.
REINGANUM, J. F., 1981, 'Market Structure and the Diffusion of New Technology', *Bell Journal of Economics*, 12, 2 (Autumn), pp. 618–624.
REINGANUM, J. F., 1983, 'Uncertain Innovation and the Persistence of Monopoly', *American Economic Review*, 73, 4 (September), pp. 741–748.
REINGANUM, J. F., 1984, 'Uncertain Innovation and the Persistence of Monopoly: Reply', *American Economic Review*, 74, 1 (March), pp. 243–246.
ROBERTS, K., 1983, 'Self-Agreed Cartel Rules', mimeo, University of Warwick.
ROBERTS, K., 1985, 'Cartel Behaviour and Adverse Selection', *Journal of Industrial Economics*, this issue.
ROBERTS, M., 1983, 'Testing Oligopolistic Behaviour: An Application of the Variable Profit Function', forthcoming *International Journal of Industrial Organization*.
ROSENTHAL, R. W., 1981, 'Games of Perfect Information, Predatory Pricing and the Chain-Store Paradox', *Journal of Economic Theory*, 25, 1 (August), pp. 92–100.

Rosse, J. N., 1970, 'Estimating Cost Function Parameters without Using Cost Data', *Econometrica*, 38, 2 (March), pp. 256–275.
Rothschild, R., 1981, 'Cartel Problems: Note", *American Economic Review*, 71, 1 (March), pp. 179–181.
Salant, S. W., Switzer, S. and Reynolds, R. J., 1983, 'Losses from Horizontal Merger: The Effects of an Exogenous Change in Industry Structure in Cournot–Nash Equilibrium', *Quarterly Journal of Economics*, 98, 2 (May), pp. 185–199.
Salop, S., 1979a, 'Strategic Entry Deterrence', *American Economic Review*, Papers and Proceedings, 69, 2 (May), pp. 335–338.
Salop, S., 1979b, 'Monopolistic Competition with Outside Goods', *Bell Journal of Economics*, 10, 1 (Spring), pp. 141–156.
Sandmo, A., 1971, 'On the Theory of the Competitive Firm under Price Uncertainty', *American Economic Review*, 61, 1 (March), pp. 65–80.
Sattinger, M., 1983, 'Value of an Additional Firm in Monopolistic Competition', mimeo.
Sauermann, H. and Selten, R., 1967, 'Ein Oligopolexperiment', in H. Sauermann (ed.), *Beitrage zür experimentellen Wirtschaftsforschung*, 1, Tübingen, pp. 9–59.
Schelling, T., 1960, *The Strategy of Conflict* (Harvard University Press, Cambridge, Mass.).
Scherer, F. M. et al., 1975, *The Economics of Multi-Plant Operation* (Harvard University Press, Cambridge, Mass.).
Scherer, F. M., 1976a, 'Predatory Pricing and the Sherman Act: A Comment', *Harvard Law Review*, 89, 5 (March), pp. 868–890.
Scherer, F. M., 1976b, 'Some Last Words on Predatory Pricing', *Harvard Law Review*, 89, 5 (March), pp. 901–903.
Scherer, F. M., 1981, *Industrial Market Structure and Economic Performance* (2nd Edition, Rand-McNally, Chicago).
Schmalensee, R. L., 1978, 'A Model of Advertising and Product Quality', *The Journal of Political Economy*, 86, 3 (June), pp. 485–503.
Schmalensee, R., 1978, 'Entry Deterrence in the Ready to Eat Breakfast Cereal Industry', *Bell Journal of Economics*, 9, pp. 305–327.
Schmalensee, R., 1979, 'On the Use of Economic Models in Antitrust: The ReaLemon Case', *University of Pennsylvania Law Review*, 127, 4 (April), pp. 994–1050.
Schwartz, M. and Reynolds, R. J., 1983, 'Contestable Markets: An Uprising in the Theory of Industry Structure: Comments', *American Economic Review*, 73, 3 (June), pp. 488–490.
Selten, R., 1965, 'Spieltheoretische Behandlung eines Oligopolmodells mit Nachfrageträgheit', *Zeitschrift für die gesamte Staatswissenschaft*, 121, pp. 301–324 and 667–689.
Selten, R., 1978, 'The Chain Store Paradox', *Theory and Decision*, 9, 2 (April), pp. 127–159.
Selten, R., 1979, 'Experimentelle Wirtschaftsforschung', *Reinisch-Westfälische Akademie der Wissenschaften, Vorträge*, 287, pp. 41–72.
Selten, R., 1982, 'Einführung in die Theorie der Spiele mit unvollständiger Information', in *Information in der Wirtschaft*, Schriften der Vereins für Socialpolitik, Gesellschaft für Wirtschafts- und Socialwissenschaften, Neue Folge Band 126 (Duncker und Humblot, Berlin), pp. 81–147.
Shaked, A. and Sutton, J., 1982, 'Relaxing Price Competition through Product Differentiation', *Review of Economic Studies*, 49, 1 (January), pp. 3–14.
Shaked, A. and Sutton, J., 1983a, 'Natural Oligopolies and International Trade', in H. Kierzkowski (ed.), *Monopolistic Competition and International Trade* (Oxford University Press, Oxford).

SHAKED, A. and SUTTON, J., 1983b, 'Natural Oligopolies', *Econometrica*, 51, 5 (September), pp. 1469–1484.
SHAPIRO, C., 1983, 'Premiums for High Quality as Returns to Reputations', *The Quarterly Journal of Economics*, 98, 4 (November), pp. 659–679.
SHUBIK, M., 1982, *Game Theory in the Social Sciences*, Concepts and Solutions (MIT Press, Cambridge, Mass.).
SIMPSON, P. and WATERSON, M., 1984, 'Cartel Problem: The Incentive to Lie about Costs', mimeo, University of Newcastle.
SLADE, M., 1984, 'Conjectures, Firm Characteristics and Market Structure: An Analysis of Vancouver's Gasoline—Price Wars', mimeo, University of British Columbia.
SPENCE, A. M., 1975, 'Monopoly, Quality and Regulation', *Bell Journal of Economics*, 6, 2 (Autumn), pp. 417–429.
SPENCE, A. M., 1976, 'Product Selection, Fixed Costs and Monopolistic Competition', *Review of Economic Studies*, 43, 2 (July), pp. 217–236.
SPENCE, A. M., 1977, 'Entry Capacity, Investment and Oligopolistic Pricing', *Bell Journal of Economics*, 8, 2 (Autumn), pp. 534–544.
SPENCE, A. M., 1978, 'Tacit Co-ordination and Imperfect Information', *Canadian Journal of Economics*, 11, 3 (August), pp. 490–505.
SPENCE, A. M., 1979, 'Investment Strategy and Growth in a New Market', *Bell Journal of Economics*, 10, 1 (Spring), pp. 1–19.
SPENCE, A. M., 1980, 'Notes on Advertising, Economies of Scale, and Entry Barriers', *Quarterly Journal of Economics*, 95, 3 (November), pp. 493–507.
SPILLER, D. and FAVARO, E., 1984, 'The Effects of Entry Regulation on Oligopolistic Interaction: The Uruguayan Banking Sector', *Rand Journal of Economics*, 15, pp. 244–254.
SPULBER, D., 1981, 'Capacity, Output and Sequential Entry', *American Economic Review*, 71, 3 (June), pp. 503–514.
STAHL, K., 1982, 'Differentiated Products, Consumer Search, and Locational Oligopoly', *Journal of Industrial Economics*, 31, 1 (September), pp. 97–113.
STERN, N., 1972, 'The Optimal Size of Market Areas', *Journal of Economic Theory*, 4, 2 (April), pp. 154–173.
STIGLER, G. J., 1964, 'A Theory of Oligopoly', *Journal of Political Economy*, 72, 1 (February), pp. 44–61.
STOECKER, R., 1980, *Experimentelle Untersuchung des Entscheidungsverhaltens im Bertrand-Oligopol* (Pfeffersche Buchhandlung, Bielefeld).
SUMNER, D., 1981, 'Measurement of Monopoly Behaviour: An Application to the Cigarette Industry', *Journal of Political Economy*, 89, 5, pp. 1010–1019.
TELSER, L. G., 1966, 'Cutthroat Competition and the Long Purse', *Journal of Law and Economics*, 9, 2 (October), pp. 259–277.
TELSER, L. G., 1972, *Competition, Collusion and Game Theory* (Aldine-Atherton, Chicago).
ULEN, T. S., 1983, 'Railroad Cartels Before 1887: The Effectiveness of Private Enforcement of Collusion', *Research in Economic History*, 8, pp. 125–144.
VICKREY, W., 1961, 'Counter-speculation, Auctions, and Competitive Sealed Tenders', *Journal of Finance*, 16, pp. 8–37.
VIVES, X., 1983, 'Duopoly Information Equilibrium: Cournot and Bertrand', Department of Economics, University of Pennsylvania.
VON UNGERN-STERNBERG, T., 1984a, *Zur Analyse von Märkten mit unvollständiger Nachfragerinformation* (Springer-Verlag, Berlin-Heidelberg-New York).
VON UNGERN-STERNBERG, T., 1984b, 'Marktschutz und legaler Schutz auf Märkten mit Qualitötsunsicherheit', *Abhandlungen des Vereins für Socialpolitik*.
VON UNGERN-STERNBERG, T. and VON WEIZSÄCKER, C. C., 1981, 'Marktstruktur und Marktverhalten bei Qualitätsunsicherheit', *Zeitschrift für Wirtschafts- und Sozialwissenschaften*, 101, pp. 609–626.

von Ungern-Sternberg, T. and von Weizsäcker, C. C., 1985, 'The Supply of Quality on a Market for "Experience Goods"', *Journal of Industrial Economics*, this issue.
von Weizsäcker, C. C., 1980a, 'A Welfare Analysis of Barriers to Entry', *Bell Journal of Economics*, II, 2 (Autumn), pp. 399–420.
von Weizsäcker, C. C., 1980b, 'Barriers to Entry: A Theoretical Treatment' (Springer-Verlag, Berlin-Heidelberg-New York).
Ware, R., 1984, 'Sunk Costs and Strategic Commitment: A Proposed Three-Stage Equilibrium', *Economic Journal*, 94, 374, pp. 370–378.
Waterson, M., 1983, 'Economies of Scope within Market Frameworks', *International Journal of Industrial Economics*, 1, pp. 223–237.
Williamson, O. E., 1977, 'Predatory Pricing: A Strategic and Welfare Analysis', *Yale Law Journal*, 87, 2 (December), pp. 284–340.
Wolinsky, A., 1983, 'Prices as Signals of Product Quality', *Review of Economic Studies*, 50, 4 (October), pp. 647–658.
Wolinsky, A., 1984, 'Product Differentiation with Imperfect Information', *Review of Economic Studies*, 51, 1 (January), pp. 53–61.
Yarrow, G., 1985, 'Welfare Losses in Oligopoly and Monopolistic Competition', *Journal of Industrial Economics*, this issue.

AUTHOR INDEX

Aaftink, J., 139
Akerlof, G. A., 163
Anderson, J., 11n
Appelbaum, E., 9, 10n
Areeda, P., 77n, 78, 89n
Arrow, K. J., 163
d'Aspremont, C., 44n
Aumann, R. J., 7n

Baker, J., 9, 60, 65, 68n, 69n, 74n
Basar, T., 6
Baumol, W. J., 15n, 77n, 89n, 128
Bradburd, R. M., 142n
Brander, J., 116, 123
Bresnahan, T. F., 9, 10, 12, 60, 61n, 63n, 65, 68n, 69n, 74n, 157
Brodley, J. F., 77n, 80n, 87, 88, 89
Brown, D., 17
Bulow, J., 9

Caves, R., 8n
Chamberlin, E. H., 34, 59n, 61n
Chern, W., 9
Clarke, R. N., 5, 6, 8n
Comanor, W., 122
Cowling, K., 8n, 63n, 122, 147, 152
Crawford, V., 6n
Cubbin, J., 10, 63n, 136
Cyert, D., 12n

Dansby, R., 12n
Dasgupta, P., 15, 16, 18, 93, 94
DeGroot, M., 12n
Demsetz, H., 8n
de Palma, A., 2n
Dickson, V., 10n
Dixit, A. K., 13, 14, 15, 17, 116, 127n, 136, 147, 150, 151
Dixon, H. D., 4, 16, 115, 120, 123, 124, 126
Dolbear, F., 4

Easley, D., 2n, 82n, 86n
Eaton, C., 15
Eisenberg, B. S., 6n
Eizinga, K. G., 66n
Ellison, R. I., 67n
Encaoua, D., 14

Farrel, J., 124
Favaro, E., 11
Fisher, F. M., 115
Fouraker, L., 4
Friedman, J. W., 4, 7n, 8n, 10n, 22n, 24, 48
Fudenberg, D., 7n, 95n

Gal-Or, E., 6n
Geroski, P., 8n, 10n, 11, 12n, 15, 17
Gilbert, R. J., 15, 16, 93, 94
Gollop, F., 10, 11
Green, E. J., 8, 31, 32, 33n, 34, 47, 52, 56, 58
Greer, D. F., 66n, 77n
Grossman, G., 17n, 115

Harberger, A., 122, 147, 152, 161
Harris, C. J., 16, 95, 100n, 111
Harsanyi, J. C., 3n
Hart, O. D., 13, 14
Hatten, K. J., 67n
Hay, D., 15
Hay, G. A., 77n, 80n, 87, 88, 89
Heal, G., 17
Ho, Y. C., 6
Hogarty, T. F., 66n
Hoggatt, A. C., 4, 7n
Holahan, W. L., 3n
Hotelling, H., 15

Ingham, A., 17n
Ireland, N. J., 17n, 135n, 139, 142n
Ishii, Y., 133, 136, 137
Iwata, G., 10

Jacquemin, A., 15
Joskow, P. L., 63n, 77n, 89n
Just, R., 9

Kamien, M. I., 96n
Keithahn, C., 66n
Kelton, W. D., 66n
Klein, B., 164
Kleton, C. M. L., 66n
Klevorick, A. K., 77n, 89n
Koenker, R. W., 135, 141

AUTHOR INDEX

Koller, R. H., 87
Kreps, D. M., $2n$, 4, 16, $41n$, 79, 90, 91, 154
Krugman, P., 145

Lambin, J., 14
Lancaster, K., 13, 14, 17
Lee, L.-F., 12, 15, 47, 48, 54
Leffler, K., 164
Leibenstein, H., 122
Lipsey, R., 15
Loury, G., 15
Luce, R. D., $22n$

MacAvoy, P., 64
McConnell, J. D., $66n$
McGee, J. S., 77, 79, 88
McKinnon, R. I., 19, $33n$
MacLeod, W. B., 4, $8n$
Maddala, G. S., 56
Marris, R., 13
Marshall, A., 122
Masson, R. T., $82n$, $86n$
Milgrom, P., $2n$, 79
Meade, J., 17
Mueller, D., $8n$, 13, 122, 147, 152
Myerson, R., $36n$

Nelson, P., 163
Nermuth, M., $2n$
Newbery, D., 15, 16, 93, 94
Novshak, W., 5, 13

Ordover, J., $77n$, $89n$
Ornstein, S., $66n$
Orr, R., 64
Osborne, D. K., 2, 6, $32n$

Palfrey, T. R., $6n$
Perloff, J., 13, $14n$
Perry, M. K., 135, 141
Pfeiderer, P., 9
Phlips, L., 13, 17
Plott, C. R., 4
Porter, R. H., 8, 12, 31, 32, $33n$, 34, 47, 50, 51, 52, 54, 55, 56, 58
Posner, R. A., 6, $77n$, 89, 155
Prescott, E., 15
Pugel, T., $8n$

Raiffa, H., $22n$
Rees, R., $7n$

Reinganum, J. F., 15, 16, $94n$
Reynolds, R. J., $82n$, $86n$, $89n$
Roberts, J., $2n$, 79
Roberts, K., 1, 34, 35
Roberts, M., 10, 11, $12n$
Rosenthal, R. W., $79n$
Rosse, J. N., 9
Rothschild, R., $3n$

Salant, S. W., $60n$, $94n$
Salop, S., 13, 14, 15
Sandmo, A., 133, 136, 137
Sattinger, M., 13
Sauermann, H., 4
Scheinkman, J. A., 4, 16
Schelling, T., 15
Schendel, D. E., $67n$
Scherer, F. M., $8n$, $33n$, $77n$, 89
Schmalensee, R. L., 14, 15, $77n$, 89
Schwartz, M., $89n$
Schwartz, N. L., $96n$
Selten, R., $3n$, 4
Sertel, M. R., 139
Shaked, A., 14, 15
Shapiro, C., $17n$, 124
Shubik, M., $2n$
Siegel, S., 4
Simpson, P., 34
Slade, M., $11n$
Sobel, J., $6n$
Sonnenschein, H., 5, 13
Spence, A. M., 4, 15, 17, 48, 135, 147, 148, 165
Spencer, B., 116, 123
Spiller, D., 11
Stahl, $2n$
Stern, N., 14
Stigler, G. J., 1, 19–21, $31n$, 32, 33, 47, 51, 58, $59n$
Stiglitz, J. E., 13, 15, 17, 136, 147, 150, 151
Stoecker, R., 4
Sumner, D., 9
Sutton, J., 14, 15

Telser, L. G., 48, 79, 85
Thisse, J., 13
Tirole, J., $7n$
Turner, D. F., $77n$, 78, 89

Uhl, K. P., $67n$
Ulen, T. S., 49, 51, 55
Ulph, A., $12n$, $17n$

von Ungern-Sternberg, T., $2n$, $17n$, 164, $171n$, 172

Vickers, J. S., 16, $95n$, $100n$, 111
Vickrey, W., 44
Visscher, M., 15
Vives, X., $6n$

Ware, R., 15
Waterson, M., $8n$, 34, 135

von Weizsäcker, C. C., $17n$, 165, $171n$, 172
Wilde, L., 15
Williamson, O. E., $89n$
Willig, R., $12n$, $77n$, $89n$
Wilson, R., $2n$, 90, 91, 154
Wolinsky, A., $17n$

Yarrow, G., $123n$

SUBJECT INDEX

adverse selection, 33–45, 163, 164, 172
advertising, 13, 14, 67, 69, 75, 76, 147, 152
antitrust policy, 60, 77–8, 86–90, 147
auction mechanism, 44

balanced temptation equilibrium, 22, 24
bargaining power, 36, 37, 39, 43, 44
Bayes assumption, 35
Bayes rule, 53, 91
Bayes–Cournot assumption, 6
behavioural rules, 82
Bertrand equilibrium, 16, 63, 157
Bertrand outcome, 48, 116, 123, 135
Bertrand strategies, $4n$, $6n$, $13n$, 60, 61
bidding games, 94–5

capacity, 15, 66, 70, 76, 120, 130, 150, 153
capacity choice models, 16
Chamberlinian equilibrium, 143
cheating, 2–3, 4, 7–8, 19–32, 34, 47–51, 56, 58, 171
Cobb–Douglas technology, 124, 125, 126
collusion
  agreements, 1, 22, 32, 47, 48, 51–3
  bilateral, 60, 74
  cartels, 12, 33–45, 47–58, 155
  equilibrium, 21, 22, 24
  explicit, 2, 34, 35
  gains from, 51, 59–76
  and information, 1–8, 33, 39–43
  and the law, 33
  model, 11
  number of firms, 51, 55, 58
  side payments, 33, 35, 43–5
  and uncertainty, 47–51, 55
  welfare loss from, 147–61
communication costs, 33
competitive equilibrium, 4, 31, 32, 43, 49, 115, 120
concentration, 11, 47, 66, 67, 115, 130
conjectural variations, 10–12, 134, 135, 144, 154
Consistent Conjectures model, 11, 157
consumer surplus, 122, 141, 142, 165
cost function, 9, 48, 116, 117, 130, 134, 140, 147, 157, 158

Cournot equilibrium, 16, 22, 31, 36, 63, 115, 116, 120, 123, 124, 125, 126
Cournot model, 4, 11, 12, 36, 123, 125, 157
Cournot strategy, 43, 60, 61
Cournot–Nash equilibrium, 2, 3–6, 7–8, 25, 154, 157
Cramer's rule, 137, 140
critical level of sales, 19, 20, 24–32

defection, 19, 22, 24, 32, 48–51, 57
demand curve, 9, 14, 43, 59–75, 121, 149, 154, 155, 165
demand, market, 5, 21, 128, 134
demand uncertainty, 142, 144
demographic variables, 67–9
distribution of income, 18
Dominant Firm model, 11
duopoly, 2, 4, 15, 19–32, 85

economies of scale, 13, 17, 18, 67, 135, 142, 145, 149
efficiency, 36, 38, 80, 122–8, 143, 144, 145
elasticity
  conjectural, 136, 143, 145
  constant, 123–5
  demand, 59, 60, 62–71, 73, 74, 116, 121, 123, 124, 145
  price, 148
  substitution, 139
  supply, 124, 125
empirical analysis, 8–12, 18, 54–8, 66–73
enforcement, 19–32, 47, 50, 53, 87, 89
entry, 14–17, 52, 55–6, 93–103, 116, 135, 161, 164
  and antitrust policy, 88–90
  barriers, 14, 88
  costs, 8, 155
  expectations, 78
  free entry, 133, 150, 153–5
  and information, 78–86
  and strategic investment, 127–30
  equilibrium, 10, 41, 48, 50, 60, 82, $85n$, 102, 115, 116, 119, 120, 121–6, 133, 158, 164, 166, 168
  balanced temptation, 22, 24
  Bertrand, 16, 63, 157

Chamberlinian, 143
collusive, 21, 22, 24
competitive, 4, 14, 31, 32, 43, 49, 115, 120
consistent conjectural, 157
Cournot, 16, 22, 31, 36, 63, 115, 116, 120, 123, 124, 125, 126
Cournot–Nash, 2, 3–6, 7–8, 25, 154, 157
duopoly, 15
enforcement, 20–1, 31
first-best, 17
free-entry, 153–5, 158
general, 147
industry, 68
instantaneous entry, 86
market, 20, 28, 30
monopolistic competition, 14, 133, 134, 136–45, 150, 151
Nash, 2, 3, 6, 8, 9, 21, 23, 24, 31, 32, 80, 82, 115, 118–19, 135, 150, 154, 159, 160
oligopoly, 63
sequential, 86, 90–2
signalling, 4
strategic investment, 123–30
symmetric, 124
two-stage dynamic, 115
zero-entry, 86
zero-profit, 147, 158, 160
experience goods, 163–72
extrapolations principle, 164

factor bias, 123, 147, 155–60
firm, theory of, 133
First Mover Advantage, 14–17

game theory, 1, 79
games
  bidding, 94–5
  duopoly, 19–32, 85
  incomplete-information, 78
  monopolistic competition, 134–44
  multi-stage strategic, 16
  oligopoly, 2–3
  one-shot, 48, 79, 154
  price-output, 154–61
  price-setting, 16
  Prisoners' Dilemma, 2–3, 7, 40–1
  sequential equilibrium, 90–2
  strategic investment, 117–31
Germany, 172

GNP deflator, 75
good will mechanism, 164–72
government intervention, 172
government regulation, 48

Herfindahl index, 52, 53, 55
horizontal differentiation, 13, 18

incentive constraint, 27, 37, 38, 44
incentive device, 43, 44, 45
income effect, 148
industry equilibrium, 68
information, 1, 5, 33–5, 43, 52, 86, 87, 90, 134, 168
  asymmetric, 36, 43
  and experience goods, 163–71
  imperfect, 1–8, 53, 78–86, 165–6, 170
  perfect, 16, 33, 43, 81, 176
  pooling, 5–6
  private market, 5, 39
instantaneous entry equilibrium, 86
interest rate, 7, 22, 29, 48, 171
Interstate Commerce Commission, 51
investment behaviour, 1, 16, 18, 115–30

Japanese Flat Glass industry, 10
Joint Executive Committee, 12, 47, 49, 51–5, 58
joint-profit maximization, 1, 2, 4, 8, 12n, 20, 22, 33, 43, 49, 50, 135, 147, 159

Leontief technology, 123, 125
Loschian markets, 8n

market equilibrium, 20, 28, 30
market failure, 151, 153–6, 160, 166, 171
market power, 59, 60, 64, 65, 66, 70, 73, 147
market share, 115, 153–5
mergers, 9, 59–76
minimum efficient scale, 149, 150, 152, 153–5
monopoly, 10, 15, 78, 79, 128, 153, 155
  natural, 128, 129, 153
  patent races, 93–113
  power, 8, 130
  predation, 78–92
  pre-emption, 14–17
  welfare, 122–3, 147–61
monopolistic competition, 14, 133–45, 147–61, 165, 166, 170, 171
moral hazard, 33–5, 52, 163, 164, 172

SUBJECT INDEX

Nash equilibrium, 2, 3, 6, 8, 9, 21, 23, 24, 31, 32, 80, 82, 115, 118–19, 135, 150, 154, 159, 160
Nash strategy, 78, 81, 134, 167, 169
non-price competition, 13–18

observation lag, 48, 52
oligopoly
  asymmetrical models, 11
  empirical analysis, 1, 8–12, 18, 54–8, 66–73
  and information, 1–8
  natural, 14, 18
  non-price competition, 13–18
  pre-emption, 14–17
  pricing behaviour, 8–12, 47–58
  solution concepts, 9, 10, 11, 16, 63, 96
  welfare loss, 155–61
one-shot games, 48, 79, 154

patenting, 15–17, 18
patent races, 16, 93–113
pre-commitments, 15–17, 120, 123
predation, 52, 77–90
pre-emption, 1, 14–17, 18, 93, 94, 100
preferences, 13–14, 33, 34, 134, 148, 150, 154
policy, 1, 86–90, 161
price-output games, 154–61
pricing behaviour, 2, 6–8, 8–12, 13, 14, 17, 18, 19, 23, 32, 34, 73, 115–30, 151, 164
product differentiation, 9–10, 13–14, 17, 59–76, 133–45, 147, 148–9, 150–5
product quality, 9, 14, 15, 17–18, 152, 163–72

Ramsey solution, 128–30
rational behaviour, 1, 2, 16, 20, 33, 50, 77, 135
reaction function, 4, 48, 60, 64, 157
recontracting, 36, 39, 44
research and development (R & D), 14, 16, 18, 95, 108, 115, 116, 147, 152
retaliation, 2, 20–1, 22, 24, 25, 31, 32, 48
returns to scale, 17, 116, 143
"revelation principle," 36n
risk, 133, 136, 137, 139, 141, 142
Robinson–Patman Act, 89n

scale effects, 13, 17, 18, 67, 116, 135, 142, 143, 145, 149, 150, 152, 153–5, 158, 161
secret price-cutting, 2, 19, 32, 34, 48, 50, 52
self-correcting mechanisms, 172
self-interest, 33
sequential competition, 14–17
sequential equilibrium games, 90–2
Sherman Act, 51, 87n, 89
side-payments, 33, 35, 43–5
signalling equilibria, 4
Stackelberg model, 11
strategic behaviour, 18, 94, 95, 109, 115–31, 155
structure-conduct-performance theory, 147
supernormal profits, 147, 155
Sylos postulate, 15
symmetric equilibrium, 124

taxes, 9, 17
technology, 121, 123, 125
trade associations, 6
trigger strategies, 34, 48, 49

UK car industry, 10
uncertainty, 47–51, 55, 133–45, 163
utility, 134, 136, 137, 142, 143, 148, 149, 150, 151, 152, 165
utility-output, 149–61
US antitrust guidelines, 60
US automobile industry, 9
US brewing industry, 59–76
US coffee-roasting industry, 10, 12
US computer industry, 115

varying conduct models, 12
vertical differentiation, 9, 14, 15

welfare, 6, 116, 127–30, 134, 138, 139, 165, 166, 170
  and factor bias, 157–60
  loss, 9n, 115, 122, 123, 125–7; under monopolistic competition, 141–5, 147–61; under oligopoly, 6, 17–18, 155

zero-entry equilibrium, 86
zero-profit equilibrium, 147, 158, 160